Chihuahuas

3rd Edition

by Kim Campbell Thornton and Jacqueline O'Neil

Chihuahuas For Dummies®, 3rd Edition

Published by: **John Wiley & Sons, Inc.,** 111 River Street, Hoboken, NJ 07030-5774, www.wiley.com

Copyright © 2023 by John Wiley & Sons, Inc., Hoboken, New Jersey

Media and software compilation copyright © 2023 by John Wiley & Sons, Inc. All rights reserved.

Published simultaneously in Canada

For general information on our other products and services, please contact our Customer Care Department within the U.S. at 877-762-2974, outside the U.S. at 317-572-3993, or fax 317-572-4002. For technical support, please visit https://hub.wiley.com/community/support/dummies.

Wiley publishes in a variety of print and electronic formats and by print-on-demand. Some material included with standard print versions of this book may not be included in e-books or in print-on-demand. If this book refers to media such as a CD or DVD that is not included in the version you purchased, you may download this material at http://booksupport.wiley.com. For more information about Wiley products, visit www.wiley.com.

Library of Congress Control Number: 2023930139

ISBN 978-1-394-15680-1 (pbk); ISBN 978-1-394-15681-8 (ebk); ISBN 978-1-394-15682-5 (ebk)

SKY10041267_011323

Contents at a Glance

Table of Contents

CHAPTER 6: **What's on the Chi Menu?** 97

Introduction

Today you can't turn on the TV or browse in a gift shop without seeing Chihuahuas. From fashion centers to flea markets, they've become one of the nation's most popular pets. But just because these critters attract attention with their incredible cuteness isn't enough reason to run out and get one. You wouldn't ask the prettiest cheerleader or the best football player to marry you when you don't even know their name, would you? That's why we wrote this book: to introduce you to the charming, adorable Chihuahua breed. Whether you're a potential new owner or have enjoyed the companionship of Chihuahuas for years, this book can help you and your dog make the most of your relationship.

About This Book

Chihuahuas For Dummies, 3rd Edition, is designed to be a complete reference guide. In it, we tell you everything you need to know about selecting, raising, and training a healthy, well-mannered Chihuahua. And although we promote prevention — not only in health matters but also by proposing positive training methods right from the start — we explain how to deal with problem behaviors your dog may have already picked up.

But wait. Maybe you don't have a dog yet and you're reading this book because you wonder if a Chihuahua is the breed for you. Well, you've come to the right place! This book covers the unique Chihuahua personality and gives honest answers about both the pleasures and problems of living with a Chihuahua. Ohmygosh! What if you read those sections and then decide a Chihuahua isn't your dream dog after all? In that case, we just saved you a bundle of money and years of enduring a match that wasn't made in heaven. It's important to think about how *your* personality will blend with the unique disposition of this diminutive breed.

We wrote this book to make living with a Chihuahua easy and fun. Whether you have one Chi or half a dozen, this book simplifies daily care, explains how to train your dog in a kind and positive manner, and helps you recognize health problems, feed your dog appropriately, and have fun together.

Conventions Used in This Book

To make this book even easier to understand, we've included a few conventions:

>> *Italic* text indicates new words or terms that we define, or for emphasis.

>> **Boldfaced** type helps you remember the most important points when reading bulleted lists or numbered steps.

>> We use monofont to set apart websites and e-mail addresses.

>> Occasionally, we write "Chi" instead of spelling out "Chihuahua." We do this to make for faster reading, not because it's a nickname for the breed. It isn't.

Because Jackie's degree is in English and Kim's is in journalism, we know that the accepted way to refer to an animal is "it," but neither of us can stand "it" when talking about a member of a family. So, we get around this by using gendered (he/she) or gender-neutral (they) language. We use "they" as a singular and a plural pronoun, usage that actually dates to the 14th century and earlier, so no lectures about how it's incorrect. It's not. And occasionally, we'll refer to specific Chihuahuas, like Jackie's chi, Manchita, or Kim's chi, Gemma.

Foolish Assumptions

Before writing this book, we had to think about who we were writing it for, so we made some assumptions about you, dear reader, and the type of book you need. Here they are — are we close?

>> You like dogs in general, and the Chihuahua is one of the breeds you like in particular. You're thinking about making one a part of your family. But first you want to know more about the breed, the pros and cons of living with a Chihuahua, and how to select your ideal dog.

>> You've already taken the plunge. Your Chihuahua puppy is coming home soon and you want to know what they need right away and how to take care of them.

>> Your Chihuahua puppy is home, but doggone it, they wake you up during the night and can't seem to get the hang of housetraining.

>> Your Chihuahua is an adult. You want to read this book in your comfy recliner, but that darn dog claimed it. Lately, your chi growls and nips whenever anyone tries to sit in it. And don't even think about touching their food dish!

>> Your Chihuahua is well behaved and super smart. Everyone agrees that they're special, and now you want your dog to try obedience, agility, or maybe a dog show. Or perhaps you're considering training them to be a therapy dog.

>> You don't have and don't want a Chihuahua, but your cousin just got one and her birthday is coming up!

Icons Used in This Book

The pages of this book are peppered with icons in the margins. Besides adding a little salsa, they also give you a quick bite of Chihuahua information. Here's what's on the menu:

TIP

You'll see this icon quite often. It contains advice on Chihuahua care and training techniques and provides shortcuts to simplify life with a dog.

REMEMBER

There are certain tidbits of information we'd like you to keep in your memory bank for the duration of your time as a Chihuahua owner. This icon highlights this information.

WARNING

Whoa! This Chihuahua is on full alert. This information helps you to keep from skidding into common but potentially serious mistakes.

TECHNICAL STUFF

Every species has its own language and characteristics. These icons define the terms that dog owners in general, and Chihuahua owners in particular, need to know. You also find some interesting dog lore and some fun trivia.

Beyond the Book

In addition to what you're reading now, this product comes with some access-anywhere goodies on the web. Check out the free Cheat Sheet for interesting information on what to expect from Chihuahuas, what to buy for them, signs of a healthy Chihuahua, and a schedule of routine care. To get this Cheat Sheet, simply go to www.dummies.com and search for "*Chihuahuas For Dummies* Cheat Sheet" in the search box.

Where to Go from Here

Don't you just hate it when you pick up a book that you're sure has the information you need but it doesn't give you a clue where to find it? Well, we won't do that to you. This book is organized for your convenience — whether you want to "read all about it" or simply find a trick you can teach your Chihuahua to do so they can show off when Aunt Amelia visits.

You can start wherever you want to and easily find the information you need. Do you want to know how to raise an outgoing, social Chihuahua? Turn to Chapter 9. Are you concerned about house training? Chapter 10 will help you handle that. Are you Chihuahua shopping? Chapter 4 will help you find a good breeder.

If you're still wondering if a Chihuahua (or any dog) is right for you, read Chapters 1 and 3. They tell you what you need to know about dog ownership in general and living with a Chihuahua in particular.

There's no need to read this book from cover to cover unless you want to. Flip through it at will. Let the table of contents and the index guide you quickly to the info you need. Happy reading!

1

Is a Chihuahua Your Canine Compadre?

IN THIS PART . . .

Consider the ups and downs of living with a little dog.

Find out all you ever wanted to know about the Chihuahua's distinctive personality and body structure.

Decide whether a Chihuahua is right for you and your lifestyle.

Chapter **1**

Sharing Your Digs with a Dog: A Big Decision

Can money ever buy you love? Sure. Just use it to buy a Chihuahua. Your Chihuahua won't waffle about making a permanent commitment to you. In fact, expect your Chi to envelop you in affection, do their best to protect you, and maybe even improve your health. No kidding! Scientific studies show that a pet's companionship alleviates stress and helps people relax. In many cases, dogs (and other pets) get credit for lowering their owners' blood pressure. However, although most Chihuahua owners are crazy about their pets, a few wish they had never brought a dog (or *that* dog) home.

We don't want Chihuahua ownership to disappoint you, so in this chapter, we talk about the ups and downs of living with dogs in general, and Chis in particular. Is this portable pet with the king-size heart the right breed for you? In this chapter, you find the answer.

Deciding if and Why You Want a Dog

If you are *dog-deprived,* you know it. You greet all your friends' dogs by name, eye every dog you see on the street, and sometimes even ask strangers if you can pet their pups. Maybe you surf through your favorite breeds on the internet or browse through the dog magazines at the bookstore. Do you have a list of possible puppy names in your head? You're already a *dog-goner.* It won't be long before other dog-deprived people are asking to pet your new puppy.

Ideally, you're drawn to dogs, and playing with them makes you feel good. But your reason for buying a dog may be less than ideal. For example, maybe you're lonely or bored, and you hope a dog can fill the void. The truth is, a little fur wrapped around a pleasant personality (like the dog named Manchita in Figure 1-1) spices up a bland life if you let it. Being loved by a dog is fulfilling in itself, and you can take it a step further and become involved in dog activities (see Chapter 12) that can bring you excitement, new friends, and a sense of purpose. So what's the problem? The glitch is that dogs purchased to relieve monotony often are ignored when the novelty wears off.

REMEMBER

Before buying a Chihuahua, you must decide if you'll always appreciate your pet or if you just crave some instant entertainment. Still not sure? Ask yourself this: "Am I ready to love a dog for the duration (possibly 15 or more years for a Chihuahua), or will a cruise to the Caribbean be just as effective for banishing my boredom?"

Getting a dog is a big decision. After all, dogs are dependent, make demands on your time, cost money, and inhibit your freedom. Is your pet worth it? Absolutely. That's why there are more than 83 million pet dogs in the United States. But just because dogs and people have been best buddies through the ages does not necessarily mean you need to run out and get a puppy right away. Maybe the Chihuahua life isn't right for you; maybe it is right for you, but not right now. Hopefully, you'll find out by taking a look at what living with a Chihuahua entails and the matchmaking tips in the following sections.

TECHNICAL STUFF

Chihuahuas are either smooth or long coated. Smooths have short hair that's soft and shiny (see Figure 1-1). Long coats have (you guessed it) long hair that may be straight or wavy (see Chapter 3 for more).

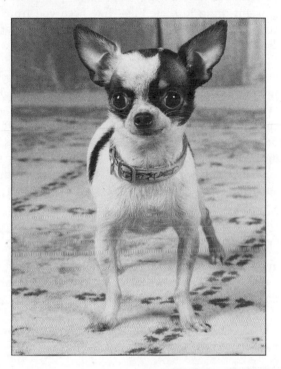

FIGURE 1-1: This Chi (named Manchita) is a smooth-coated Chihuahua.

Doggy Dependents Aren't Tax Deductible: Chi-Care Duties

Like a child, a Chihuahua relies on you for food, housing, education, affection, toys, and veterinary care — and the IRS won't even let you declare your pet. Unlike a child, your puppy won't ever become independent. Your Chi won't fix their own dinner, brush their own hair and teeth, or pay their own vet bills. Instead, they'll depend on you for their health and happiness all their life.

Fortunately, most dog owners enjoy the small chores that make up daily dog care. For some, interacting with their dogs is a restful transition from a too-busy day. Others say that their dogs keep the nest from feeling empty and add laughter to their lives. And when you have a doggy dependent, you're always the most important thing in their life. They need you from puppyhood through old age. They don't graduate, get a job, marry, or move halfway across the country.

You should discuss division of labor with your family before getting a dog, but don't expect even the most logical schedule to be carved in stone. In the end, someone — one person — must take responsibility, making sure your Chihuahua is fed, watered, groomed, trained, exercised, and taken outdoors when they indicate a need to eliminate. Because you're the one reading this book, I bet that someone is you. Will you relish or resent the responsibility?

Considering the long-term cost

Can you afford a dog? We're talking not only about the price of the dog (which can range from $1,000 to $2,500 or more for a Chihuahua puppy), but also the price of upkeep.

Some breeds — Chihuahuas, for example — don't eat much, but they still need the following:

» *Quality* food (see Chapter 6)

» Puppy shots, an annual checkup, and vaccinations and deworming as needed (see Part IV)

» Minor surgery to spay or neuter (see Chapter 13), and potentially, removal of retained baby teeth, a procedure that is often performed at the same time as spay/neuter surgery

» Medication to prevent heartworm, fleas, ticks, and other parasites (see Chapter 14)

» A crate, grooming equipment, a collar and leash, dog dishes, and a variety of toys and treats (see Chapter 5)

And although Chis tend to be healthy, yours may rack up a big bill if they're ever in an accident and require emergency surgery or a week in a veterinary ICU. (Purchasing pet health insurance when they're a pup can help ensure you can cover such costs without a qualm.)

If all of those things fit your budget, lifestyle, and personality, then you are absolutely ready for and can afford a Chihuahua. Let's take a look at what you can expect.

Placing your Chi in your daily schedule

So you're doing fine financially, but maybe you're working crazy hours to reach the next rung up the corporate ladder. In that case, your Chihuahua's excited antics when you come through the door can be just the ticket to turn your mood from office mania to bemused tranquility. Forget fuming over a frustrating meeting. Your dog needs to be walked and fed, and both of you will look forward to snuggling through a sitcom or two. Just keep in mind that no matter how frazzled you are, and no matter how late it is, your dog still needs your attention and affection. If you and your Chi live alone, especially, you're their entire world.

Chapter 5 and the chapters of Part 3 deal with setting up a schedule for your Chi and socializing and training your little buddy.

TIP

Some offices allow employees to bring well-behaved pets to work. Jackie's Chihuahua spent many hours in the office when she worked for the American Kennel Club (AKC) in New York City. Sure, that's a special case, but while they walked to work, they saw plenty of other pooches accompanying people carrying briefcases. Dogs in the office are even more common these days.

Fitting your Chi into your family's future

Your spouse's feelings about having a dog, your kids' ages, your activity level, and your travel plans are important considerations when deciding whether to make a Chihuahua part of your family. Bringing home a dog when your spouse doesn't want one or you're always busy with the kids is unfair to everyone. So is buying a breed your other half hates. In some cases a reluctant spouse grows to love the dog, but often one partner never quite comes around. Having to defend your dog on a daily basis gets old fast, and you don't need that. Furthermore, no dog deserves to be dumped at the pound because everyone got tired of the hassles at home.

Are you hoping to settle down and start a family in the near (or distant) future? Some breeds (Chihuahuas are one of them) are long lived, so with luck, you can plan on your dog being with you for your wedding and the births of your babies. But as sweet as that sounds, it may not be a good thing. Will your spouse also love your dog, or will they consider your Chi excess baggage?

WARNING

Another potential problem is that some breeds (Chihuahuas included) don't thrive around toddlers. It's a no-fault, lose–lose situation. While tiny dogs such as Chihuahuas are referred to as Toy breeds, they are living beings who aren't made for rough play. Chihuahuas are too delicate to be safe in the hands of young children, whose motor skills are still developing, so they're not suited to homes with kids under the ages of six or seven. Imagine how long your poor Chihuahua puppy would last if a toddler tripped over them or swung them by one leg like a stuffed teddy.

Picking up after your Chi

REMEMBER

When you live with pets, you are responsible for their well-being. That means you have to maintain a safe, healthy environment.

Before you commit to caring for another living being, consider how you do on your own. For example, what kind of housekeeper are you? Is your home casual and relaxed — the kind of place where friends gather to munch popcorn and stream movies? Or is your house so immaculate that family members remove their shoes before stepping on the cream-colored carpet? If any of this sounds like you, throwing a dog into the mix might not be the best idea (unless you are willing to change your habits.)

Puppies aren't perfect. Chances are you'll have to clean up some accidents while housetraining your Chihuahua. Not only that, but they'll shed at intervals (or constantly) all their life (see Chapter 7). Long after they're reliably housetrained — maybe years after you've moved into your dream home — they can get sick and upchuck on the new sofa. When that happens, will you view the mess as a minor annoyance or a major tragedy? (The chapters of Part 3 deal with socializing and training your little buddy.)

WARNING

Even though a Chi's poops are small, they can make a big mess on the bottom of someone's shoe. Don't forget to clean up after your dog every time you walk them (see Chapter 8). In many places, it's the law!

Viewing the Chihuahua as a Toy Breed

Let's say that after reading about the ups and downs of dog ownership, you decide that you want a canine companion. Right on! You're going to love living with a dog — that is, if your dog lives up to your expectations. Dogs are capable of doing an extraordinary number of things, but they are specialists in a sense, and no one breed does it all. A wrong match between dog and owner usually brings misery, like a bad marriage, while a good match means years of satisfaction and fun.

Some Toy dogs, such as the Toy Poodle, are downsized versions of their larger cousins. Others, like the Miniature Pinscher, have been around longer than the larger dogs that resemble them. Chihuahuas aren't a scaled-down version of any breed. They are a true Toy dog, developed solely to be companions to people. The following sections give you more details on this breed (for more, head to Chapters 2 and 3).

What's terrific about Toys

What do all the Toy breeds have in common? They're living proof that great things really do come in small packages. Here's the upside of a Toy dog:

>> **Toy dogs are small.** They fit anywhere and can get enough exercise in a small apartment if that's where you live.

>> **Toy dogs are cuddly and love human attention.** They form extremely strong bonds with their people, and many are content to warm a lap for hours.

>> **Toy dogs are portable.** They're ideal for people who travel a lot and like to take their dogs along with them.

>> **Toy dogs love to show off.** Most of them enjoy learning new things when they're taught with positive-reinforcement techniques.

>> **Toy dogs often are welcome where larger breeds are not.** For example, some condo associations limit the size of pets.

>> **Toys are real dogs.** They're intelligent and affectionate, with bold, fun-loving temperaments. Many of them make alert watchdogs.

TOY BREEDS ON PARADE

The American Kennel Club (AKC) currently recognizes 197 dog breeds and divides them into 7 groups, depending on the function each breed originally performed. The Chihuahua is a member of the Toy Group — a collection of small companion dogs. The AKC recognizes the following Toy breeds:

- Affenpinscher
- Biewer Terrier
- Brussels Griffon
- Cavalier King Charles Spaniel
- Chihuahua (smooth or long coat)

- Chinese Crested (hairless or powderpuff)
- English Toy Spaniel
- Fox Terrier (Toy)
- Havanese
- Italian Greyhound
- Japanese Chin
- Maltese
- Manchester Terrier (Toy)
- Miniature Pinscher
- Papillon
- Pekingese
- Pomeranian
- Poodle (Toy)
- Pug
- Russian Toy
- Shih Tzu
- Silky Terrier
- Yorkshire Terrier

According to AKC statistics, the top three most popular Toy breeds in 2021 were Yorkshire Terriers (13th among all breeds), Cavalier King Charles Spaniels (15th), and Shih Tzu (22nd). Toy Poodles also are popular, but knowing where they rank is impossible because all three varieties (Standard, Miniature, and Toy) are counted as one. Poodles as a whole, though, are the 5th most popular breed overall.

TECHNICAL STUFF

In the lingo of the dog fancier, the Chihuahua is considered a *natural dog*. That means their coats aren't trimmed, shaved, stripped, or plucked, and their ears and tail are left the way nature made them — not cropped or docked (in the style of the Miniature Pinscher, among others). In dog-fancier slang, that makes the Chihuahua a *wash-and-go breed*.

Potential problems with portable pets

Toy dogs need careful owners. Depending on your nature, that's one potential downside of owning a Chihuahua. Although most Chis think they're tough, they're more vulnerable to injury (especially being stepped on or tripped over) than larger dogs. Here are some other concerns:

>> When people with Toy dogs overdo carrying and cuddling and skimp on training, their pets become spoiled. And that can turn them into tiny tyrants or nervous wimps.

>> Toy breeds are social. Developing that typical Toy spirit means they need plenty of social interactions with a variety of people from puppyhood on.

>> Toy dogs neglected during puppyhood, or whose breeders aren't vigilant about health testing, socialization, nutrition, and veterinary care, may suffer myriad physical and/or mental problems at maturity.

>> Some people dislike Toy dogs and may make rude remarks about your Chi when you walk them. If you answer at all, smile and say something like, "Shh. He thinks he's a wolf."

>> Toy dogs are real dogs. Like every other breed, they need training and guidance. In other words, if you don't train your Chi, your Chi will train you.

Making a Match with a Chihuahua

All the Toy breeds make exceptional companions to the right people, but they aren't interchangeable. The 23 breeds come in a variety of shapes, coat types, and colors, and their temperaments and activity levels vary from lazy and laid back to extremely active. Is the Chihuahua the right breed choice for you? Here's a synopsis of what a Chi can and can't bring to a relationship. (And for more on the Chihuahua look and disposition, see Chapters 2 and 3.)

>> **Chihuahuas are perfect pets — for some people.**
Because they thrive on togetherness, a Chihuahua is the
ideal dog for someone who's home a lot and spends some
time sitting. That's because Chis love to sit beside you, or
better yet, on your lap. If you work from a home office, or if
some of your favorite activities are watching television,
reading, or surfing the net, your Chihuahua will be in pooch
paradise. They're also an excellent family dog, provided the
children are gentle and older than seven. But if you're on
the go all the time and can't make space in your schedule
to accommodate an accomplished lap warmer, this isn't
the breed for you.

>> **Chihuahuas aren't running dogs.** They enjoy a brisk walk
around the block when the weather is nice, but if you want
a jogging or hiking companion, check out some of the
larger breeds. No, a Chihuahua isn't wimpy when it comes
to exercise. Remember that they take several strides to
keep up with just one of yours.

>> **Chihuahuas are alert watchdogs with a bark much
bigger than they are.** But they aren't guard or attack dogs,
no matter what they think.

>> **Chihuahuas are loyal and loving.** They believe in family
first and are vigilant and discriminating when you have
visitors. Your friends *may* become their friends after they
get to know them.

>> **Chihuahuas are easy to groom whether they have a
smooth or a long coat.** If you're looking forward to fussing
with hair, many other Toys have thicker, longer coats.

>> **Chihuahuas are housedogs.** They can't tolerate cold or
rainy weather, garages, drafty basements, or life outdoors
in a doghouse.

>> **Chihuahuas are super short.** That means you, your
family, and your guests must watch where you walk. Don't
worry. It becomes second nature in a day or two. But when
you or your children have friends over, you must remind
them to be careful not to accidentally step on or kick your
tiny dog.

>> **Chihuahuas play games with you (you can find some in Chapter 8).** They may learn to fetch a small ball or chase a small flying disc, but they won't be able to handle any rough stuff. If you want a tough dog that plays hard, get a larger pet.

>> **Chihuahuas can be great travelers.** Most Chihuahuas adapt well to the open road and love to watch the world go by from the passenger seat of a car, recreational vehicle, or semi (lots of truckers have Chihuahuas as road companions), safely ensconced in a carrier with a view, of course (see Chapter 5).

>> **Chihuahuas must be taught manners, the same as any other dog.** Little and cute loses its charm fast when your Chi develops bad habits.

>> **Chihuahuas are natural-born showoffs with a good memory.** After they learn a trick or two, they'll be proud to perform for your friends (if they're familiar with them).

>> **Chihuahuas are sensitive.** They try to comfort you when you're sad and dance for joy when you're happy. They won't feel secure in a house full of friction.

>> **Chihuahuas are delicate.** They need your protection from bigger dogs, even if they don't think so. And not just when they're on the ground. Big dogs have been known to snatch tiny ones right out of their owners' arms (yes, that's rare, but we thought we should warn you).

WARNING

Do you tend to get physical when you're angry? If so, it's best not to have any pet, especially not a Chihuahua. The first hot-tempered blow a Chihuahua receives will probably be the last.

>> **Chihuahuas are intelligent and highly trainable.** In fact, they're capable of becoming competitive in active events like agility, obedience, and more (see Chapter 12).

Loyal, intelligent, trainable, portable, and incredibly cute to boot! If all those endearing Chihuahua charms have you captivated, you have plenty of company. In 2021, Chihuahuas ranked in the top 40 breeds registered with the American Kennel Club, coming in 37th out of 197. The little guys are big on popularity!

Chapter **2**

What's Behind That Unique Chihuahua Look?

P lenty of little dogs have compact bodies and expressive eyes (like the Toy breeds; see Chapter 3), so what makes a Chihuahua unmistakably a Chihuahua? Details. A whole bunch of details combine to create a dog that looks and acts like a Chihuahua and nothing but a Chihuahua.

This chapter focuses on appearances and gives you the official (honest!) description of Chihuahua perfection. A canine blueprint called a breed standard outlines exactly what a Chihuahua should look like and how one should act. No Chihuahua is perfect, of course, but the standard sets out what breeders strive for and gives buyers an idea of what they should expect to see.

Looking for Yourself: The Classic Chihuahua

You may already have a mental picture of a Chihuahua from watching the old television ads that show Gidget, the Taco Bell dog (see Figure 2-1), mouth a polite request for a little grub.

FIGURE 2-1: The head of the best-known Chihuahua ever on television.

Next to diminutive size, the Chihuahua's most recognizable feature is an apple-domed head, which you can plainly see on a cutie named Manchita in Figure 2-2. Chihuahuas have big eyes, brimming with intelligence, an inquiring gaze, and erect ears, a bit bigger than you might expect, that add to their alert expression. On top of many Chihuahua heads, practically invisible but easily discernable through touch, is the *molera* — a soft spot similar to the one found on newborn babies. The molera is also called the *fontanel.*

A Chihuahua's body is surprisingly sturdy. Although Manchita's feet are dainty, her legs are muscular and swift. Her back is level, she's a little longer than she is tall, and she carries her tail confidently — either in a semicircle or in a loop over her back.

The apple-shaped head and a few other features pretty much define a Chihuahua's distinctive appearance, but building a complete little superdog takes much more anatomy. Although knowing the details is important to successfully showing your Chihuahua (see Chapter 12), you don't need to know the finer points to love and enjoy your pet. So if you want details, stick with us. But if anatomy isn't your thing, you can skip the following section.

FIGURE 2-2: This pup, named Manchita, presents the classic Chihuahua look: apple-shaped head, prominent leg muscles, level back, and confident tail.

Striving for the Picture-Perfect Chihuahua

Believe it or not, a blueprint exists for building a picture-perfect Chihuahua (and every other American Kennel Club registered breed). The blueprint is called the *Official Standard for the Chihuahua.* Of course, no dog is perfect (just as no person — not even a Miss America — is perfect), so no matter how charming a Chihuahua appears, the knowledgeable eyes of a good breeder or dog show judge can always find room for improvement. Even the best breeders always have something to strive for.

Breed standards are serious stuff. Selecting breeding partners with the standard in mind is how breeders produce generation after generation of dogs that look and act like Chihuahuas. The best breeders try to produce dogs that come as close to matching the standard as possible, and dog-show judges select winners by comparing how closely each competitor matches the breed standard. (Head to Chapter 12 for more info on dog competitions.)

In Figure 2-3, you see dog lingo describing the external features of the Chihuahua. This is a handy diagram to refer to as you cruise through the details in the following sections. Pretty soon, you'll be able to speak the language of *dog people* — breeders, show exhibitors, and judges.

General appearance and demeanor

The Chihuahua is a graceful, alert, swift-moving, and compact little dog with a saucy expression and terrier-like qualities of temperament.

A Chi is compact, feels solid in your hands, and appears well proportioned. They aren't long of body or lanky or too tall. Like a terrier, they're confident, animated, spirited, curious, and interested in everything happening around them.

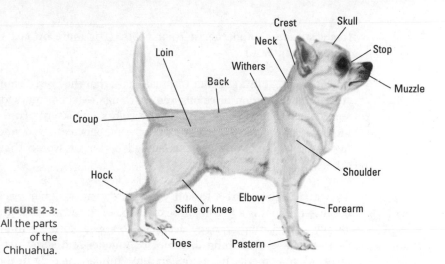

FIGURE 2-3: All the parts of the Chihuahua.

Coat and Color

Chihuahuas come in two varieties — *smooth coat* and *long coat.* If a Chi has a smooth coat, the hair is short and close to the body, and they may or may not have an *undercoat* — a protective layer of shorter fur underneath the outer or top coat. A smooth Chihuahua with an undercoat appears more thickly coated and usually has a furrier tail and a ruff of thicker hair around the neck. If a Chi has no undercoat, the hair is sparser. In fact, it may be so thin that the dog appears nearly bald on parts of the head, ears, chest, and belly.

A long-coated Chi has an undercoat, and the outer coat is between 1 and 1½ inches long. They also have the following characteristics:

» Their ears are decorated with longish hair called *fringe* or *feathering.*

» They have an abundant ruff around the neck.

» They have long hair called a *plume* on the tail.

» They have wispy hair on the back of the legs.

» They sport *natural pants* — long hair on their buttocks.

Aside from that, they should look exactly like a smooth Chihuahua, because the two varieties have the same conformation (body structure) underneath their coats. (For more on coats, jump to Chapter 3.)

One of the great things about Chihuahuas is that they can be any color or combination of colors and markings — solid, marked, splashed, take your pick. Among the colors or patterns commonly seen are black, black and tan, cream, chocolate, red, and fawn and white. None are considered better or worse than others.

WARNING

Any time someone tries to sell you a puppy at a higher price because the coat is a "rare" or "exotic" color, be aware that it's simply a marketing strategy designed to appeal to the human desire to have something different or unique. And some patterns, such as merle, have appeared in Chihuahuas only in the past couple of decades. If breeding is not done carefully, the genes linked to the merle pattern can result in the birth of puppies that are deaf and blind. Your puppy should never have two merle parents, known as a double merle breeding. That's one very good reason to choose a breeder and puppy carefully.

Size and proportion

A Chihuahua is a well-balanced little dog, weighing not more than six pounds (to qualify for the show ring). Their bodies are *off-square,* to quote the official standard — they should be slightly longer when measured from point of shoulder to point of buttocks than they are tall at the *withers,* or the top of their shoulders. Somewhat shorter bodies (in length) are preferred in males. A Chi's height is the distance from the highest point of their withers to the floor; their length is the distance from the point of the shoulder to the point of the buttock. (Refer to Figure 2-3 to see all the technical terms applied to the dog.)

TECHNICAL STUFF

The reason a little more length is desired in females than it is in males is because females need the extra space to carry puppies.

A proper Chihuahua has a balanced appearance, meaning that every part of the body is in proportion. Legs that are too long or a head that is too small can give a Chihuahua an awkward appearance instead of the graceful and dainty look they're known for.

A SOFT SPOT FOR CHIHUAHUAS

Many historians contend that the Chihuahua is a native Mexican breed (see Chapter 1), but others argue that the breed originated in the Mediterranean — particularly on the island of Malta. According to proponents of the Malta theory, a tiny dog with a molera (a soft spot on the head) became established there and traveled on trading ships to European ports. To back up the theory, these historians point out that many paintings produced by European masters include small dogs resembling the Chihuahua. The most famous of these paintings is a fresco in the Sistine Chapel, created by Sandro Botticelli around 1482. Part of a series illustrating the life of Moses, *The Youth of Moses* includes a little dog with a round head, big eyes, large erect ears, and other distinct Chihuahua characteristics. The painting was completed ten years before Columbus dropped anchor in the New World, so it's a sure bet that Botticelli never saw or heard of a Mexican dog, yet he painted something incredibly close to a Chihuahua.

In general, many breeds are considered *square*, meaning that their height is the same as their length. But Chihuahuas are supposed to be just a little longer than they are tall.

Head

To meet the standard, the shape of a Chihuahua's head should look sort of like an apple — rounded but not completely round. Breeders prefer eyes to be large, set well apart, radiant, and shiny — not close together, protruding, smallish, or dull. For perfect proportions, the middle of the eyes lines up with the lowest part of the ears. The following sections break down the rest of the head.

Ears

If a Chi has ideal ears, they'll be at a 45-degree angle to the head when resting, but they'll come to attention, held high, when the dog is alert. A Chihuahua may flatten their ears against their skull when moving fast or when something makes them uneasy.

How a dog's ears stand (for example, relaxed or alertly erect) is called *ear carriage.*

Chihuahua ears must be left as nature made them. *Cropped ears* (surgically shaped or shortened ears) aren't permitted on Chihuahuas in the show ring (and shouldn't be done for pet dogs either). Broken ear cartilage, resulting in a droopy or lopsided ear, is grounds for disqualification from showing, but a floppy ear doesn't stop a Chihuahua from being a fantastic companion.

Muzzle (snout)

The standard calls for a muzzle, or *snout,* that's moderately short, but that doesn't mean shorter is better. A super-short muzzle is incorrect in the Chihuahua, because extremely short muzzles can cause breathing problems and crowd the teeth. Crowded teeth are a big problem in such a tiny mouth and can cause dental problems that are expensive to fix. It's not unusual for Chihuahuas and other Toy breeds to have retained baby teeth that cause crowding when adult teeth start to push their way in. If your Chi puppy has only a few retained teeth, they can be removed at the same time that spay or neuter surgery is performed, but in complicated cases your pup may need a referral to a veterinary dental specialist.

Teeth

If a Chi's upper front teeth meet tightly outside the lower front teeth, the dog has a *scissors bite;* if the upper and lower incisors (front teeth) meet flush with each other when the mouth is closed, the bite is *level.* The scissors bite is the strongest bite and is considered ideal. The teeth wear down faster when the bite is level.

Neck, topline, and body

Ideally, a Chi's neck is of medium length. Too short a neck may be the result of improperly placed shoulder blades, which prevent the dog from moving well (see the section "Gait" later in this chapter). If the head appears to be attached directly to the shoulders, they'll look unbalanced and front-heavy.

On the other hand, an extremely long neck may be a sign that the dog lacks substance (appears weak). It may be accompanied by a lanky body and legs that are too long. You should look for graceful lines. All the dog's parts should be well balanced in relation to one another.

A Chi's *topline* flows along the top of the back from the withers to the root of the tail (where the tail meets the body). Ideally, the topline should be level or straight, without a dip in the middle or a downward or upward slope. The body should appear rounded rather than flat along the sides; a Chihuahua needs a roomy rib cage to house the heart and lungs.

A dog's *conformation* is the shape of the body from the top of the head to the tips of the toes and tail. It encompasses balanced body proportions and size, both of which need to be correct for the breed.

Tail

Figure 2-4 illustrates the Chihuahua's three correct tail positions as well as what a sorry tail tuck looks like. When a Chihuahua puts their tail between their legs, something is wrong. The dog may be timid, frightened, cold, or sick.

A cropped tail or bobtail disqualifies a dog from the show ring, but again, that's an opportunity for you to have a great pet.

Forequarters

Well-laid-back shoulder blades are important in a Chihuahua. (Sloping shoulders can also be described as *well-laid-back*.) That means the shoulder blade, or *scapula*, connects the upper-arm bone with the vertebrae with an obvious backward slope from its bottom end (at the arm) to its top (just in front of the withers). Why are well-laid-back shoulder blades important? Because sloping shoulder blades allow a Chi's front legs to have a good range of motion. Shoulders that lack this slope are called *straight shoulders*. They're faulty because the upper end of the shoulder blade is too far forward — crammed right into the dog's neck. Besides making the neck look too short, straight shoulder blades shorten a dog's gait by limiting the forward reach of their front legs.

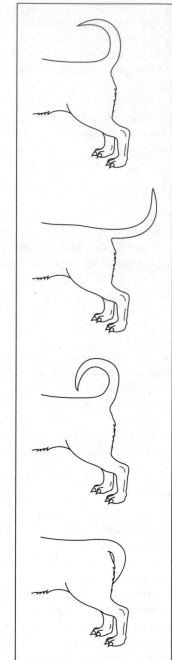

FIGURE 2-4:
Three
correct tail
positions —
and one
sorry tail
tuck.

Here are some more forequarter considerations on the Chihuahua:

>> Ideally, a Chihuahua's front legs should be straight while the toes point forward. Being bowlegged is a fault, as is an *east-west front* (toes pointing to either side) or *toeing in* (toes pointing toward each other).

>> Feet that are elongated like a rabbit's foot or rounded like a cat's paw aren't desirable. Instead, paws should achieve a happy medium between the two, with toes separated but not *splayed* (flat and spread apart).

>> The *pasterns* are the lowest points on a Chi's front legs, just above the feet. They need to be slender and straight.

Hindquarters

To give you a little taste of dog talk, the perfect Chihuahua's rear end is officially described as "Muscular, with hocks well apart, neither out nor in, well let down, firm and sturdy. The feet are as in front." Have you got that? Well the first word, "muscular," is obvious, and what the rest of it means is that a Chihuahua's hind leg has an upper and lower thigh, separated by the *stifle*, or knee joint, which is located on the frontal part of the dog's hind leg (don't forget Figure 2–3). The upper and lower thighs need to have sufficient muscle. Between the stifle joint and the foot is the *hock joint*. Hock joints that are much lower than the middle of the hind leg are better. *Well let down* means the hock joint is close to the ground. Chihuahuas and other small dogs are prone to an orthopedic condition called *patellar luxation*, in which the kneecap slips out of place, causing the dog to walk with a "hitch" or "skip." The kneecap, or patella, should be in the center of the stifle.

Rear legs that are absolutely parallel when viewed from behind are ideal. Hocks turning toward each other, known as *cowhocks*, and hocks turned outward (bowed or spread) are faulty.

A Chi with minor cowhocks may go through life with no problems at all, excelling at dog sports such as agility, but one with severe cowhocks may tire easily when walking or develop joint problems later in life.

Gait

If you walk at a normal pace, a Chihuahua should easily be able to keep up with you by moving along at a smart trot. When they gait properly, they waste no motion — no high-stepping hackney or goose steps. Their feet don't turn in toward each other or wing out to the side. Their movement is lively but effortless, and only their legs are involved. Their back (*topline* in dog lingo) should remain level and not roll from side to side, bob up and down, or appear concave (dip in the topline) or convex (roached back).

One way to check your Chi's movement is to watch while someone else trots them squarely toward you and away from you on a leash. If their movements are ideal, you'll see only the front legs as they approach you and only the rear legs as they move away. When watched from the side, the front legs should reach out but stay close to the ground, and the rear legs (which actually power the dog) should have good drive. None of the legs should interfere with each other. If you're not sure about rear drive, watch them trot away from you again. Can you see the pads of the back feet? If so, they probably have plenty of drive.

When a Chihuahua stands relaxed, the front feet may turn ever so slightly away from each other, toward either side, and still be correct. In fact, if they point perfectly in front when the dog is in a casual stance, chances are they'll point toward each other (toe in) rather than straight ahead when the dog moves.

Temperament

A Chihuahua should be bright, bold, and saucy, but that just scratches the surface. Chihuahua temperament deserves a full chapter. Read all about it in Chapter 3.

Hitting the Chihuahua Standard (or not)

The truth is, no dog — not even an AKC champion — matches every word of the standard. Show dogs just have to come pretty close, or their careers end early. An incorrect bite won't affect your Chihuahua's ability to chew, and Chihuahuas who are fiddle-fronted (bowlegged with the toes turned out) are still agile and enjoy going for brisk walks.

If you've just read about the Chihuahua standard and discovered that your precious pet isn't perfect, don't worry. As long as their faults don't affect their health and mobility, only a top breeder or judge will know (and they'll never tell).

DIGGING UP THE MEXICAN CONNECTION

Chihuahuas are lap warmers, and their purpose is companionship. But in tougher times — before people owned pets for pure pleasure — every creature had to have a function. "Just for fun" didn't cut it. Historians are still uncertain about the precise origins and uses of the earliest Chihuahuas, but legends about their beginnings abound — a combination of fact and fantasy that makes the dog world's littlest breed one of its biggest mysteries.

Relics from ancient Mexico include sculptures of small dogs that archaeologists discovered while studying the remains of the Mayan, Toltec, and Aztec cultures. Although some of the statues (you can see them at the National Museum in Mexico City) don't look much like modern Chihuahuas, and little is known about the Mayans, some relics from the Toltecs have aroused researchers' attention.

The Toltec people lived in Mexico during the ninth century, and possibly even earlier. They had a dog called the Techichi, which some historians believe is the ancestor of today's Chihuahua. Stone carvings of these dogs exist at the Monastery of Huejotzingo (on the highway between Mexico City and Puebla), and they look much more like the modern Chihuahua than the statues that are believed to be of Mayan origin.

REMEMBER

Naturally, it's most important that dogs used for breeding comply with the standard, because their quality is reflected in the next generation. Breeding to their own standard is what makes each breed of dog unique. If breeders ignore the details, soon Chihuahuas, Papillons, Miniature Pinschers, and other Toy dogs will resemble each other, and the individual breeds will gradually fade away. Chapter 4 covers the ins and outs of choosing a breeder, and Chapter 16 provides questions you can ask a breeder to make sure they've taken the proper steps to produce the best dogs.

IN THIS CHAPTER

» Examining Chihuahua traits and attributes

» Exploring a Chihuahua's relationship with other people and dogs

» Comparing coat lengths

» Focusing on male and female personalities

» Dealing with challenging dispositions

Chapter 3

Perusing the Particulars of Chihuahua Charm

What makes the world's smallest dog one of our nation's most popular pets? The Chihuahua's perky personality, of course. Yes, these unique dogs have more going for them than a serious case of the cutes. Chihuahuas are protective despite their size and react appropriately to their owners' moods. They are affectionate, travel well, and adore creature comforts.

In this chapter, we talk about the traits of typical Chihuahuas — complete with all their characteristics and quirks. We discuss how Chihuahuas usually interact with their families and how they react to other animals; the personality differences between Chihuahuas with short and long coats; and what must go right so your Chi can mature with the personality traits typical of the breed.

Getting Acquainted with this Little Dog's Big Personality

The breed standard for Chihuahuas describes their temperament as "terrier-like." What does that mean? Well, most small terriers are feisty and brave to a fault. Terriers are alert to their surroundings, quick to defend home and family, and positive that they're tougher than the biggest dog on the block, making them alert watchdogs and energetic, playful companions. Chihuahuas share many of those qualities.

Of course, as with any breed, Chihuahua personalities vary. Lots are feisty or outgoing, but plenty of others are gentle and demure. To make sure there's not a mismatch between you and the pup you take home, tell the breeder about your personality, lifestyle, and what you're looking for in a dog to help ensure that you and your Chi become best friends.

The following sections break down the individual characteristics of the Chihuahua.

Petite protectors

When your Chi trots down the street with you, they appear animated and confident — a bantam rooster with proud posture.

Most Chihuahuas don't realize that they're small. Given the opportunity, they may approach big dogs in play, and occasionally — especially if the large dogs are invading their territory — they may react aggressively.

WARNING

Although a tiny terror, barking and running full force, sends some gigantic dogs packing, this situation isn't safe. People with Toy breeds must exercise caution around strange dogs, because even the friendliest medium-sized dog can seriously injure a small one during rough play, and big dogs may respond in kind to a Chihuahua's challenge to prove who's the toughest.

That same bravado makes Chihuahuas good watchdogs. They're alert and have keen hearing, and they possess a bark that's loud and shrill for their size. To top it off, they can tell the difference between a family member's footsteps or a stranger's stride nearing the door, and they know when a vehicle other than the family car pulls up to the house.

Chihuahuas have an unjust reputation for excessive barking. Most bark an alarm when a stranger approaches, but when properly trained (see Part 3), they won't be any noisier than most other breeds.

Comfort-loving creatures

Chihuahuas are masters of the art of relaxation. Indoors, your Chi will play bathing beauty, stretching out on the carpet right where a sunbeam shines through the window. On gray days, they'll seek out another source of warmth, napping near a heating vent or in their own bed — that is, if your lap isn't available.

TIP

You'll know your Chihuahua is a little chilly when they curl up into a ball with their nose under one leg. Dogs do that because it allows them to breathe in air preheated by the warmth of their bodies. Inhaling the warm air helps keep them cozy.

Heat-seeking house dogs

Most Chihuahuas (some exceptions live in semitropical climates) prefer indoor living to the great outdoors. Lovers of warmth and softness, they consider cold concrete and dewy grass hardships to be endured, not enjoyed. (If your Chi is a smooth coat, they chill easily, sometimes shivering from ear tips to toes. See the later section "Comparing Long and Smooth Coats.") They also hate rain and snow, and it's no wonder. Imagine being so low to the ground that every step you take splashes cold water onto your bare belly! Of course, you must take your pet outside no matter what the weather so they can eliminate on schedule (see Chapter 10). (Chapter 5 covers accessories you can purchase that help keep your Chi comfortable.)

On cold days, it's amusing to see how fast some Chihuahuas get their business over with so they can rush back to their warm homes. When Jackie lived in New York, she carried Manchita to the curb during winter; otherwise, Manchita squatted the second her toes touched the sidewalk!

Spirited, but not hyper

Although they're playful, Chihuahuas aren't super-active little dogs. In fact, most of them don't have an especially high activity level.

Rather than racing around the living room, your Chi prefers spending part of their day on your lap or burrowed beneath a blanket. Their attitude about exercise is easygoing — ready to play when you are but content to relax when you aren't in an active mood.

As Chihuahuas mature, they tend to take on the same activity level as their people. The same dog that acts frisky when around their active family will turn into a contented cuddler when grandma and grandpa dog-sit.

TIP

Even though Chihuahuas prefer human company, properly trained adult dogs can occupy themselves for hours without looking for trouble or demanding attention. The chapters of Part 3 cover training exercises, including helping your dog feel comfortable when alone.

Unusually adaptable

Chihuahuas thrive in living quarters ranging from country estates to studio apartments. Don't worry about stairs or elevators; after you introduce your pup to them (see Chapter 9), they will handle them just fine.

Because Chihuahuas are so small, they don't need fenced yards or kennel runs to get their exercise. You can give yours a few toys (see Chapter 5) and they'll play active games right in the living room. Or better yet, you can join in the fun, and both of you will get some exercise. We suggest some games you can play together in Chapter 8. But don't assume that your Chi won't enjoy playing outdoors at all. If you have a safely fenced yard and are there to supervise so that a hawk or owl doesn't swoop down to carry off a Chihuahua snack, it's more than likely your Chi will have just as much fun racing around and chasing squirrels as any other dog.

TIP

For extra protection against raptors or coyotes, you can purchase a protective coat, such as the CoyoteVest.

Chihuahuas are good travelers and adjust to moving better than many breeds. They feel at home wherever their people are. That attitude, plus their small size, makes Chihuahuas ideal for people who move frequently and for retired couples who crisscross the country in RVs.

WARNING

If you move often, remember that finding rental housing that allows dogs can be difficult. Jackie's daughters faced that problem when they took Manchita to college, but they solved it by taking her along to meet potential landlords. When one landlord saw how petite and polite Manchita was, he made an exception. And the girls did their part by keeping her in a well-equipped playpen (the type meant for an infant) when they weren't home to supervise (see Chapter 5).

Sensitive supporters

Chihuahuas can sense their owners' moods and will react accordingly. When you arrive home after receiving a promotion, your Chi will recognize right away that something wonderful happened and dance around you with glee. But they'll also sense when you're sick or sad, and they'll try to be consoling. Stories abound about Chihuahuas that stopped playing and had to be reminded to eat and even eliminate when family members were bedridden with serious illnesses. These companions tried to spend all their time with the sick persons.

Quick studies when trained with TLC

Although housetraining any dog (see Chapters 10 and 11) can seem like a time-consuming chore, the training you give your Chi should be pure pleasure for both of you. Chihuahuas love being center stage and are eager to learn — provided that the training is gentle, upbeat, and complete with plenty of positive reinforcement (read: praise and treats). Because they're so people oriented, Chihuahuas have longer attention spans (when they're past the puppy stage) than many other breeds. If you make training fun, your pup will focus their big eyes on you and pirouette happily every time you praise them.

After learning a new trick, your Chi will never forget it. They may, however, try to improvise. Some Chis are so clever that as soon as they perfect a trick, they invent a new way to ham it up. Many Chihuahuas are successful in competitive sports such as obedience and agility. You can read all about those activities in Chapter 12.

Building Furry Friendships

Although they can be sociable, Chihuahuas don't extend the paw of friendship to anyone and everyone they meet. They like to take their time getting to know people first. Here's what to expect and how to advise newcomers about getting on your Chihuahua's good side.

Cautious compadres

Typical adult Chihuahuas are sassy with strangers and discriminating about making new friends. Few Chihuahuas, no matter how well socialized they are, run up to a houseguest and vie for attention. Instead, your Chi makes sure you know a stranger is in the house by barking at the intruder until you say "Enough!" or "Quiet!" (see Chapter 10). After that, they'll probably take a position with a view of your visitor from across the room for several minutes until deciding that the person deserves canine company. Then their likely approach will be a slow and gradual offering of furry friendship — provided that your guest lets the dog make the first move and resists the temptation to grab at them.

TIP

To speed up the buddy-making process between your friends and your dog, tell your guests to ignore your Chi until the dog approaches them. Then they can reciprocate by tickling the dog on the chest or under the chin. These actions are less threatening than reaching over the Chi to pet their head. Chihuahuas don't like it when strangers swoop down on them from above like hungry hawks. If your friends squat down and let your Chi check them out, they'll soon become best buddies.

ENVIRONMENT BEATS HEREDITY

Although caution in choosing friends is a Chihuahua trait, not every adult Chihuahua is persnickety about meeting new people. Jackie's three-pound Chi, Manchita, made a merry dash into the arms of anyone who showed interest in her. When she was a puppy, Jackie's daughters were teenagers who had friends coming and going daily. All the kids fussed over Manchita during her formative months, so she grew up believing that every human was a potential petting machine.

A Chihuahua probably will make friends much faster on neutral ground (such as a park) than in their own home, because they won't feel the need to defend their territory.

Close companions

Awake or asleep, Chis want to be near you. They are affectionate animals and will dog your footsteps as you move from room to room. Don't downplay the Chihuahua need for togetherness! People new to the breed can find it overwhelming. Some breeds always seem in search of mischief, but typical adult Chihuahuas are content with the company of their people (see Figure 3-1 for an example). After your Chi grows out of the busy puppy stage, they're happiest when you and they are close — preferably touching. An accomplished cuddler, the Chihuahua lies on your lap for as long as you'll let them, helping you relax as you scroll through your phone or watch television. They adore being stroked when you have a free hand, and a gentle massage transports them to puppy paradise. Don't be surprised if they roll over to beg for a belly rub!

After all that togetherness, your Chi may not want you to leave them, even at bedtime. Many Chihuahuas sleep in their owners' bedrooms, but not necessarily in their beds. You can train them to snooze in their own soft bed or crate, which is where they'll curl up when the lights go out (see Chapter 10). It's safer than sharing space with them in your bed. Sure, they'd rather snuggle up with you, but they can easily get hurt if they fall off the bed or you roll over onto them during the night, especially if your Chi is ultra-small.

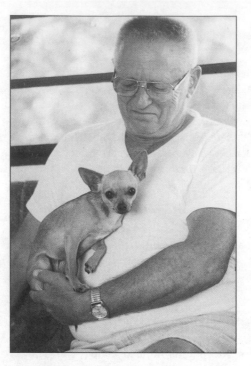

FIGURE 3-1:
Chihuahuas
need
affection
and thrive
on
together-
ness.

Chihuahuas are one of the longest-lived breeds. And that's great news for the humans who love them!

**TECHNICAL
STUFF**

Friend to (most) other critters

Your Chihuahua may sass strange dogs when out for a walk (basic manners training cures that; see Chapters 9 and 10), but they should get along with the other pets in your home. After you make the introductions (see Chapter 5) and the pets get used to each other, your Chi likely will curl up with your cat, ignore your caged birds, and become buddies with your bigger dog.

Don't be surprised if they show a jealous streak over who gets the most attention, though, shouldering aside other pets to get the notice they consider their due. It's not unusual for Chihuahuas to become the family's top dog despite their tiny size. Be sure to supervise the animals closely until they get used to each other and obviously get along.

WARNING

You should keep little critters like hamsters, gerbils, geckos, and small birds out of your Chi's reach, or pouncing on them may be just too tempting.

One Chihuahuaism is that the breed recognizes and almost always welcomes other Chihuahuas. Even though your Chi may seem sassy or even scared around strange dogs, in most cases they'll become ecstatic at the sight of another Chihuahua, and the two will quickly make friends.

Comparing Long and Smooth Coats

When deciding whether you want a long-coated or a smooth-coated Chihuahua (see Chapter 2), you should consider more than just the length of coat you want to cuddle. That's because the differences are more than skin deep. In general (with some exceptions), slight personality differences exist between the two coat types. Here are the more obvious differences:

>> **Long coats can handle the cold better.** Although no Chihuahua can stand the cold for long, many long coats enjoy a short walk in brisk weather and may even play in the snow (provided it's only a couple of inches deep). Not the case with smooth coats. Chihuahuas with short hair are miserable in cold weather and should wear a sweater outdoors on chilly days, even when going for a short walk (see Chapter 5).

>> **Smooth coats cuddle closer.** A short-coated Chi will enjoy feeling the warmth of your body on their nearly bald belly as they lie on your lap while you read or watch television. Their long-coated counterpart wants your company, too, but is more likely to sit beside you rather than on you. Differences also are noticeable if you decide to bed down with them. A smooth coat curls up under the covers, and a long coat usually lies on top of the blankets. (That said, Kim's long-coated "Chihuameranian" loved to burrow under the covers, and Kim came to enjoy her tiny canine footwarmer at night.)

>> **Long coats shed less.** No, that isn't a misprint. Long-coated Chihuahuas shed seasonally — usually twice a year. During those periods, they lose a lot of hair quite quickly. But a few good brushings, plus vacuuming the carpets and furniture, put an end to the problem for several months (see Chapter 7). Smooth coats, on the other hand, shed old hair and replace it with new hair all the time. Consequently, a few tiny hairs will always work their way into your clothes, furniture, and carpets.

>> **Smooth coats are wash and go dogs.** Unless they are show dogs, who may get some special trimming to perfect their outline, smooth coats are good to go with a quick weekly brushing and occasional bath. Long coats can benefit from occasional visits to the groomer to clean and neaten their neck ruff, "pants," and tail plume, or you can bathe and trim them yourself as needed.

>> **Long coats are a bit more reserved.** Smooth coats often are more outgoing and accept new friends faster than long coats. Although long coats like attention, too, they tend to be a little more reserved and need more time to warm up to friendly strangers.

TECHNICAL STUFF

Long coats and smooth coats often are *littermates*, which means they're brothers and sisters born in the same litter. According to an old wives' tale, at least one long-coated Chihuahua appears in every litter of smooth coats — a gift from Mother Nature to keep short-coated littermates warm. Although this is a sweet story, it doesn't always happen that way. Besides, smooth-coated pups don't need the help. They do just fine by cuddling up to their mom and to each other.

Observing Male and Female Traits

You can find plenty of Chihuahua lore concerning which sex makes the better pet. Some people favor males while others extol the virtues of females. The truth is that the personalities of a puppy's parents are a much better indicator of potential temperament than which sex the pup happens to be. Even so, you should be aware of a few characteristic differences between the sexes before you decide on the dog you want:

>> Unspayed females have heat cycles (usually twice a year), and during that time they can leave blood on your clothing and furniture if you don't have them in dog pants (sort of like a diaper). And even if your female is indoors almost all the time, neighborhood males still can smell her enticing scent and serenade her. You can't let her out of your sight when she's in season, or it could result in an unwanted pregnancy — or worse if her suitor is big enough to injure her.

>> An unneutered male has a sex drive that makes him follow a female's sexy scent until he finds her — no matter how big she is or how many larger dogs also are competing for her favor. Consequently, he can become quite the escape artist and put himself in life-threatening situations. And if he can't escape, he may instead become affectionate with a throw pillow or someone's shin (see Chapter 11).

>> Male and female Chihuahuas are equally affectionate and appealing, and initially take about the same amount of time to housetrain. But many males (if they haven't been neutered) disregard their training when they get old enough to lift their legs and mark their property (a sign of sexual maturity) and may regress to urinating in the house. You can correct the problem by catching it early and returning the male to his crate-training puppy schedule (see Chapter 10) for a few weeks. If that doesn't do the trick, you can find help for hard cases in Chapter 11. Neutering can also help reduce the incidence of marking in the home in mature dogs.

TIP

The good news is that spaying or neutering nullifies much of the behavior in the list above, making males and females equally excellent as pets. Chapter 13 discusses the altering procedure and its importance for your pet.

Checking a Chi Pup's Résumé

Several things must go right before a Chihuahua puppy grows up to be typical of their breed. Chihuahua puppies are most likely to mature with characteristics that people admire if they have the following advantages:

>> Well bred (comes from a breeder who emphasizes temperament and health in tandem with looks); see Chapters 1 and 2)

>> Adequately cared for on a daily basis (a clean environment and quality food, for instance)

>> Socialized by a caring breeder

>> Further socialized by their new family (see Chapter 9)

>> Raised with attention and affection

>> Taught basic house manners (see Chapter 10)

>> Never abused or neglected

If any of these necessities are missing during a dog's upbringing, or if they are neglected or abused, they may be less likely to behave like a typical Chihuahua. Unfortunately, Chihuahuas often get a bad rap from people who meet members of the breed who grew up without these benefits and decide that all Chihuahuas behave in unpleasant ways.

WARNING

The following undesirable traits frequently plague Chihuahuas who are poorly bred, undernourished, unsocialized, untrained, or unloved:

>> Timid, shy, or extremely nervous

>> Frail and sickly

>> Temperamental

>> Refuse to accept friendly strangers

>> Yappy

» Aggressive (snaps at people without warning and for no reason)

» Possessive (defends their food dish, toys, or favorite chair, even from their owners)

Oh my! That's a scary list, isn't it? I bet it doesn't sound like anything you want in a dog. Don't panic. In Chapter 4, we tell you how to avoid the unhappy traits and find a Chihuahua with the potential to grow up with all the breed's best characteristics.

2

Fitting a Compact Canine into Your Life

Choose a healthy Chihuahua with a great disposition and a perfect personality for your family.

Welcome your new pet into your life and integrate them into your routine.

Feed your pet the right food for their condition and lifestyle, from puppyhood to old age.

Keep your baby beautiful and clean with proper grooming.

Exercise your tiny dog properly to ensure safety and good health, all while having fun and strengthening your bond.

Chapter **4**

Choosing Your Ideal Chihuahua

hew! You've made the really big decisions (if you haven't, head back to Chapters 1–3). You're sure you want a dog, and you think a Chihuahua is the breed for you. But you aren't finished yet. Now you have to make the most important decision of all — picking the one special Chihuahua to share your life.

Easy now. Don't rush. Picking your pet may be your only opportunity, outside of marriage, to actually choose a member of your family! Not all Chihuahuas and Chihuahua providers are created equal, so in this chapter, let's go looking together. We can help you find a good breeder and a healthy dog with that charming Chihuahua character, as well as help you understand all the paperwork involved in the process, such as the sales contract, AKC registration applications, and pedigrees.

Buying from a Breeder

The first step toward finding a fabulous four-legged family member is locating a respected breeder. The best Chi breeders usually specialize in Chihuahuas, devoting years to preserving the breed's finest traits (see Chapter 2). Good breeders are usually members of the Chihuahua Club of America (CCA; www. chihuahuaclubofamerica.com), and perhaps local dog clubs as well. Whether they have just a few adult dogs or a large kennel, their breeding stock is excellent, they give their puppies plenty of affection, and they probably exhibit at dog shows (see Chapter 12).

Breeder isn't a bad word (though there are some bad breeders). Without great breeders, you wouldn't have the joy of living with your Chihuahua. Responsible breeders pour their heart and soul into producing puppies who are happy, healthy, beautiful examples of their breed. They love them and want the best for them throughout their lives. A good breeder can be your best friend as you bring up your Chihuahua pup as well as for the rest of their life, and if you ever can't keep your dog, the breeder will take them back in a heartbeat, no matter what their age, and make sure they're cared for.

Here are several general suggestions to help you find a good kennel in your area: After you find one, the following sections take you all the way through the process, from visiting a breeder to picking out your puppy:

>> **Visit the Chihuahua Club of America website** (www. chihuahuaclubofamerica.com) **to find the regional Chihuahua club closest to you (click on CCA Member Clubs) or a list of member-breeders**. If you're in Canada, go to the Chihuahua Club of Canada website: https:// chihuahuaclubofcanada.ca/. British Chihuahua fans can learn more through the British Chihuahua Club: https:// www.the-british-chihuahua-club.org.uk/.

>> **Talk to local veterinarians (see Chapter 13).** They know which breeders in your area have healthy dogs with terrific temperaments.

>> **Find the all-breed kennel club nearest you.** Almost every sizable city has an all-breed kennel club. A search of the American Kennel Club's website (www.akc.org) can help you find one or more such clubs in your area (click on Find a Dog Club at the bottom of the page). Local dog trainers may also be able to point you toward one. Contact the all-breed club to find out if any of its members are Chihuahua breeders.

>> **Go to a dog show.** Good breeders travel many miles to show their dogs, and they'll be glad to talk to you after they finish competing. (Don't approach them before they've gone into the ring!)

REMEMBER

Dog shows are fun and educational even if you have no interest in showing your dog. With luck, you'll see several Chihuahuas in the show ring. Watching them may help you decide what traits appeal to you. If several of your favorites come from the same breeder, you know where to look first. Find out from your local all-breed kennel club or the AKC when shows are scheduled in your area (see Chapter 12 for more).

Visiting the breeder

Most reputable breeders cherish their Chihuahuas as a hobby, not a business. They're proud to show you their facilities and tell you about their dogs. Just be sure to contact them ahead of time to set up appointments. Breeders don't keep regular business hours like pet shops do, and their facilities are almost always attached to their homes. Meeting a breeder and seeing their dogs is a lot like visiting someone socially.

TIP

Making a list of what you want in a Chihuahua and letting the breeders know your criteria before you visit simplifies things. For example, tell the breeder if you're set on a male or a female, a smooth or a long coat, a certain color, and whether you plan to show your dog (see Chapter 12). That way, a breeder can save you a trip if they don't have what you want, and they may be able to send you to another kennel where your dream dog awaits. Try visiting a few breeders and seeing several puppies before making a decision. It's hard not to fall for the first cute puppy you see, but doing your homework and being patient will help you find the best pup for you and your family.

Evaluating breeders and their dogs

Locating a Chihuahua breeder and setting up an appointment is only the first step. Just because you locate a breeder doesn't mean they are reputable or right for you. Here's how to make sure you've found a good breeder (see Chapter 16 for more evaluation advice):

» If you see puppies of several different breeds on the premises, or notice that the puppies are treated like merchandise, don't purchase a puppy from that kennel. The best breeders specialize in one or two breeds. They usually exhibit their dogs at shows or compete with them in dog sports rather than simply breeding to produce a never-ending stream of puppies. They may breed a litter only once every couple of years.

» Healthy puppies come from clean kennels. Check out the floor or grass the puppies are playing on. Has it been washed or pooper-scooped recently, or is it covered with miniature messes? Sneak a peek at the food and water dishes. Is the food dish clean, or is ancient goop stuck to the sides? Is the water clear or has yellow slime invaded the bottom of the dish? Use your nose. Sure, you'll catch a whiff of fresh puppy poop, but if the stench is stale or overwhelming, don't buy from that kennel, even if you feel sorry for the dogs.

» The puppy play area shouldn't be bare; puppies should have toys to play with or even an entire puppy play area with mobiles, obstacles to climb, tunnels to run through, and more. Toys and play stimulate puppies physically and mentally, motivating them to exercise, have fun together, and learn.

» Pay attention to the breeder's adult dogs in the home. Are they nice to be around or yappy and annoying? Whatever they're like is probably what your pup will be like too.

» A good breeder knows the puppies' personalities inside out and should gladly discuss them with you. They're proud of their breeding and spend enough time with their dogs to know them well.

>> A good breeder should give you the third degree about how you'll care for one of their pups (see the following section). Don't be insulted! They want to be sure that a Chi is the right breed for your family and that you'll give the puppy a good home. Steer clear of money-hungry puppy vendors who pretend Chihuahuas are ideal pets for everyone. It simply isn't so.

>> Chihuahua puppies need to stay with their dam (female parent) and littermates until they're 12 weeks old. Beware of any breeder who's willing to let pups leave for their new home sooner than that. Toy puppies benefit from spending extra time with their mother and littermates, learning how to be good dogs as well as how to be good companions to people. At 12 weeks, they are often more confident and friendly, bigger, and better prepared to adapt to their new home. Bonus: a good breeder will have already started socializing and housetraining them for you.

>> A good breeder will tell you that if you ever have to give up your Chihuahua, for any reason or at any age, they will take the dog back and find them a new home.

>> A good breeder may feed you endless data about how to raise and care for a Chihuahua. You may get annoyed by all the *you shoulds,* but cut the overprotective breeder some slack. You're talking to a caring person who willingly shares information and who someday, when you need advice, will be willing to help.

Do you like the breeder? Okay, maybe not for a best friend, but well enough to call on if you need advice about health or training? Or do you hope you never need to talk to the breeder again? If you have a bad feeling about the breeder, the facility, or any of the dogs, trust your intuition and look elsewhere for your puppy.

Oh gee, why the third degree?

All responsible breeders will grill you about your intentions and your situation, so don't be surprised or insulted when you're asked about your lifestyle. Instead, be glad you found a breeder who truly cares about the puppies' welfare. It all evens out in the end. After all, you should be evaluating the breeder while they assess you.

Here are some questions breeders may ask you, and why they want to know:

>> **What made you decide on a Chihuahua?** The breeder is making sure you chose the breed because you truly like Toy dogs and especially Chihuahuas — not just because they're "stylish" or you think a little dog costs less to feed or is easier for your two-year-old to tote around.

>> **Have you had dogs before? What happened to them?** Good breeders want their puppies to have loving, permanent homes. If you've never had a dog before, the breeder probably wants to fill you in on the facts of dog ownership just to make sure you know what you're getting into. If you had a beloved dog who eventually died of old age, the breeder will be happy to sell you a puppy. But if your previous dog ran loose and got killed by a car or died of a disease you could've prevented through vaccination or appropriate care, a responsible breeder likely won't sell you a dog.

>> **What are your work hours? How much time do you spend at home?** The breeder wants to be sure the puppy will get enough attention. Puppies must be fed and walked on a regular schedule to become housetrained (see Chapters 8 and 10).

>> **How old are your children? Are they gentle with animals?** Tots and Chihuahuas aren't a good match. Toddlers are too young and uncoordinated to safely handle small dogs, and Chihuahuas are too tiny for rough handling. Teasing by youngsters also turns nice dogs into holy terrors.

>> **Do you have a fenced yard?** Although fenced yards make dog ownership easier, many Chihuahua owners live in apartments or condos and exercise their dogs by walking them on leash (see Chapter 9). Tell the breeder how you plan to exercise your Chihuahua and the steps you'll take to keep them safe from cars, bigger animals, and other risks.

>> **Is everyone in your family looking forward to getting a Chihuahua?** It isn't fair to the Chihuahua if someone in the family despises little dogs but was outvoted. A dog can sense the disdain immediately; the person may go so far as to sabotage socialization or training. Everyone should be on board the Chihuahua train before you bring one home.

>> **What do you expect from your Chihuahua?** Tell the breeder if you want a dog solely as a companion or if you also want to show your dog or compete in dog sports. Will your Chihuahua live only with adults, or do you have kids in the family? Will your dog live at home or travel in your RV or big rig? Will you have your pet spayed or neutered, or are you considering using the dog for breeding?

REMEMBER

The more the breeder knows about your plans for the pup, the better they can help you make a selection. After all, the breeder has observed the litter since birth and knows each puppy's personality. You may be surprised and delighted by their matchmaking skills.

SMALL SIZE DOESN'T MEAN SMALL PRICE TAG

Just because Chihuahuas are little, don't expect the purchase price to be less than what you'd pay for a larger dog. Chihuahuas have small litters, and the cost of breeding them (including stud service, health testing, and possibly a Caesarean section) is high. Raising healthy, outgoing Toy dogs takes a lot of time and energy. Nonetheless, good breeders don't expect to make a profit. They do it for love, not money.

When tempted to buy a bargain puppy, remember that the purchase price is only a small part of what you'll spend on your dog during their lifetime. It's smarter to pay more and get a dog who makes your heart sing. (For more on pricing and other basics, refer to Chapter 1.)

Getting the pick of the litter

Gotta have the pick of the litter! But which one is it? Everyone wants the pick of the litter, but it's a different puppy for different people:

> To the show exhibitor, the pick is the puppy who comes closest to the description of the ideal Chihuahua in the breed standard (see Chapter 2).
>
> To the woman who lives alone in the city, the pick is the puppy who alerts instantly to strange sounds.
>
> To the young couple with kids in elementary school, the pick is the largest and liveliest puppy.
>
> To the retired couple in the condo, the pick is the quiet puppy who loves to cuddle.

The truth is, the pick is the puppy who appeals to you — provided they're healthy and have the right temperament to share your lifestyle (see Figure 4-1). If you're dealing with a show breeder but have no intention of showing, you don't need the puppy the breeder considers the pick of the litter. Chances are the breeder won't sell that pup to you anyway! But one of that pup's brothers or sisters may make you the perfect pet.

FIGURE 4-1: Pick a puppy who appeals to you on first sight but check health and disposition before making a purchase.

REMEMBER

At the best kennels, show puppies and pet puppies come from the same litters. In fact, the last choice in a top breeder's litter may be of higher quality than the first choice in a mediocre litter.

TIP

If you want to buy a puppy with show potential, don't be surprised if the breeder insists on keeping that one until they are six months old. That's perfectly normal. Why? Because it takes that long to be positive (well, almost positive, anyway) that a puppy has what it takes to become an AKC champion.

Whether the breeder is allowing you to pick out your own puppy (sometimes they don't!) or you are asking the breeder for input, the following sections offer helpful suggestions to guide you on the big day: puppy picking day!

Playing with all the puppies

Have a plan when meeting the puppies, or canine Cupid will sting you with an arrow and you might end up with the wrong one. The following suggestions help you choose a puppy with your head as well as your heart:

>> **Trust your instincts.** Did one puppy catch your eye immediately? Do you keep going back to that one even though you want to give them all equal time? Are you already naming that pup in your mind? First impressions are important, and love at first sight can last a lifetime. Just take the time to make sure your furry favorite is healthy and has a pleasing personality.

>> **Be observant.** Watch the puppies play together for several minutes without human interference. (Chihuahua litters are small, so you can probably observe two to four littermates interacting with each other.) Your best bet is a puppy in the middle of the pack — neither the bossy pup nor the scaredy-cat.

>> **Eye the eyes.** The puppy's eyes should be bright, alert, and clear of mucus. Don't mistake clear tears for mucus. Many Chihuahuas (and other Toy breeds) have tear ducts that are too small, so tears occasionally fall from their eyes. A telltale sign is a small water stain at the inner corner of each eye. This isn't a sign of sickness, but you shouldn't

convince yourself that the stains will fade away as the puppy matures. More than likely, the dog will always sport the tear stains, but this won't affect their health or happiness.

>> **Check the coat.** Bald may be beautiful on your husband, but it's a bad sign on a puppy. A healthy coat is glossy and smooth to the touch, with no bald patches. Smooth coats without an undercoat may have thin hair on their temples and practically bald bellies, but no puppy should have skin showing through on the back or sides.

>> **Know the nose.** The puppy's breathing should be quiet and rhythmic, and the nostrils free of mucus.

>> **Watch the puppies move when they play.** Despite a bit of baby clumsiness, puppies should appear quick, bouncy, and agile. Puppies standing up straight on legs that look strong enough to carry their bodies is a good sign.

>> **Check the teeth and running gear.** If a show career is in your puppy's future, don't forget to check their teeth for a *scissors bite* (the upper-front teeth meet tightly outside the lower-front teeth). And although it isn't easy to do with a tiny puppy, try to evaluate their *gait* (the way they move at a trot) by watching them move both straight toward you and directly away from you. Front legs moving parallel with each other as they trot toward you and rear legs moving parallel with each other as they trot away are good signs. Study the breed standard (see Chapter 2) before selecting a potential show dog.

REMEMBER

When choosing your Chihuahua, avoid orphan puppies a litter of only one, because hand-raised orphans and solo pups get everything they want instantly. Consequently, they don't learn how to handle frustration or how to get along with other dogs. In general, puppies raised by their *dams* (their mothers), along with at least one littermate, make better companions.

Snagging some one-on-one time

After watching the litter play together, it's time to meet your favorites up close and personal. But first you need to know how to hold a puppy. Novices often hold puppies high, with their back legs dangling, but dogs hate being held that way. Instead, when lifting a puppy (or an adult Chihuahua, for that matter), use both hands. Place one hand under the chest and brace their bottom in your other hand, and then cradle the puppy close to your body. Little puppies are wiggly and a fall can be fatal, so keep your grip gentle but firm. And don't let your fingers push the pup's elbows outward or squeeze their front legs together, because either error could damage the dog.

WARNING

Never lift a puppy by its front legs. Not only is it painful, but it also can cause permanent injury to the puppy's shoulders.

TIP

Sit on the floor to play with the puppies during this first meeting. You'll enjoy it more because you won't have to worry about dropping a pup, and the breeder's blood pressure will normalize.

Now you're ready to see how well each puppy relates to people — especially you. Follow these steps to meet your potential pups:

1. **Ask if you can take your favorite puppy or puppies out of sight (one puppy at a time) of the breeder, their dam, and their littermates so you can check out their temperaments.**

   Begin by giving each puppy at least two full minutes to survey their surroundings (time it or you won't wait long enough). Watch their attitude while they explore. Are they curious or fearful? Lively or laid back?

2. **Sit down and try coaxing the pup into coming to you.**

   When they do, praise them. Then get up, move away slowly, and try talking them into following you. If they do, that's a good sign that they enjoy human company, including yours.

3. **Show the puppy a small ball or other dog toy just the right size for them, and roll it about 3 feet away from (never toward) them.**

   Do they seem interested? If they don't respond right away, that's okay. It may take three or four tries before they understand the game. Do they eventually chase or follow the rolling toy and examine it when it stops moving? That's a good sign that they learn quickly, aren't afraid to try new things, and are willing to play on your team. If they pick up the toy in their mouth and carry it part of the way back to you, that's even better.

4. **Pick up the puppy and cradle them upright, held securely against your body.**

   They should feel strong (for their size) and solid in your hand. The puppy may struggle briefly, but should soon relax and enjoy the attention, maybe even sniffing or licking you. These are signs that they have a good temperament and have been well socialized by the breeder.

5. **Try a little TLC before giving up.**

When you pick up the puppy, do they stiffen with fear or struggle nonstop? Neither reaction is good, but don't give up too soon. The puppy may just need a little more time. Talk to them while stroking them soothingly. Does that tight little body relax? Good. If not, they may have missed out on early socialization. Pick another puppy.

No matter how super a puppy looks and tests, make sure some chemistry exists between you. During your first couple of months together, both of you go through a period of adjustment. But a Chihuahua who charms a smile out of you makes all the adjustments seem minor.

Preparing for potential problem pups

Not every puppy will ace your tests from the previous sections. Here are some signs that may warn you away from a pup:

>> **Don't buy an unhealthy puppy.** This could include a skinny puppy or one with pimples or raw patches on the skin, excessive dander, mucus seeping from the nostrils or the corner of the eyes, or diarrhea.

>> **Please don't purchase a puppy out of pity.** When an active litter of puppies vies for your attention but one hangs back or hides in a corner, they aren't an abused baby in need of comfort. If the breeder neglected or mistreated the pups, every one of them would shy away from people. The truth is, that puppy has a temperament problem. Yes, they may improve a little with time and a lot of socialization

(see Chapter 9), but their apprehensive attitude is probably a permanent problem.

>> **Go for impy, not wimpy.** Don't pick a puppy who shies away from littermates' games. It's tempting to take home a little underdog, but resist as hard as you can. Pups who allow themselves to be terrorized by their littermates seldom become confident pets.

>> **Avoid anxious Annie.** Don't buy a puppy who runs away or crouches fearfully in one spot when you take them out of sight of the breeder and four-legged family. It's okay if it takes the pup a couple minutes to get their bearings, but after a few moments, expect them to show some interest in their surroundings and be curious about you.

A puppy who tests well probably will make someone a wonderful pet, but that someone may not be you. How do you feel when you play with the pup? Are they the tiny soul mate you've been searching for? Or are you thinking of buying them only because they tested well and you're tired of Chihuahua shopping? When you're tempted to think that way, remember that you're choosing family. Keep looking until you know you've found your canine counterpart.

Meeting the extended family

When looking at a litter of puppies, ask to see their dam and any other close relatives who live with the breeder. With luck, you may get to meet the puppies' granddam, a couple of aunts or uncles, or even an older brother or sister from a previous litter. You may also see the sire, but don't be disappointed if he lives far away from the breeder. If the sire isn't on the premises, the breeder should be able to show you his pedigree and pictures or videos of him.

A mature female dog is called a *bitch*, no matter how sweet she is! And when used for breeding, she's a *brood bitch*. The mother of a litter of puppies is the *dam*; the father is the *sire*.

The more of your potential puppy's close relatives you meet, the better. Why? Because their attitudes and appearances give you a good indication of how the puppy may turn out. Choose a puppy from a breeder whose dogs are enjoyable to be around.

Considering online purchases

What if the breeder you're considering buying from lives in another city or state and you can't meet them or their dogs in person? Is it safe to buy a Chihuahua pup sight unseen?

The answer is . . . maybe. Pets are big business and in short supply, and that means scammers abound. Here are some tips to help you sort out who's good and who to avoid:

» Don't be swayed by a pretty website. Get references from other buyers and a veterinarian and check them out. If you know someone in the area where the breeder lives, ask them to meet the breeder and dogs and give you a report on cleanliness and friendliness.

» Use your Google skills to confirm the breeder's claims. Are they really a member of the parent club? Do they post their dogs' health information on websites such as Orthopedic Foundation for Animals (ofa.org) and Canine Health Information Center (akcchf.org)? How long have they been at their current address?

» Do breeders have any complaints lodged against them by the USDA (which oversees commercial breeders) or the Better Business Bureau? Search their name, address, and phone number in combination with the words "scam" or "complaint."

» Ask the breeder to email photos or videos of their dogs, as well as copies of health certifications. Set up an online meeting with the breeder in the presence of their dogs and puppies. Scammers usually can't meet that requirement and will turn you down.

» Red flags include the following phrases, which indicates the breeders are churning out puppies for profit with no care for their future well-being: "Next-day delivery," "puppies always available," "low, low prices," "sale," "champion bloodlines," "teacup," "rare," and "extra-tiny." See the nearby sidebar "The teacup lie" for more information on deceptive marketing.

>> Avoid offers for free Chihuahuas "if you pay shipping" or from sellers who want payment in the form of gift cards, wire transfers, money orders, or mobile payment apps, all of which are nonrefundable. These are frequently scams and your pup will never arrive.

REMEMBER

If you make contact with a breeder through an online ad, use the info presented earlier in this chapter to figure out if you've found a good one. Pretty websites can hide a multitude of sins, so don't let them blind you to a breeder's or puppy's flaws.

It's a jungle out there, but you can indeed find good breeders on the internet if you are careful about vetting them first.

Reading sales contracts

Good breeders will provide a sales contract to buyers. The contract spells out the conditions of the sale. The contract, and/or a separate agreement, may include items such as the following:

>> Whether the puppy is to be spayed or neutered and by what age (see Chapter 13 for more details on the latest recommendations)

>> Whether the puppy's AKC registration will be full or limited (see the end of this section)

>> How soon you should have the pup checked out by your veterinarian to rule out genetic problems

>> An explanation of the breeder's responsibility if a genetic problem turns up

>> Whether you're expected to exhibit the pup to their championship should they grow up show quality (if you buy a pup with show potential)

>> An explanation of the breeder's responsibility if you plan on showing your pup but they aren't show quality at maturity

Surveying the Doggie in the Window

Chihuahua puppies are frequently sold in pet shops. In this section, we tell you why you should proceed with extreme caution when you see a cute puppy in a pet shop.

Be wary about buying a puppy from pet shop. The darling "Doggie in the Window" can cost you a small fortune if you run into hereditary health problems, for instance.

The pet shop itself isn't necessarily the problem. The puppies may be clean and well nourished, have toys to keep them occupied, and receive petting and attention frequently from the employees. The problem is where they came from before arriving at the pet shop. Good breeders plan matings carefully, breed to the standard, socialize their puppies, and, after all that, want to check out every potential puppy owner. But people who sell puppies to pet shops breed only to make money. They choose breeding partners out of convenience rather than quality and willingly sell entire litters to middlemen without caring who ends up with the pups. Sometimes their facilities are dirty, and they usually have far too many dogs to give any of them individual attention, let alone good socialization, which is so essential to a puppy's development. And that's a serious problem.

Lack of human attention early in life results in puppies who are nervous and shy, and a dirty habitat during the formative weeks can make the puppies hard to housetrain. Sure, time and affection help, but the bottom line is this: No matter how hard you try, you can't cure bad breeding. Know what you're getting into if you decide to bring one of these puppies home. If you want to rescue a Chihuahua, check out the "Adopting from a Shelter or Rescue Group" section.

TECHNICAL
STUFF

Dog lovers have a name for the over-crowded, filthy facilities that breed litter after litter and sell hundreds of poorly bred puppies every year. We call them *puppy mills.*

Classified canines

Should you check out the ads for Chihuahua puppies in your local newspaper? That depends on what's on your Chihuahua wish list. With the right knowledge, you may find a nice pet through the classifieds, but don't look there if you want a show dog.

TIP

Although both parents you see through a classified ad visit may be healthy Chihuahuas with excellent dispositions, it's better to have plenty of knowledge about picking puppies before trying to select a pet from the litter. See the section "Pick of the litter" for plenty of advice on picking out the right puppy.

REMEMBER

If you dream of owning a show champion, buying from an established breeder is your best shot at success. Why? Because puppy sellers who advertise only in the paper or online, and not through the dog journals, probably bred their pets to their friends' pooches without studying the standard (see Chapter 2) or comparing pedigrees.

Navigating the Ups and Downs of Choosing a Mature Chihuahua

Sometimes a puppy isn't the right choice. They're a lot of work! If you're not sure you're up for a pup, consider adopting an adult Chihuahua. Why would you want an adult dog? There are lots of good reasons to go this route.

Even though puppies are precious, they're also babies. And like infants, they're sloppy eaters, go potty often, and sleep a lot — but not always on your schedule. They need constant supervision for weeks or months, or else they may teethe on the table legs and leave puddles (or worse) on the carpet.

A mature dog may be easier on your schedule. And although not every mature Chihuahua is housetrained, and unsupervised young adults may still exercise their choppers on the chair legs, grown dogs have bigger bladders and longer attention spans than puppies, so they tend to learn house rules quickly.

Most important? After a brief period of adjustment, an adult Chihuahua bonds to a new owner just as strongly as a puppy does.

But isn't acquiring an adult dog kind of like buying a used car? Isn't the adult just someone else's problem looking for a new place to happen? In some cases, maybe, but certainly not always.

Practically perfect adult dogs often find themselves homeless because of factors out of their control — a divorce or death in their families, family members' allergic reactions to dog hair, or owners moving and being unable to find dog-friendly housing, for instance. Many breeders also won't breed their bitches past a certain age and are happy to place them in loving homes. And lost or abandoned Chihuahuas often are available for adoption through rescue or humane organizations.

WARNING

All adult dogs have a past, so every member of the family should meet an adult Chihuahua before making a decision to buy or adopt. That's because something in the dog's past may have caused them to love men but hate women (or vice versa) or become defensive around children.

Selecting an adult Chihuahua is a lot like choosing a puppy but without some of the guesswork, because their personality and habits are already formed. Here are some tips to help you sift through the problem pets and single out your future best friend:

>> When meeting a mature Chihuahua, remember that you're a stranger and adult dogs are more discriminating than puppies. Don't force your attention on the dog. Instead, sit

down and talk to the owner for a few minutes until the dog warms up to you.

>> Check for general good health by looking at the dog's eyes, nose, coat, skin, and movement. Eyes should be clear and bright and the nose free of mucus. A shiny coat should cover the body and skin should be smooth and supple, without bumps, lumps, or pimples. Movement should be easy and animated — not stiff or labored.

>> You and the dog need to appeal to each other. Give them time to accept you and then pet them if they allow it. Do they relax and enjoy your company, or are they fearful, reactive, or aggressive? Ask the owner to place the dog on your lap. Are they content to cuddle? Or are they scared stiff or frantic to escape?

>> Ask if you may put a leash on the dog and take them for a walk. Encourage the dog to walk beside you with soft, happy talk. Do they trot down the street with you willingly, or do they freeze in place, cry, balk, or try to make a break for home?

>> Perform the smile test. Does looking at this dog make you smile? That's good chemistry, but it should work both ways. After the dog knows you, do they wag their tail and dance a few happy steps when you talk to them? Liking each other is the most important criterion of all.

TIP

Many dogs are protective of their homes but warm up to friendly strangers easily on neutral ground. Moving to a neutral site is worth a try if you like everything about an adult Chihuahua but they don't seem to like you.

Understanding Pedigree versus Purebred

Fun fact: all dogs have a pedigree, whether they're purebred or not. Honest. A *pedigree* is nothing more than a list of ancestors, just like a family tree. A mixed breed's grandparents may be a Miniature Pinscher, a Chihuahua, a Yorkshire Terrier, and a Toy

Poodle, and that's the dog's family tree. The dog has a pedigree, but isn't a purebred.

TECHNICAL
STUFF

What is a *purebred*? It's a dog descended from dogs who were all the same breed. A purebred Chihuahua has two Chihuahuas for parents, four Chihuahuas for grandparents, eight Chihuahuas for great-grandparents, and so on, as far back as records can be traced.

The following sections dig deeper into the topics of registration and pedigree.

Deciphering full or limited registration

The American Kennel Club (AKC) gives breeders the option of selling a puppy with either full or limited registration. A Chihuahua with full registration, if bred to another Chihuahua with full registration, will have puppies eligible for AKC registration (full or limited, depending on the breeder's wishes). Dogs with limited registration may be lovely to look at and delightful to live with, but they should be spayed or neutered, not bred. And if they are bred, their puppies aren't eligible for AKC registration.

TECHNICAL
STUFF

Dogs with limited registration may compete in AKC (and other dog clubs') obedience and agility events, but they're not eligible to compete in conformation (see Chapter 12).

If the puppy you fall for has been selected by the breeder for limited registration, ask why. Usually, it's because of some small fault that won't matter to you anyway unless you're planning to show and/or breed your dog.

Registering your new dog

When you purchase a dog who's AKC registrable, you should receive a registration application that has been filled out and signed by the seller. The form includes a section for the new owner (congratulations, that's you!) to complete. Do it ASAP (because the price goes up if you wait too long) and send the application to the American Kennel Club (the address is on the form), along with the required fee. As soon as your dog's paperwork is processed and recorded, you'll receive a registration certificate. That's what allows your dog to compete in AKC conformation events or other dog sports.

REMEMBER

Thousands of eligible dogs aren't registered even though their owners think they are. That's because their owners put the registration applications in a safe place but never read them. That official-looking piece of paper is only an application. It means your dog is *eligible* to be AKC registered. For the dog to actually *be* registered, you must fill out the form and send it in with the required fee.

TIP

Don't be surprised if the breeder/kennel where you purchase your Chihuahua wants to include the kennel name as part of your dog's registered name. Breeding good dogs is an art form, and putting a kennel name on a top-quality dog is the same as an artist signing their work. If you buy your dog from Talko Chi Town Kennels and want to name her Susie, her registered name may be Talko Chi Town Susie. In dog-show lingo, Susie is her *call name*. But even if Susie isn't part of her registered name, you can still call her that at home.

WARNING

If a seller doesn't have a registration application for your puppy but assures you that one is coming, proceed with caution. If you trust the seller enough to buy on that basis, ask for a bill of sale signed by the seller that includes your dog's breed, date of birth, sex, color, the registered names and AKC numbers of the pup's sire and dam, and the full name and address of the breeder. That way, if you don't receive official paperwork in a week or so, you can write to the AKC and fully identify your dog.

Don't be shy about requiring this info to be included in the sales agreement. According to AKC rules, anyone who sells dogs eligible for AKC registration must provide complete identification in writing. If you want a registered dog and the seller can't give you the registration application or every bit of the necessary information, pass up the puppy.

Adopting from a Shelter or Rescue Group

You love the idea of having a Chihuahua, but you also want to give a second chance to a dog who needs it. Adopting from a shelter or a Chihuahua rescue group gives you the opportunity to do both.

You may be surprised to learn that, depending on where you live, Chihuahuas are frequently found in local animal shelters. Places where Chihuahuas are popular include California, Arizona, Texas, and Florida. The little dogs may end up needing a new home if they were purchased by people who didn't do their homework about the breed and aren't a good match for them or whose lives have changed and they can no longer keep their pets, much as they may love them.

TIP

Ask at nearby shelters if Chihuahuas come in regularly and put your name on a notification list if possible. Check the shelter's website daily to see if any Chihuahuas have come in; little dogs are popular and they go fast!

If the dog was relinquished by a family, shelter personnel may be able to provide you with the dog's age, health information, personality quirks (good with kids, for instance, or likes to chase cats), and whether they're housetrained or know tricks.

You can also seek out a Chihuahua-specific rescue group. The Chihuahua Club of America has links to Chihuahua rescues, or you can simply do a web search for Chihuahua rescue and your city or state. Petfinder.org is also a good resource that allows you to search by breed and location.

Rescue groups typically place dogs in foster homes until they can be adopted. That's a plus because the foster family can advise you about what the Chi you're considering is like in a home environment.

Look for a dog who is calm and confident, recovering quickly from startling sounds or situations. If you are able to take the dog on a walk outside the shelter or foster home, watch how they react to passersby. Acceptable responses range from indifference or caution to curiosity or friendliness. A dog who seems afraid may need extra time to adjust to a new home.

WARNING

No matter where you adopt, expect to find primarily adult dogs. A "shelter" or "rescue" that always has puppies available may be a commercial breeder (read: puppy mill) in disguise.

REMEMBER

If you adopt a Chihuahua, the rule of paw for giving them time to adjust is 333: three days to decompress in your home; three weeks to settle in and get used to your routine as well as to begin displaying their true personality; and three months for them to realize they are "home."

Giving a home to a senior Chihuahua can be one of the greatest, most rewarding experiences of your life. Kim adopted Gemma, a 13-year-old Chihuahua mix, and had four very happy years with the tiny dog with the huge personality until Gemma succumbed to cancer.

CHIHUAHUAS WITHOUT CREDENTIALS

If you adopt your Chihuahua from a rescue group or animal shelter, they'll probably come to you without papers. Does this matter? Only if you want to compete in AKC events, such as obedience or agility (see Chapter 12).

The American Kennel Club allows purebred dogs with no papers to compete in obedience and agility if they have *Purebred Alternative Listing* (PAL) numbers. A form for you to fill out is available at www. akc.org, or you can call AKC Customer Care at 919-233-9767 and ask a representative to send you a PAL form.

IN THIS CHAPTER

» Scheduling an appropriate arrival

» Protecting your puppy (and your belongings)

» Going shopping for your Chihuahua

» Sailing through the first 48 hours

» Resisting the freedom fantasy

Chapter **5**

Welcome Home, Little Amigo

t's almost new dog day! You can feel the excitement in the air. We bet you can hardly wait to bring your puppy home, but first you need to do a little organizing. This chapter helps you decide when to bring your Chihuahua home and tells you how to keep your pup's curious tongue out of toxic things. It also helps you decide what your new dog needs and doesn't need so you won't be tempted to buy every toy and food option in the pet supply store!

Are you wondering how to handle your Chihuahua when they're the new dog on the block? How to guide your children or grandkids into a good relationship with their new pal? How to introduce your Chihuahua to your other pets? What you'll do during those uncertain first couple days? How you'll keep your Chi safe and free from escape temptation? Don't worry. That's all here, too.

Timing the Homecoming Just Right

The best time to bring home a new dog is when nothing new is happening at your place. Wait until the repair people are finished, the relatives have gone home, and the holiday season is over. This gives your Chi quiet time to get to know you and adjust to their new home.

If your Chihuahua is a holiday gift from your spouse to you or vice versa, find a way to present *the gift* without bringing *the dog* into chaos. Settle for a photo of the dog under the Christmas tree or beside the Hanukah candles. If you have kids at home, gift-wrap a collar and leash, a food and water dish, and dog toys to go with the photo (see the later section "Shoppin' 'til You Drop: Gathering the Chi Goods"). Bring the dog home only after the parties are over and the decorations have been boxed. A normal home has enough gizmos to tempt a puppy into trouble. Halls decked out for the holidays can be downright dangerous.

WARNING

Don't ever give a dog as a present unless you're absolutely sure the recipient wants one and that the breed you picked is their favorite. Better yet, before actually making the purchase, invite the potential owner to meet the pup and check out the chemistry between them.

TIP

Dogs are social animals, so being alone in a strange place makes a Chihuahua feel lonely and insecure. It's better if you can bring them home when you have a long weekend or can take a few days off so you can be around to help them settle in. Is a regular weekend the best you can do? Bring them home as early as possible on Saturday morning. Don't opt for Friday night, because bedtime without their dam (mother) and littermates is the hardest time for a puppy, and they'll feel better if they have a whole day to acclimate first.

Puppy-Proofing Your Chi's Room

Until they're housetrained (see Chapter 10), the right place for your Chihuahua (when no one can supervise) is in one easily cleaned room of your home. Most people find the kitchen ideal, unless yours is exceptionally large. In that case, a bathroom may be suitable.

Your Chi's room must be puppy-proofed for their safety. Puppies are curious, and because they don't have fingers to feel things, they try to taste everything (no matter how yucky the things may smell to you). Keep all cleaning agents, pesticides, antifreeze, and other household and garden chemicals out of your puppy's reach. Cover electrical cords within your Chi's reach with tough plastic covers, available from home improvement stores, to prevent them from chomping down on them and receiving a shock—or worse.

Place a wire mesh baby gate across the doorway; this works better than a solid door, which isolates the puppy, adding to their loneliness and frustration, and leads to incessant barking, temper tantrums, and tiny tooth prints in the door. Make sure the mesh is strong enough to withstand sharp teeth and that the mesh pattern is too small for the dog to chew through or get caught in.

TIP

If you can't give your Chi the run of an entire puppy-proofed room, a baby's playpen with mesh sides or a wire, plastic, or nylon pet exercise pen (available at pet supply stores or online) is a good (and portable) alternative.

Do you have houseplants? Identify each one (not just the ones in the puppy-proofed room) and look them up to find out if they're toxic (or take a leaf to a nursery and ask). Many popular houseplants are deadly when ingested, including holiday plants such as holly, amaryllis, and those merry mistletoe berries. Placing all plants, even the safe ones, out of your dog's reach is a good idea, because no puppy can resist playing with a plant. But extra precautions are necessary with the poisonous plants. They shed leaves and berries even though they may be hanging high, and your Chi is bound to pick them up. Your best course of action? Get rid of them or decorate with artificial plants.

A ROCK IN A HARD PLACE

The variety of things that puppies and dogs will put in their mouths and swallow is astounding, so it's important to keep anything small out of reach, even if you don't think it's something a dog would be interested in. When Jackie's Chi Manchita was a puppy, she earned the nickname Hoover because she behaved like a vacuum cleaner, inhaling everything in her path. One day while they were out walking, Manchita snatched up a small rock and swallowed it before Jackie could get it out of her mouth. The next day, she strained to eliminate, couldn't pass the rock, and became sick. Luckily, the veterinarian was able to dislodge it by medicating her at both ends. Otherwise, the 2½-pound puppy would have faced emergency surgery!

TIP

If you like your nonpoisonous houseplants right where they are, and you want your Chihuahua to know to leave them alone, spray them with a product called Bitter Apple, which has a harmless but unpleasant taste meant to make objects undesirable for puppies to chew on. It is also useful for preventing pups from chewing on furniture, electrical cords, and other dangerous items.

WARNING

While Bitter Apple usually works, some dogs just find that it adds to the flavor.

When young and unsupervised, your Chi will try to teethe on everything they can reach, from your bedroom slippers to your shower curtain — even a box of dishwasher detergent, if you leave the cupboard door ajar. But keeping their curious mouth out of mischief isn't as hard as it sounds. You can secure closet and cupboard doors and flip the shower curtain up over the rod, for instance. After you have your dog for some time, these actions will become second nature.

Shoppin' 'til You Drop: Gathering the Chi Goods

You've puppy-proofed your Chi's special room and your home, and you have a long weekend coming up to welcome your new pet (see the previous sections). You'll be ready for Chihuahua life as soon as you go shopping. Your Chi needs a few things right away.

Wait until you see the colorful display of dog toys, collars, leashes, food and water dishes, car safety seats, and even canine clothing in the pet store. It's tempting to buy twice what you need. How will you know what's necessary and what isn't? The shopping list in this section explains each item so you can get the perfect one for your Chi.

Essentials for your new Chihuahua

The following shopping list contains the essentials you need for your new Chihuahua:

>> Two dishes — one for water and one for food (Get a couple of extras for when your Chi's dishes are being washed, which should be a daily occurrence.)

>> Puppy (or dog) food (Ask the breeder what they've been feeding so your puppy won't get an upset tummy from a rapid change in diet.)

>> Harness or flat collar and leash (never a choke chain)

>> Grooming equipment

>> Three or four toys

>> Dog crate (which can double as a containment device in the car)

>> Dog bed (optional)

>> Soft carrier or pet seat for car rides (optional if you use a crate for this purpose)

>> Warm sweater (if you live in a chilly climate or keep the air conditioning running)

>> Pooper-scooper and poop bags

>> Identification

>> Doggie toothbrush and toothpaste

>> An excellent veterinarian

Practical dishes

What's a practical dog dish? One that's easy to clean and hard to tip over. Dishes made of stainless steel, stoneware, and porcelain are good choices because they are sturdy and can go in the dishwasher. Some dishes are wider at the bottom than at the top and others are weighted; these are good features because it makes them impossible to tip over, even if your Chi likes to play with the bowl. (They'll probably still splash water out of the water dish, though.)

WARNING

If you buy ceramic dishes for your Chihuahua, make sure they were made in the United States. Some foreign glazes still contain toxic stuff, including lead. Look for ceramics that are well glazed (read: glossy).

Place your Chi's dishes where they won't slide around the floor while they eat and drink. A corner usually works well. You can lay down a small rug or puppy placemat to help dishes stay in place as well as catch dropped food or soak up water spills.

Chihuahua chow choices: What should your Chi eat?

Kibble? Soft-moist? Biscuit? Canned? Chopped or chunky? Paté? Are you confused yet? Don't be. Feeding your dog a good diet is easy as well as important — so important that it has its own chapter in this book. So instead of giving Chihuahua chow your best guess, turn to Chapter 6. It explains how to choose food that will meet your Chi's nutritional needs during every stage of their life.

Collars, harnesses, and leashes (oh my!)

Many veterinarians recommend using a harness instead of collar because small dogs who pull hard against the leash can be prone to a condition called *tracheal collapse*. It causes them to develop a honking cough or severe symptoms such as difficulty breathing. That's because the cartilage that makes up the trachea can be easily damaged by the pressure that occurs when a dog strains against the collar. A harness helps by relieving pressure on the neck. Even better, teach your Chihuahua to walk nicely on leash without pulling, under the guidance of a trainer who uses positive-reinforcement techniques.

TIP

Wait until you bring your puppy home before buying a collar or harness so you can get one that fits perfectly.

Your Chihuahua's collar should apply no pressure as it encircles the neck, but it shouldn't be so loose that it slips over their adorable apple head. Don't buy a collar that's too large so your puppy can grow into it, either. Collars that are too loose are a choking hazard if they become caught on something.

Shop for a flat collar, made of nylon webbing or leather that fastens with a buckle and has a D ring for attaching a leash. The benefit of this type of buckle collar is that you can adjust it as your puppy grows. Some nylon collars have plastic quick-release buckles similar to those used on camera bags and fanny packs, and they come in a variety of attractive designs.

Check the fit of your Chi's collar weekly. Puppies grow rapidly, and you must replace or adjust the collar right away if it feels tight. Depending on the style of collar you choose, a puppy can go through two or three collars before reaching maturity, so keep that in mind when pricing collars.

What's a collar without a lead? Simply an accessory! The length of your Chi's lead should be between 5 and 6 feet. Leather, nylon, or other flexible fabric leads are preferred. Avoid expandable leads that allow a dog to get several feet away from you. They are trip hazards for other people and can allow your pup to wander into trouble before you can stop them. A traditional lead is the safest choice, especially in crowded places. (To find out how to lead train your puppy, see Chapter 9.)

WARNING

Don't buy a leash or collar made of chain. Chain is too cumbersome and can hurt your Chihuahua's legs if they get tangled in it. And don't buy any type of training collar (they also come in nylon and webbing) with a ring at both ends that tightens up when you or your dog pulls away. Commonly called *choke collars*, these harmful and unkind training devices should be avoided. They can injure your Chihuahua's throat if used improperly as well as damage your bond with your puppy. You never want to use anything that would hurt him.

Grooming gizmos

Smooth Chis have easy-care, wash-and-wear coats, so for their grooming, you can get by with purchasing the following:

>> A quality shampoo that's pH-balanced for dogs

>> A natural-bristle brush

>> A toothpaste formulated for dogs

>> A soft toothbrush made for small dogs or human babies

>> A doggie nail clipper

Long-coated Chis are also easy to maintain, but they require a few more things in addition to the previous tools:

>> Both you and your Chi will appreciate a coat conditioner formulated for dogs. Besides making their coat a cinch to comb after shampooing, it will keep it soft and silky.

>> A hard rubber comb is a must for keeping mats out of a Chi's coat — especially behind the ears.

>> If you don't use the comb often enough (don't worry, it takes only a minute or two), you'll probably need a mat splitter to put your Chi's coat back in good condition.

>> Find a good groomer as well. It's easy for long-haired Chis to become matted behind the ears or on the pants or belly without your ever noticing.

Chapter 7 tells you how to use your grooming gizmos to keep your dog's skin and coat healthy.

WARNING

Don't buy a nylon or metal comb or a brush made with anything but natural bristles. Natural products do the least damage to a dog's coat. If you comb your dog during the winter with a nylon or metal implement, you'll probably zap him with static electricity. They'll hate it and won't want to be groomed anymore.

Toys for toys (dogs, that is)

Think of your Chihuahua's toys as essentials, not extras. They need something safe to gnaw on while they're teething (and just for fun) and a couple of toys available to play with the rest of the time. Although your Chihuahua may continue chewing after they grow up, they'll no longer sink their fangs into everything they can reach the way teething puppies do. Be glad your mature Chi still likes to chew (see Figure 5-1). Besides keeping them content, chewing promotes healthy gums and teeth.

Toy dogs need chews and playthings that are small enough for them to manipulate but big enough that they can't swallow them. Rawhide chew toys are traditional favorites, but they're not easily digested and can be a choking or obstruction hazard. If you're going to give your Chi a tiny rawhide, choose one made in the U.S. (which has stricter manufacturing standards), and let your dog enjoy it only when you're there to supervise. Replace it with something safer when you're not around. We think there are better chew choices.

FIGURE 5-1: Adult Chihuahuas can be serious about their chew toys.

Chew toys made of hard rubber are generally safe in a Toy dog's mouth even when no one is home. Chihuahua puppies, and many adult dogs, prefer the softer and equally safe gummy-nylon chews. Keep the "kneecap rule" in mind: If you wouldn't want to be hit in the knee with a particular toy, it's too hard for your dog to chew.

On the other hand, squeaky toys (featherweight rubber or plastic doodads with squeakers inside) are popular with pups but safe only when you're supervising — or better yet, when you join in the fun. Squeaky toys are easily chewed open (yes, even by a Chihuahua), and the squeaker inside is dangerous when swallowed. But you don't have to deprive your Chi of a squeaky toy. Instead, buy one but keep it out of reach. Get it out once every few days as a special treat, and watch the fun when your pup play-kills it.

WARNING

Don't use old leather shoes, purses, or wallets as dog toys. Sure, your dog likes sinking their teeth into the well-worn, good-smelling leather, but this teaches him that leather objects with your scent on them are chew toys. That's bad news for your shoes, purses, and other accessories.

Flat, fleecy toys (shaped like animals or gingerbread people, for instance) are popular, and dogs like cuddling up to them. They're machine washable and safe as long as your Chi doesn't shred the edges and swallow some of the material. Just keep an eye on fleecy toys and throw them away if they become worn.

REMEMBER

Don't let your Chi have all their toys at once. Instead, put a few away and rotate them every couple of days. That way your dog won't become bored with their belongings. Keeping at least three toys (but no more than five) in service at one time is a good rule of thumb. Put one in their crate, one or two in their playroom (if they have one), and one or two in the room where the family gathers.

Cozy crates

Dogs descend from denning animals that spent much of their time in the relative security of their lairs, so it won't take long before your Chihuahua feels comfortable and protected in a dog crate. Some new dog owners imagine that crate confinement is cruel, but crates have saved dogs' lives and owners' tempers for decades.

If you can't give your Chi their own puppy-proofed room, a crate becomes even more essential. It keeps them from stalking snakes (that's electrical cords to you) while you're away. Because they're so curious, many dogs are bound to get into mischief — or danger — when left at home alone. Besides, coming home to a safely crated puppy is much nicer than coming home to teeth marks on table legs and a soiled carpet. Because dogs don't like to soil their beds, a crate is a big help during housetraining. It also keeps your dog out of trouble while you're asleep. (For more info on introducing your Chi to their crate and using it to house-train, see Chapter 10.)

Buy your Chi a crate that's only big enough for a full-grown Chihuahua to stand up and turn around in comfortably. Bigger isn't better for two reasons:

>> Chihuahuas enjoy the cozy comfort of a just-the-right-size den.

>> A too-large crate loses its potty-training potential.

Most crates are made of wire or of plastic with a wire door. Both types have their benefits, but we think plastic is the best choice for smooth-coated Chihuahuas. The solid sides (except for ventilation holes) keep a Chi draft free.

The inside of your Chihuahua's crate is their private place within your home, as well as their home away from home, so you should create a comfortable den. Include bedding that's easy to wash or change and not dangerous if chewed or swallowed. An old twin-bed sheet works nicely. When you're sure that your Chi can keep their crate clean (which doesn't take long if you follow the schedule in Chapter 10), you can give them a nicer "mattress." A fleecy crate pad or soft rug sample are two possibilities.

The best place to put your Chi's crate is in their puppy-proofed room (if you have one). When it comes to crate placement, caring for your puppy works on the same principle as caring for a human baby. Just visualize their puppy-proofed room as their nursery and their crate as a combination crib, playpen, and car seat. Of course, you may opt to use a real playpen or a made-for-dogs exercise pen in addition to their crate.

TIP

For the ultimate crate toy, buy the smallest Kong toy you can find (available at many pet supply stores) and stuff it with aerosol cheese, peanut butter, or canned food. This concoction will keep your Chi occupied for hours.

Road trip safety

For safety's sake, always crate your Chihuahua when taking them for a drive, even for a short distance, and secure their crate with tiedowns so that it won't slide or roll over during turns or quick stops. A crated dog has a better chance of surviving a car accident. Not only that, but you drive better without your Chihuahua vying for your attention. The following car safety tips may surprise you, but they'll help to keep your Chihuahua safe.

Your state likely has laws regulating how dogs ride in cars. In many cases, it's illegal to let them ride in your lap or to ride loose. If your Chihuahua distracts you while you're driving or is in your lap during an accident, you could both be seriously injured or killed. (And hefty fines can be painful for your wallet.) States often require pets to be restrained in a crate or carrier or with a canine seat harness (not the car's seatbelt).

WARNING

Speaking of seatbelts, they are not necessarily a safe way to keep a crate in place. Crates can be crushed when a seatbelt tightens after a collision.

The safest place in the car for your Chi's soft or hard carrier is on the floor behind the driver or passenger seat because it's less likely to go airborne. Crates or carriers are also safer in the cargo area of a station wagon or SUV, kept in place with strength-rated tiedowns or crate straps.

REMEMBER

Not all crates, pet seats, and car safety harnesses are created equal. Choose one with tested crash protection that has been certified by the independent, nonprofit Center for Pet Safety (https://www.centerforpetsafety.org/), which has established crash-test standards for pet carriers and safety harnesses.

Snuggly beds

If a crate doesn't satisfy your concept of interior design, you can let your Chihuahua graduate into an attractive doggie bed after they're housetrained (see Chapters 9 and 10). You can find dog beds styled to suit any decor. Be sure to place the bed in a draft-free area and top it with a snuggly blanket. Chis love having something to burrow under. Even better, place a bed in every room so they can always have a place to relax as they follow you around the house.

Useful canine couture

Some doggie outfits are created just to look cute, while other clothing actually serves a purpose. For a Chihuahua, it's easy to find sweaters that do both. Because Chihuahuas chill easily, your Chi may need a jacket or sweater that helps them stay warm — some even need a sweater in an air-conditioned room. Look for one that covers the chest, part of the neck, and as much of the belly as possible (see Figure 5-2). If your Chi is a female, the more of her bald belly the sweater covers, the better. When fitting your male, remember that he'll wear his sweater outdoors when he goes potty, and you won't want him to wet the material. Most canine clothes are machine washable, but read the labels just in case.

FIGURE 5-2: Manchita (pictured here) models a coat that is functional and stylish.

Pooper-scoopers

Poop-scoops are available in a variety of styles at pet supply stores. A scoop is convenient for cleaning up your yard and for cleaning up after your Chi when you take them on walks. Most scoopers have long handles, so you don't have to bend down to clean.

TIP

If you don't have a yard or if you're traveling with your Chi, you'll soon get in the habit of carrying plastic sandwich bags or a roll of plastic poop bags imprinted with cute designs. To use the sandwich bags, put a couple in your purse or pocket before walking your dog. Put your hand inside the bag, pick up the poop, turn the bag inside out to contain the poop, close the bag, and toss it in the nearest garbage can (not someone's recycle bin!). Pet product manufacturers have designed little containers to hold rolls of poop bags. Attach one to your belt or bag and you're good to go. Kim keeps a stash of bags inside every purse and every jacket pocket so she's always prepared.

Trusted veterinarian

Your Chihuahua's veterinarian is their other best friend (many veterinarians rate Chihuahuas among their favorite patients), so choose one before bringing your pup or adoptee home. How will you know which dog doc is best for your puppy? Check out Chapter 13, which covers the details of the pet/vet relationship.

ID for dogs

Your new dog should "carry" identification all the time. The puppy ID can take the form of a microchip or a collar tag. The best ID is a collar tag plus a microchip. Chapter 13 tells you all you need to know about identification and its importance.

Surviving First Contact

Time to go! You have everything you need, and now it's time to pick up your Chihuahua! Get off to a smart start by taking your crate or a soft carrier along so your puppy can ride in it on the way home. The crate is their safe sanctuary in a moving vehicle. See the section "Road trip safety," above, for more tips on your Chihuahua's ride home.

When you arrive home, give your Chi an opportunity to relieve themselves outdoors before going in (see Chapter 10). Then take them to their puppy-proofed room, put fresh water in their dish, and let them explore *their room* to their heart's content (see the earlier section "Puppy-Proofing Your Chi's Room"). You're not depriving them by keeping them from investigating your whole home right away. Too much new territory is confusing, and besides, if they're teething and not housetrained yet, giving more space to roam simply means more areas where they can get into trouble. If you don't have a puppy-proofed room, keep a close eye on them as they inspect their new digs. And when no one is supervising, put them in a crate with a toy or treat.

TIP

Make sure your Chihuahua always has access to extra warmth whenever they need it. Whether you use a crate, playpen, dog bed, or all these options, their space needs to be equipped with a sheet or blanket to burrow under. Lots of dog beds now come with hoods or covers for dogs who like to cover up.

After your Chi has a drink (and some food if it's feeding time), take them outdoors again. Then put them back in the puppy-proofed room, give them a toy, and play with them quietly. No matter how excited you are, this isn't a good time to overstimulate your puppy. Chances are, they're tired from the trip home and seeing so many new places and faces. When they give out (some puppies go from playing to sleeping so quickly that they appear to have passed out), crate them or put them in their bed and let them take a nap. They'll love sleeping on your lap, of course, and it helps both of you bond, but don't put them on your lap for every nap. Your Chi has to learn to sleep alone, too.

For the first couple of days, try to keep household activity normal, even low key. This isn't the time for your kids to jam with the band or invite friends over to practice for cheerleading try-outs. Don't start your spring cleaning, either. And remind enthusiastic family members and friends not to rush at your Chi. Unfamiliar surroundings and strange voices are enough for a puppy to get used to during the first 48 hours. After that, household activity can gradually return to normal.

TIP

Because consistency is the key when training a puppy, and because your Chihuahua arrives full of curiosity with a brain that soaks up information like a sponge, the ideal time to start housetraining is day one. See Chapter 10 to find out how.

Picking up your puppy (safely)

Sure, your Chi puppy fits into your palm; but you need to use two hands to pick them up anyway, right from the get-go. One hand goes under the chest and the other cups the rear. Check your hands the first few times to make sure your fingers don't apply pressure to the front legs — either spreading them too far apart or squeezing them together. Habitual spreading can cause permanent damage to your puppy's elbows, and repeated squeezing can harm the legs and shoulders. Best bet? Place your thumb on one side of your dog and your little finger on the other, supporting the chest with the middle three fingers. After you try this method once or twice, it should become automatic. Hold them gently but firmly (puppies wiggle) against your body with both hands so no part of them dangles.

WARNING

Never leave your puppy alone in a place where they could fall. For example, if you and your Chihuahua are watching television in the recliner and you get up to check out the fridge, place your pup on the floor until you return. When they mature, they'll be able to jump on and off the furniture without help, but that's a dangerous leap for a puppy.

Blending dogs and kids

Please don't skip this section just because you don't have any kids at home. You may have grandchildren or friends with children, and what you discover here will ensure that visiting kids and your Chi will have pleasant (and safe) visits.

Chis and young children typically aren't a good combination. Sometimes kids and dogs scare each other without wanting to. Tiny dogs fear shrill sounds and fast movements (especially swooping down on them), and youngsters come well equipped with high-pitched voices and jerky movements. When dogs feel threatened or cornered, they usually growl, warning the offenders away. But many young children don't recognize the warning or simply ignore it, and that's how bites happen. On the other hand, children fear shrill noises, too, and a Chihuahua's piercing puppy bark may make them cringe.

The truth is, kids and dogs can hurt each other. But many people have surmounted the obstacles and succeeded in raising children and Chihuahuas at the same time. How? By being vigilant and never leaving little children and Chihuahuas alone together. Using careful and calm supervision every time a child and puppy are together keeps the child and the pup from fearing or harming each other.

From about the age of three or four — depending on their individual self-control and emotional maturity — children can help you care for a Chi. Provided that you have patience and won't freak out over spilled food or water, kids can do many things, such as picking up your Chi's dirty dishes and bringing them to you and giving your Chi their water or food after you fill the dishes. Kids also get a kick out of giving dogs an occasional treat — held out on a flat hand, please.

When children are young, helping to take care of a pet should be fun — a privilege, not a responsibility. Do it yourself when you're in a hurry. Chubby little fingers sometimes spill stuff.

Children who are ready to help care for a puppy are also ready to follow some simple rules. Here are a few rules that work for your own kids and for visitors, too; you may have to create others to fit your situation:

>> Always sit on the floor to play with the dog.

>> Don't pick up the dog.

>> Don't put your face close to the dog.

>> You may pet the dog, but don't close your hand when doing so. This keeps children from squeezing or grabbing a leg, ear, or tail.

>> Don't tease or poke the dog. (You may have to explain what teasing is.)

>> Never give the dog anything to eat or play with without permission.

>> Always offer treats on the flat of your hand.

>> Don't climb into the Chihuahua's crate or playpen; that's their special place where they can go to be alone.

>> When the dog wants to leave, let them go. Don't hang on and try to stop them.

Matching older children and Chihuahuas

By the time they're third- or fourth-graders, some kids become attuned to animals. In fact, older children often have better relationships with their pets than grown-ups do because they take the time to discover the animals' body language. Responsible older kids can share in your Chihuahua's care by feeding, grooming, and walking them. And they may surprise you by teaching them a few tricks!

REMEMBER

Kids learn the most valuable lessons about pet care when it's a family affair. Don't expect a child (or teenager) to take full responsibility for your Chi, even if they promised they would when they begged you to buy the pup. Instead, give kids an excellent example (yes, that's you) to follow. Most important of all, never make threatening remarks — "If you don't do those dishes right now, I'm giving that dog away!" A dog isn't a disposable object like outgrown skates or a broken barrette. Yours deserves affection, care, and a permanent home, and threatening to give them anything less sends your child a sorry message.

WARNING

No matter how good your children are with the family Chihuahua, keep an eye on the situation when their friends visit. Other children with little or no experience with tiny pets may want to experiment ("What would happen if we fed the dog this?") or may even harbor a mean streak. And the best of kids (like yours) may find themselves helpless in the face of peer pressure.

Introducing dog to dog

The best way to introduce your resident dog to your new Chihuahua is on neutral ground so Rocky doesn't feel the need to defend their territory from Pepe. Just half a block down the street is fine if both dogs know how to walk on a leash. Your Chi must stand on the ground (not in your arms) to participate in a proper doggie introduction, so if they aren't leash trained, borrow a fenced yard or other secure area for the meet and greet.

The easiest way to accomplish a successful meeting is to ask a dog-savvy helper to take your Chihuahua to the designated place. Then you take Rocky for a walk, on leash, and meet them there. Follow these steps as you approach the meeting place:

1. **Start by walking the dogs in the same direction, parallel to each other, gradually decreasing the distance between them.** During this time, watch their body language toward each other. Their bodies and expressions should be calm and relaxed.

2. **As the dogs get near each other, start a conversation with your helper, but watch while the dogs go through the motions of meeting.** With each dog on a loose leash, let them sniff noses and rear ends. Act nonchalant so the dogs don't sense any anxiety, and don't pet either dog. Watch closely to maintain control of the situation.

3. **If either dog seems uncomfortable, rushes at the other, stares, or has a stiff tail, calmly increase the distance between them by patting your leg and giving praise and a treat for following you.** Try again in a few minutes.

4. **If Rocky displays gentleness toward your Chi, praise Rocky verbally.** Continue walking, repeating the opportunities for them to sniff each other every couple of minutes. Typical dog greetings are short and then they move on, so you're mimicking their normal behavior.

5. **When the dogs seem comfortable with each other, walk them home together if both dogs walk on leash or drive them home separately, your resident dog with you.** If your Chi is too little to walk on leash, let your friend carry the pup while you walk Rocky, praising occasionally along the way.

6. **When you get home, let them meet once more in the yard, and then have your friend take the pup in first.** Give Rocky the impression that inviting the little friend in was Rocky's idea by praising by name for being gentle ("Gooood Rocky!") and giving plenty of attention.

7. **Inside, put your Chi in the already prepared safe space or exercise pen, which contains their bed, food, water, and some toys.** Your Chi and Rocky can see each other and continue their acquaintance via smell.

Most dogs treat little puppies gently as long as they don't suddenly feel unloved. Give Rocky at least as much attention as you ever did. Ignoring Rocky creates the canine equivalent of sibling rivalry. And if ol' Roc is a big boy, the situation may be dangerous. Just imagine how a three-year-old child would react to a new brother if they're suddenly shoved aside while the baby gets all the attention.

Don't leave the dogs alone together until you're sure that they get along. Supervise closely for at least the first week. Use their crates, or keep them in different rooms, when no one is home, and have the pup sleep in a crate at night. Feed them separately to avoid any disagreements over food. This is a good idea all the time in a multidog household; eating together can be stressful for dogs, even if they like each other.

TIP

If you have more than one dog, introduce them to your new dog or puppy one at a time. Start with your calmest canine and work up to your most excitable.

Getting the last meow — why cats rule

Dogs and cats in the same household usually get along, and some even become best buddies. At first introduction, if your Chi isn't especially agitated at the sight of Kitty, the dog may become curious and try to sniff noses with the cat. If the cat sniffs back, that's a good sign. Chances are they'll be friends in no time (see Figure 5-3). While waiting for that to happen, keep a watchful eye on them when they're together. Some dogs, even little ones, have an undeniable urge to chase cats. Don't allow that. Although some cats run from Chihuahuas, others may take swipes at the tiny tormentors, which can damage your Chi's eyes and nose.

REMEMBER

When a dog and cat live together, the cat always has the advantage. Why? Because Kitty can leave an area whenever they want to. All they have to do is jump on the bed or chair out of your Chi's reach, and the dog can't annoy or cuddle the cat until Kitty decides to come near your Chi again. When your cat has had enough of your Chi (even if that happens in less than a second), let them go. You can't force friendship; it will probably occur on its own after Kitty gets used to the interloper and they learn each other's limits.

Living with furry, feathered, and scaled critters

Furry, feathered, and scaled caged pets — such as hamsters, birds, rabbits, lizards, turtles, and mice — may look like prey to your Chihuahua. Dogs (yes, even little ones) instinctively catch and kill prey. The best solution is to keep these critters out of reach and correct everything from too much interest to a menacing growl with a firm "No!" Your Chi doesn't have to make friends with these animals. It's better if your dog learns to ignore them. Most dogs lose interest in caged pets after they get used to seeing and smelling them on a daily basis. But until then, supervise your Chi every time they're in the same room with your caged critters.

Suppressing That Dangerous Fantasy of Freedom

Some dog owners think their dogs miss out on a facet of life if they never experience absolute freedom. In fact, millions of dogs die every year from accidents encountered while roaming free.

A loose dog can be crushed by cars or picked up by animal control officers or can lick poisonous substances like antifreeze (it's sweet) or lawn herbicides.

Besides being a menace to your neighbor's flowerbed, a loose Chihuahua also faces dangers like being stolen, attacked by a bigger dog, or even snatched by an owl or hawk (it happens). A small child may also handle them roughly. And if the child frightens or hurts your Chi, your dog may bite during efforts to escape. Now you're in danger of a lawsuit.

Putting your Chihuahua in a position to become a statistic isn't doing them a favor. A Chihuahua is more than a domestic animal — they're the ultimate house dog. Rather than freedom, give them what they really want: your companionship.

IN THIS CHAPTER

» **Understanding the nuts and bolts of nutrition**

» **Giving food when you first get your Chihuahua**

» **Choosing between all those bags, boxes, and cans of dog food**

» **Feeding at different ages and stages of life**

» **Steering clear of nutritional no-nos**

Chapter **6**

What's on the Chi Menu?

ust look at the pet food aisle at any major supermarket. It's stacked high with an array of kibble, semi-moist, and canned canine cuisines, not to mention refrigerated and frozen sections containing pet food — some for puppies, some for adult dogs, and some for seniors. And they all claim to offer optimum nutrition. That's only the half of it. Pet supply stores stock several high-priced but more-concentrated brands, and each proclaims its advantages. Are you confused yet? You don't have to be. Selecting a healthy diet for your Chihuahua can be easy. In this chapter, we help you choose the right meals for your Chi to feed them through every stage of their life.

Building a Healthy Chihuahua

If you have a good understanding of human nutrition, you can skip this section. Nutrients serve practically the same function in dogs as they do in people, so you already know how your dog utilizes them. For those of you who were daydreaming when your teachers talked about the body's building blocks, the following sections detail what some of the more important nutrients do for your dog.

Nutrients your dog needs

Chihuahuas, and people, need a variety of nutrients to stay healthy:

>> Carbohydrates are starches, sugars, and fiber. They aid in digestion and elimination and provide energy and the proper assimilation of fats. Excess carbohydrates are stored in the body for future use.

>> Protein can come from meat, dairy, or vegetable sources. It isn't stored in the body, so your dog needs to eat it every single day. Protein is necessary for bone growth, tissue healing, and energy for normal activity.

>> Fats are energy sources. They also add suppleness to your dog's skin and luster to their coat. However, excess fat is stored under the skin and can lead to an overweight dog.

WARNING

Fat balance is important. Too much fat leads to the same obesity problems that humans suffer, and too little robs your Chihuahua of necessary protection from changes in temperature and can make them overly sensitive to cold (as if they're not sensitive enough to cold already!).

Vitamins and minerals for a balanced diet

Humans need vitamins and minerals in their diet, and so do dogs. Here are some of the essentials and their roles in keeping your Chihuahua healthy:

>> **Vitamin A** is needed for fat absorption, as well as for a healthy, shiny coat, normal growth rate, good eyesight, and reproduction.

>> The **B vitamins** protect the nervous system and are necessary for normal coat, skin, appetite, growth, and vision.

>> **Vitamin C** isn't often mentioned in an analysis of commercial dog food or vitamin supplements because dogs synthesize this vitamin in the liver, but some breeders add it to the diet anyway.

>> **Vitamin D** is necessary for healthy bones and teeth and good muscle tone, but the vitamin must be ingested in the correct ratio with calcium and phosphorus.

>> **Vitamin E** is associated with proper functioning of muscles and internal and reproductive organs.

>> **Vitamin K** is essential to normal clotting of the blood. Most dogs can synthesize this vitamin in their digestive tracts, but if your Chi seems to bleed too long from minor cuts, mention it to your veterinarian, because it could indicate a deficiency of vitamin K.

>> **Calcium and phosphorus**, in the correct ratio, are needed to provide protection from rickets, bowed legs, and other bone deformities. They also aid in muscle development and maintenance.

>> **Potassium** is necessary for normal growth and healthy nerves and muscles.

>> **Sodium** and **chlorine** boost your Chihuahua's appetite and enable them to enjoy a normal activity level.

>> **Magnesium** is necessary to prevent convulsions and nervous system disorders.

>> **Iron** is needed for healthy blood and prevents fatigue from anemia.

>> **Iodine** prevents goiter in dogs the same way it does in people.

>> **Copper** is necessary for growing and maintaining strong bones. It also helps prevent anemia.

>> **Cobalt** aids normal growth and keeps the reproductive tract healthy.

>> **Manganese** also aids growth and is necessary for healthy reproduction.

>> **Zinc** promotes normal growth and healthy skin.

Complete and balanced dog foods contain all these nutrients in the appropriate amounts.

Feeding for the First Few Days

The only right food to feed your Chihuahua for the first few days after you bring them home is the one they were eating before you got them. Even if your new Chihuahua is an adult, make only gradual changes to their diet. They're experiencing enough newness in their life right now. Many breeders give new owners a small amount of puppy or dog food and a written schedule to get them started, but if your breeder offers you nothing, ask the following three questions about your new dog's eating habits:

>> What brand of food have they been eating?

>> What's the feeding schedule (how frequently are they fed and at what hours)?

>> How much do they eat at each feeding?

Besides using the same food, sticking to the feeding schedule your Chi is used to is best, at least for the first three days. After that, you can gradually change food and chow time until their mealtime schedule blends into your household routine.

TIP

Assuming you feed your Chihuahua in the kitchen, you may want to put a small throw rug under their bowl. Many Chihuahuas (and other dogs, too) like to eat on the rug. They accomplish this by putting a few morsels in their mouths, trotting off to the closest carpeted area, and then munching them there. If your Chi is determined to eat dinner on a comfy carpet, an area rug may (notice we're not promising anything) keep them in the kitchen.

Dogs are omnivores, which means they eat both meat and plant matter.

Changing Dog Foods

If you've ever tried to change your diet — such as going gluten-free or vegetarian, trying Paleo, keto or the like — you know that it doesn't always go so smoothly. You may not like the food. You may feel sick. But we assume you chose to change your diet for a valid reason. When changing your dog's diet, they may also have some trouble, which is why you should only change *their* diet if it's necessary or beneficial for your furry compadre. This section helps you determine if you should change your dog's food and how to do so safely.

When to change dog foods (if you must)

Look at your Chi. Is their weight right for their height? Do they have enough energy? Does their coat have a healthy glow? As the old saying goes, "If it ain't broke, don't fix it." If they eat most of their meals and have regular bowel movements, an upbeat attitude, and a healthy coat, the best dog food for your pup (at least until they reach another life stage) may be exactly the one they're eating.

However, if your Chi is too thin or too fat, lacks energy, has a dull or dry-looking coat, or suffers from constipation or diarrhea, see your veterinarian. If the vet rules out parasites or an illness, consider changing your Chi's food. As you make your decision, the following section helps you understand the countless choices you see on the store shelves.

How to change dog foods

What if you've decided on a dog food and it isn't the one your new Chi was raised on? No problem. After a few days of feeding the brand they're used to, introduce the food you've selected by adding just a little bit of it to their usual diet. Watch to make sure your pup eats it and check their bowel movements. As long as everything is fine (no constipation or diarrhea), add a little more of the new food and take away a little more of their old food every day. You can complete the transition by the end of a week as long as nothing appears wrong.

If your dog becomes constipated (has to strain to eliminate) or gets diarrhea, add more of the food your Chi was raised on and less of the new food. When the dog normalizes, try gradually changing their diet again by substituting a very small amount of the new food daily. If problems persist, consult your vet. The problem may be caused by something other than a change of food, and persistent diarrhea is dangerous to Toy dogs because they can easily become dehydrated.

Shopping for Commercial Dog Food

Good nutrition is essential to prevent dietary deficiency diseases. The right diet helps your Chihuahua fight off infections and reduces their susceptibility to physical ailments. The easiest way to feed your dog a balanced diet — giving them the nutrition they need — is to choose an excellent commercial brand and stick with it. (Always make sure fresh water in a clean bowl is available, too.) The following sections compare the many options available and help you choose the right one for your situation. We also give you the lowdown on treats and other foods you can give your pup.

Guarding against bargain brands

How about we start this section with the don'ts — as in don't buy a bottom-of-the-line dog food. Bargain dog food is seldom a bargain, either financially or health wise, for your Chihuahua. The nutritional info on the package may say it has the same percentages of protein (or other nutrients) as the better-known brands, but the amount of usable (digestible) nutrients is what's important. For example, an old leather purse is protein, but it has no nutritive value.

Generic and economy brands are made of the cheapest ingredients available, and tests have found that many of them don't contain what their labels proclaim. In fact, many are downright dangerous for Toy breeds. Why? Because smaller dogs have higher energy requirements per pound than large dogs, but because of their size, they eat only a little at a time. Consequently, they need high-quality, easily digestible food, not cheap, empty calories.

TECHNICAL STUFF

So many nutritional deficiencies have shown up in dogs fed a diet of economy or generic foods that the Veterinary Medical Teaching Hospital at the University of California, Davis, labeled the syndrome *generic dog food–associated disease.* The common evidence of the syndrome is abnormally slow growth, coat and skin problems, and skeletal abnormalities.

Comparing regular brands versus premium brands

We tell you in the previous section not to go bargain hunting, but you still must consider two other types of dog food — regular brands and premium brands:

>> **Regular brands** are the well-known names you've seen on supermarket shelves for years. Their ingredients are more digestible and made from higher-quality ingredients than the economy foods. Cost wise, they're middle-of-the-road — neither the cheapest nor the most expensive.

>> **Premium and super-premium brands** are the highest-priced dog foods, and seldom are they seen in supermarkets. Instead, they're sold at pet supply stores, pet shops, and some veterinarians' offices. What sets them apart from the regular brands? Regular brands usually use wheat, corn, or soybeans as their primary ingredient, but many premium foods use a meat source as their main ingredient. Likewise, because premium foods contain only top-quality, highly digestible ingredients, they're considered *concentrated*. That means dogs eat less of them and still get optimum nutrition.

So even though they cost more, premium brands go further than regular brands. Another advantage is that concentrated food makes for smaller, more compact stools, giving you easier cleanups. Of course, that's more important to a Saint Bernard owner than it is to you, but we thought we should mention it anyway.

I bet you think we're going to tell you to run right out and buy a premium brand. But the choice isn't that simple . . . at least not with Toy dogs. We know you want the best for your Chihuahua, and premium food is the way to go if it agrees with them. But it may not. If you try a premium brand for a few weeks and your dog starts to show signs of constipation (straining to eliminate), gradually change back to a grain-based brand. Some small dogs do best on less-concentrated food and stay more regular on it. If your Chi is one of them, find a reputable brand that keeps their bowels regular and stick with it. (For more on foods formulated for different stages of a dog's life, see the section "Finding Foods for Special Circumstances")

REMEMBER

The ingredients on a container of dog food are listed in descending order, by weight. But just because chicken is the first ingredient doesn't mean the food is mostly chicken. The next four ingredients may be wheat flour, corn meal, barley flour, and wheat germ. When combined, the plant-based ingredients probably weigh a lot more than the chicken.

Dishing up dry dog food

Dry dog food, sold in bags or boxes, is the most popular type of commercial dog food. Here are the pluses of dry food:

>> It's easy to feed and store.

>> It has a decent shelf life (three to six months).

>> It has little odor.

Now consider the minus side: Chihuahua puppies may not consume enough dry dog food to meet their energy needs, although they may eat larger servings when the nuggets are soaked and softened. Read the labels on dry food carefully, because some are meant to be consumed dry, others form gravy when moistened and are meant to be eaten slightly wet, and still others may be consumed dry or moistened.

When choosing a dry food for your Chihuahua, check the size and texture of the pieces before buying. A Chi prefers small pieces they can easily chew as opposed to large, extra-hard chunks that make it hard for them to close their little mouth. Most manufacturers make versions of their foods with kibbles sized specifically for small dogs.

Also, consider that the freshest food is the best food. After you choose a brand of dry dog food, buy it in the smallest bag or box you can find. As you get down toward the bottom of the bag, check to make sure it still smells fresh, like biscuits, rather than stale or moldy.

Some dogs, including Chihuahuas, tend to gobble their kibble, swallowing it whole instead of chewing it first. This can lead to choking and even death, so if you have an excited eater, be sure to take kibble size into account.

Popping open canned dog food

The best canned foods are made mostly of meat products, have a high moisture content, and usually contain some vegetable products, too. If you want to use canned food exclusively, read the label carefully on each food you're considering. Some canned foods provide total nutrition, but others are formulated to be mixed with dry food. If the canned food alone provides every nutrient a dog needs, the label says something like, "100 percent complete" or "Complete dinner." Whether or not the canned food is mixed with dry, we prefer the brands that offer complete nutrition.

The best thing about high-quality canned foods (those made mostly of meat) is that dogs like them. In addition, they're easily stored, have long shelf lives, and some of the top brands for Toy dogs are conveniently available in the supermarket. And because of their high water content, they also help ensure your Chi stays well hydrated.

The downside of canned dog food is that the best brands (the only ones you want for your Chi) are expensive when compared to dry food. You have to cover and store them in the refrigerator after opening. They can also have an unpleasant smell after refrigeration.

TIP

Experts say it's better to put leftover canned food into an air-tight plastic container before refrigerating rather than leaving it in the can.

Serving semi-moist or soft-moist foods

As their name implies, the moisture content of semi-moist foods is higher than that of dry food but less than canned. The result is dog food with a chewy texture. The best thing about semi-moist food is its convenience. It usually comes packaged in individual servings; however, that helps owners of average-sized dogs more than it helps you. Because the serving size is probably more than a Chihuahua eats at one time, you still must put the leftovers in an airtight bag so that they don't dry out before the next meal.

Semi-moist foods are usually priced higher than dry food but lower than quality canned food. Many dogs like semi-moist food, but the reason they eat them so eagerly makes them a minus rather than a plus in the nutrition department. Semi-moist foods contain more sugar (or sweeteners such as corn syrup) than your dog should eat. They often contain high levels of salt, as well, and a variety of artificial colors and preservatives. In short, we don't recommend semi-moist foods.

Considering other options: Raw or homemade

Increasingly popular entries in the pet food category are fresh, raw, and homemade foods. A 2022 survey of U.S. dog and cat owners found that interest in homemade cooked and raw food, commercial gently cooked food, and pet food subscription services is on the rise, following in the pawprints of commercial raw food and human-grade diets, which have been growing in popularity for at least 20 years.

Preparing a homemade raw or cooked diet can be time-consuming for people with large breeds but the small serving sizes make it a breeze for Chihuahua people. The most important thing when it comes to preparing homemade diets is ensuring that the recipe is nutritionally complete and balanced. Don't just throw together some meat and vegetables and stop there; consider consulting a veterinary nutritionist, canine nutritionist, or pet food consulting company such as BalanceIt. At the very least, consult one of the many pet food cookbooks available, favoring those written by veterinarians.

WARNING

Be aware that feeding raw diets, whether commercially prepared or homemade, does have a risk for contamination and illness for both dogs and humans. A household with small children or members who are pregnant, immune-compromised, or elderly should evaluate the risks before deciding to put (or keep) their dog on a raw diet.

REMEMBER

Always use fresh, high-quality ingredients when making food for your Chihuahua, not your leftovers or food you wouldn't eat yourself. Feed homemade meals within two or three days or freeze for future use.

Commercially prepared raw and cooked pet diets are also available. They are usually frozen or freeze-dried and must be thawed or rehydrated before serving. Some frozen raw foods are available in a kibble-style format or in small medallions that can be cut into small bites after thawing.

Making the decision

Now that you know a little about the popular types of dog food (see the previous sections), which one should you choose for your Chi? Factors to consider include quality of ingredients, digestibility, the amount of energy the food provides, your budget, and whether your Chihuahua likes it. The best food in the world won't do your Chihuahua any good if they won't eat it.

A good-quality commercial food likely contains all the nutrition a Chihuahua needs to glow with good health. Whether dry, canned, raw, or fresh, the better brands of commercial food are balanced, providing your dog with the best canine nutrition known to modern science. That's why they're healthier than anything you can create at home, providing the right balance of protein and carbohydrates, fats and fiber, and vitamins and minerals. Feeding a quality commercial food also protects puppies from the dangerous but all-too-human tendency to believe that if a little of something is good, a lot is even better. Nutrition doesn't work that way; more of some substances actually can be toxic.

Choose a food that says "complete and balanced" on the label. You should also find on the label that the food has been tested to meet the nutritional levels for dogs as formulated by the Association of American Feed Control Officials (AAFCO). Canadian pet food manufacturers also follow AAFCO guidelines. European pet food manufacturers follow guidelines set by the European Pet Food Industry (FEDIAF).

For more advice on what to choose based on your Chihuahua's stage of life, see the section "Finding Foods for Special Circumstances."

Giving treats and people food in moderation

The problem with giving your Chihuahua table scraps is that tiny tummies can't hold much food at a time, and no matter how nutritious your dinner is for humans, chances are your dog's food is much better for them. Also, dogs that eat table scraps usually lose their taste for dog food completely.

WARNING

Don't give your Chihuahua food directly from the table or they'll become an accomplished beggar. If you have healthy leftovers like chicken or pot roast (not scraps like the fat you trimmed off your steak), you can serve them mixed with your Chi's dinner. First chop or mash them well and then mix them in with their regular ration. If you get lazy and leave them chunky, the dog will inhale them first and walk away from the rest of their meal.

Most of your dog's calories should come from their regular meals. The rule of paw is that only 10 percent of a dog's daily calories should come from treats. For a Chihuahua, that's not very much, so go easy on the snacks! Many companies make miniature dog biscuits or treats just the right size for Toy dogs.

Some dogs even enjoy an occasional cooked vegetable cut into Chihuahua bite-sized pieces, such as carrots, yams, green beans, or peas. Tiny digestive systems don't do well with raw veggies, so offer them only when they're well cooked and have cooled to room temperature. An occasional bit of hardboiled egg is good, too, but raw eggs are a no-no. Treats that are good for training include tiny pieces of cheese (provided that your dog isn't lactose intolerant) or chicken.

WARNING

Many dogs love a bit of cheese for a treat, but some of them can't handle dairy products because of lactose intolerance. They suffer from diarrhea and gas cramps when they dine on dairy. The only way to find out if your dog can handle cheese is to try it, so offer just a tiny tidbit at a time until you're sure that they can digest it without problems.

Finding Foods for Special Circumstances

Many of the major dog food companies offer special formulas (dry or canned) for every stage of a dog's life. And that's a good thing. Dogs have different nutritional requirements at different times, just like people. The following sections break down the different stages or options and their nutritional requirements.

Grub to grow on

Whether you choose dry food, canned food, or a combination of the two, your Chihuahua needs to eat a diet formulated for puppies (often called a *growth formula*) until they're one year old. Growth formulas contain more protein and fat than adult diets. Puppies need extra protein for growth and extra fat to maintain their energy levels.

Maintenance meals

After your Chi celebrates their first birthday, you can switch gradually to a commercial adult (*maintenance*) food (clearly labeled as such). You can use it until they're an oldster, provided that it keeps them healthy inside and out. A poor coat usually is the first sign that your dog's diet is letting them down. And depending on their activity level, you may want to adjust amounts a little bit over the years to keep them from gaining or losing weight. Due to the high occurrence of dental disease in Chihuahuas, a food designed for oral hygiene in small or toy breeds is a great choice for adult maintenance or as a regular treat.

Provisions for performers

If you decide to enter your Chihuahua in dog shows or train them for high-energy events such as obedience or agility competitions (see Chapter 12), consider feeding them a performance diet. Most performance foods have higher protein and fat percentages than maintenance foods, making them similar to puppy food. Some exhibitors simply keep their dogs on top-quality puppy food as long as they're competing.

Low-calorie cuisine

When it comes to weight issues, prevention is the best policy. Make sure your Chihuahua exercises enough, eats a regular diet of dog food (not table scraps), and doesn't get a treat each and every time they beg. If they start getting pudgy anyway, a variety of reduced-calorie dog foods are available to help them slim down. Most of them contain lower percentages of protein and fat and higher amounts of fiber than normal maintenance diets, as well as all the micronutrients in the correct ratios. This can make feeding reduced-calorie foods a better option than simply reducing the amount of normal adult kibble.

Although the fiber in a reduced-calorie diet helps your dog feel full on less food and the lower fat content helps them lose weight, other weight-loss options should be considered, too. The best option is increased exercise, with your veterinarian's guidance. If that doesn't do it, try feeding a little less of their regular food at each feeding, such as a level measure instead of a heaping measure. Start by giving 90 percent of their normal ration for a month. After that, if you don't see any improvement, talk to your veterinarian about a low-calorie food.

Senior specials and specific health concerns

Special diets are available for senior and geriatric dogs but if your Chi is a healthy oldster, changing chow may not be necessary.

REMEMBER

It's a myth that senior dogs need less protein in their diet to protect their kidneys. If anything, they need higher-quality protein to maintain good health.

When your Chi becomes a golden oldie (around age 10 or 11), try feeding them so they maintain the same weight they carried in healthy middle age. You can adjust the amounts, or even how the food is presented, to keep your senior Chi in top condition.

If they have less of an appetite than they used to, try tempting them with a few easy options:

>> For starters, warm up the food to enhance the smell. That's often all it takes to stimulate an old dog's appetite.

>> Another option is treating them as though they're in their second puppyhood by feeding small meals at frequent intervals.

>> If that doesn't help, try soaking the dry food until it softens, which makes a difference when sore teeth or gums are the problem.

>> The final option is mashing tasty goodies, like boiled chicken, cooked ground beef, or cottage cheese, into their regular dinner.

It's only fair to tell you that special foods spoil your pet and make them expect the same treatment at every meal! But then, that isn't so terrible. If your Chi is well into their teens, a little spoiling may make both of you feel better.

Most breeds are considered seniors when they're older than seven, but because Chihuahuas are so long lived (usually well into their teens), they aren't considered oldsters until their ages reach double digits.

If your Chihuahua has a specific health problem — such as diabetes, heart disease, renal failure, pancreatitis, or certain skin ailments — your veterinarian may prescribe a food formulated especially for dogs with that issue. Such diets are available only through veterinarians, because the formulas are so different that they aren't good for healthy dogs. If your veterinarian recommends a specific diet for your Chi, the vet will want to monitor the dog's progress to make sure they're doing well on it.

To supplement or not to supplement

You may also wonder if your puppy, adult, or senior Chihuahua would benefit from vitamin or mineral supplements, the same way you might pop a daily multivitamin. No matter what age, if your Chi is eating a complete and balanced diet, there's no need for them to take a vitamin as well. Doing so could even unbalance their diet.

The only time a pet multivitamin might be important for your dog is if you're feeding a homemade diet and need to provide a micronutrient supplement mix to ensure that it's complete and balanced. Another exception is if your dog has a specific health condition that responds to vitamins. For instance, your veterinarian may prescribe vitamin B12 for certain gastrointestinal issues or vitamin D3 for chronic kidney disease.

If you do give your dog supplements, be sure you're giving them vitamins made specifically for pets; the amounts in your own vitamin pills would be way too much for your Chihuahua!

Over supplementation with vitamins and minerals can be dangerous — even toxic. Check with your veterinarian before adding supplements to a balanced dog food.

Setting Puppy Feeding Schedules

Depending on your Chihuahua's age at the time, the breeder probably fed them between three and five times a day. The younger and tinier the puppy, the less they can eat at a time and the more often they need nutrition. As they grow older, they'll chow down on larger amounts at a time and therefore will need less frequent meals.

TIP

Most Chihuahua puppies need four meals a day when they move into their permanent homes, but they won't have to eat that often forever. How do you know when to cut back to three feedings? Easy: Your Chi will tell you. They'll simply start ignoring all or most of the food at one of their meals (usually when they're around three months old). After they leave most of one meal several days in a row, cut out that feeding. Give slightly larger portions than before, but offer food only three times a day.

At around six months old, your Chi will lose interest in another meal (usually the middle one). Now it's time to increase the portions again and feed only two meals a day, between 10 and 12 hours apart. Many large dogs wolf down a big dinner once a day and do just fine, but that doesn't work with a little dog. A Chihuahua's energy requirements are big and their belly is small, and too much elapsed time between meals can cause a dangerous drop in blood sugar.

As a starting point, offer your puppy a minimum of half a cup of food at every meal. If they finish it quickly, lick the bowl, and look for more, you can increase the amount. No tried-and-true rule exists for how much a puppy needs to eat, and appetites vary. Your eyes are your best gauge. They tell you if your pup is gaining or losing weight or staying just right.

Don't let your Chi keep the food dish for longer than 15 minutes. If they haven't finished the meal by then, remove it until the next feeding. This will help them learn to eat when they're fed.

WARNING

Don't try to teach your Chihuahua to clean their plate by giving the same stale meal at every feeding until they finish it. That won't teach them to eat and may make them sick. A dog needs fresh food in a clean bowl at every meal.

Filling an Adult Chi's Belly

How much should you feed your Chihuahua? The feeding guidelines on the bag or can are a good starting point, but your Chi may need more or less than the recommended daily amount. It's okay to experiment. Give a little less if they're getting chunky and a little more if they're looking thin. Depending on their size, though (some Chis range up to 12 pounds), you can expect a Chihuahua to eat anywhere from ¼ cup to ¾ cup daily.

Adult Chihuahuas do best on twice-a-day feedings. If you feed a healthy, parasite-free Chihuahua properly, they'll maintain the same weight month after month, along with bright eyes, a shiny coat, healthy skin, steady nerves, and enough energy. If something is missing from their diet, or if they consume too many calories, you'll notice. Poor nutrition displays itself through coat and skin problems and sometimes a lack of energy, and excess calories lead to obesity.

WARNING

Watch out for weight gain! Most Chihuahuas are good eaters. In fact, some Chihuahua owners have to watch their pets' weights to prevent obesity. Please don't let your Chihuahua get fat. It's bad for their bones and organs. Obesity does as much damage to dogs as it does to people. It's a major health problem in dogs in the U.S., Canada, and Europe.

After you find a high-quality dog food that your dog enjoys and obviously does well on, you have no reason to change. Your Chi won't get bored with the same food every day like you would and doesn't need to discover new shapes, colors, or sizes in their bowl at frequent intervals.

Avoiding Dangerous Foods

The following list presents a rundown of forbidden foods for Chihuahuas; some items may surprise you:

>> **Chocolate, onions, or any highly spiced, greasy, or salty foods:** Chocolate contains theobromine, a substance that's poisonous to dogs. Onions (raw or cooked) can also be

toxic, and spicy sauces and junk food lead to upset stomachs.

Children often want to share their treats with their pets; unfortunately, their favorites usually include chocolate chip cookies, brownies, and chocolate ice cream. You must let your kids know that chocolate, in all forms, is off limits to your Chihuahua.

» **Bones:** Bones from cooked chicken, turkey, and pork chops can splinter and slice open your dog's intestines. Raw meaty bones do not have this issue, but there is still a risk of a dog choking on them or swallowing a piece of bone that then causes an obstruction. If you choose to give your Chi a raw bone, let them have it only while you're there to supervise.

» **Beer, wine, or any other alcoholic beverage:** Alcohol poisoning is deadly, and it doesn't take much to poison a little dog. Also, be careful not to leave leftover cocktails where your Chi can find them.

» **Grapes and raisins:** These have been known to cause kidney failure in dogs. The dogs become critically ill, and many die even with aggressive treatment programs.

» **Macadamia nuts:** Some dogs have had serious reactions from eating macadamia nuts. And the high levels of fat in other nuts such as almonds, pecans, and walnuts can give your Chi a bellyache at best, complete with vomiting and diarrhea, and a case of pancreatitis at worst.

» **Xylitol:** Many baked goods, candies, some peanut butter, chewing gum, and other items are sweetened with xylitol, a natural sugar alcohol that's often used as a sugar substitute. It's highly toxic to dogs and ingesting it could mean a hospital stay or even death for your Chi. Read labels to make sure packaged items you give your dog, such as peanut butter, aren't sweetened with xylitol, which may also be called birch sugar.

» **Cat food:** Feed your cat out of your Chihuahua's reach. Dogs love cat food, but it contains more protein and fats than they can handle.

>> **Spoiled or moldy stuff:** Don't even consider giving your dog the leftover piece of chicken that you ignored for several days in the fridge. And be careful that they don't snatch it out of the garbage. The bad food's enticing odor will attract them. If the food is too old for you to eat, it's just as dangerous for your pup.

Of course, you wouldn't even think of feeding your Chi any of the following dangerous items, but we mention them because it's important always to keep them out of a dog's reach:

>> **Baking powder and baking soda:** If you spill some, clean up the mess before your Chi can lick it. These agents can cause myriad problems in dogs, including congestive heart failure.

>> **Coffee grounds or coffee beans:** These items can cause caffeine toxicity. (Chocolate-covered espresso beans are double trouble!)

>> **Fruit seeds, pits, and stones:** The seeds or pits of certain fruits such as apples, peaches or apricots contain cyanide, which is poisonous to people and pets. Most people have the good sense not to eat them, but pets may consider them chew toys.

Chapter **7**

Grooming the Body Beautiful

You want some really good news? Less than five minutes of daily grooming keeps your Chihuahua squeaky clean, even if they have a long coat! But the benefits of grooming go way beyond time considerations. Brushing, for instance, helps their skin and coat stay healthy by stimulating circulation and the secretion of natural oils. It also removes dirt, dead hair, and dander — dead skin cells to which some people are allergic.

Grooming also makes a Chi more lovable. After all, whether their coat is sporty smooth or luxuriously long, nice, clean hair is appealing for petting and hugging. No one likes to snuggle with a smelly, matted dog who is frantically scratching.

In this chapter, we talk about how just a few minutes of your time can keep your Chihuahua's coat enticing to the touch, as well as how you can care for their ears, teeth, nails, and eyes, and give them a bath as needed.

Keeping the Shine in Your Chihuahua's Coat

Grooming your Chi's coat daily is ideal and takes just minutes, but if that isn't possible, three times a week is the bare minimum. Caring for their coat gives you a chance to look for lumps and bruises, scratches and skin infections, and for signs of external parasites like fleas and ticks (see Chapter 14). Everything is easier to treat when discovered early.

TIP

Although most ticks are easy to spot on a smooth's sleek coat, they're a little harder to find on a long coat. Favorite hiding places are in the ears, just behind the ears, between the toes, in the thick neck hair, or in the rump area just in front of the tail. To uncover fleas, run your hand along your Chi's coat in the opposite direction from the way it grows. You may not see any of the minuscule pests move, but tiny black specks on the skin will tell you that fleas are having a free lunch courtesy of your Chihuahua. If you see the telltale specks, ask your veterinarian to recommend a treatment program (see Chapter 14) and use the products exactly as recommended.

The following sections give you some general coat care advice, discuss grooming tables, and take you through the process of brushing your Chi's coat.

TECHNICAL STUFF

A Chihuahua's coat grows in cycles. As it grows, it should look glossy, but eventually it stops growing, dries out (doesn't look quite as shiny), and finally is shed. The cycle takes a little more than one-third of a year, or about 130 days, but it varies considerably between Chis. In fact, smooth coats shed some hair all the time. Dogs that spend a lot of time outdoors always shed their winter coats in the spring because the amount of natural light affects the hair growth cycle, but because Chis are house pets and don't always grow winter coats, they tend to shed on their own personal schedule.

Starting early

How soon do you start grooming your pretty puppy? As soon as they settle in — just a day or two after you get them (see Chapter 5). Condition your Chihuahua from puppyhood to accept grooming as a fact of life, and they'll soon learn to like it. The best way to teach your Chi to enjoy grooming is to touch them all over frequently and reward them for being touched. Show them the grooming tools and let your pup get used to them before you use them. Talk to your Chi softly as you work (go on, tell them how handsome they are!). If they become fidgety, attract their attention with some tasty treats or a favorite toy and continue grooming gently. Soon the sessions will become routine, especially if you groom the same areas in the same order every time. Play soft nature sounds or music during grooming time for a complete spa experience. If lions, elephants, gorillas, and other zoo animals can learn to cooperate for grooming and medical care — and they do! — so can your Chihuahua.

TIP

If your pup is adamant about not wanting you to touch a certain part of their body — their feet, for example — don't force the issue. Instead, use the peaceful ploy presented at the beginning of Chapter 9.

Finding a place to groom

You can groom your Chihuahua on your lap or another surface with traction if they cooperate (see Figure 7-1), but some Chi owners prefer placing their dogs on grooming tables. Special tables just for grooming are available through pet supply stores, at booths at dog shows, or in animal supply catalogs. They even come in small sizes for Toy dogs.

TIP

You can also create your own grooming table. Any tabletop does well as long as it's the right height for you to work at and stands absolutely steady, without even a hint of a wobble. The top of a washing machine or dryer, for instance, can double as a grooming surface. Provide traction by placing a rubber mat or nonskid throw rug on top of the area. And never turn your back when your dog is on the table, especially if you're using a grooming noose or other tether.

Brushing up a hairdo

Whether your Chi is a smooth or a long coat (see Chapter 2), you'll wear less of their hair and they'll stay cleaner and need fewer baths if you brush them regularly. Just before brushing, give them a full-body massage. They'll love it because it feels good, but it serves a functional purpose, too: You're actually stimulating the skin and examining them from head to toe at the same time. Figure 7-1 shows a Chi undergoing such an examination. Now you're ready to brush.

FIGURE 7-1: During grooming, examine your dog from head to toe.

Doing short hair

For short-haired Chis, grab a natural-bristle brush or rubber curry brush such as a Zoom Groom, or for Chis who shed heavily, a deshedding tool such as a SleekEZ. Use a soft slicker brush and a metal comb for a long-haired Chi. Follow these steps:

1. **Place your dog so they face away from you on your lap or on the grooming table. (If they're on your lap, you might want to wear an apron over your clothes.)**

2. **Start brushing the body against the lay of the hair, from just in front of the tail to the top of the neck.**

Giving a few strokes in the opposite direction of hair growth is the quickest way to loosen dead hair. Do the same along each side.

3. **Brush the back, sides, neck, and legs in the same direction as the hair grows.**

4. **Gently turn them upside down in your lap or on the table and brush the chest, belly, and underside of the neck.**

5. **Place them right-side up and, if they're a smooth coat, finish by brushing the tail.**

6. **Praise them for being so cooperative and give them a treat!**

That's all there is to it unless it's toenail-trimming day. We explain how to handle that procedure later in this chapter.

Doing long hair

If your Chihuahua has a long coat, you need a rubber comb for the finishing touches after you complete the general steps (see the preceding section). With your Chi right-side up, comb the ear fringe and the long hair on the legs (see Figure 7-2 for an example of a groomer making her way to the legs). Be gentle, but make sure you get all the way to the skin. Next, brush the tail and then comb it. Simple as that — unless the coat is (horrors!) matted.

TECHNICAL STUFF

Chihuahua long coats have their own lingo. The hair on their legs is called *furnishings*, the tail hair is *a plume*, and the fine hair falling from their ears is called *fringe*.

Mats (balls of hair you can't get a comb through) seldom occur on a dog groomed daily, but when they do, they usually show up just behind the ears. (Of course, leg hair and tail hair is also susceptible to matting.) You can loosen minor mats with your fingers by separating each hair patiently until the mat is gone. An implement called a *mat splitter* (available at pet supply stores) usually is necessary for major mats. The splitter loosens the mat while removing the worst of it. Use it gently or it can hurt your Chi's skin and make them wary of grooming.

If your long-coated Chi has gone ungroomed for too long, your best bet is to go to a professional groomer. The pro will bathe your pup, remove the mats, trim their toenails — basically, the groomer will put your Chi's coat back in shape so you can easily care for it yourself.

REMEMBER

Do your clothes and furniture look furry? Don't blame your Chi. All that dead hair would be on your grooming brush rather than your navy suit if you brushed them daily.

Ears Looking at You, Chi!

Don't forget the perky ears when giving your Chihuahua the grooming once-over. Healthy ears are pinkish on the inside, and their edges are smooth. They don't have nicks, splits, or places along the edge where the hair is stuck together as if smeared with dark glue. When something is wrong, your nose may be the first to know. That's because nasty odors or discharges are early signs that ear mites have set up camp. These pests live in the ear canal, irritating your Chihuahua's sensitive ears and producing a dry, rusty-brown or black discharge.

Even if no unusual odor or discharge is present, suspect something if your Chi paws at their ears, shakes their head, or stands with their head unnaturally cocked to the side. Ear mites are easily banished and ear infections quickly cured when discovered early. As soon as you see any of these signs of trouble, visit your veterinarian.

REMEMBER

Are your dog's ears driving you crazy because they're erect one day and flopped over the next? The ears may be all over the place because your Chi is teething. Chi ears generally stay up by the time pups are six months old, but if your Chi's ears are still hanging like a hound dawg's by the time they're eight months old, you may as well learn to like it. They're going to stay that way! Dogs with floppy ears can be more prone to ear infections, so give ears a regular sniff and a good look to make sure they don't smell stinky or look inflamed, which are signs of infection.

Keeping Those Pearlies White

According to the American Veterinary Medical Association (AVMA) and the World Small Animal Veterinary Association (WSAVA), 80 percent of adult dogs develop gum disease by the time they're two to three years old. That is outrageous and unnecessary. If you brush your Chihuahua's teeth three or four times a week (daily is better), you can keep plaque under control and gum disease at bay.

The following sections dig a little deeper into brushing your Chi's teeth and preventing other oral issues.

Brushing tiny teeth

If you can, start brushing your Chi's teeth when they are a puppy so they can become accustomed to the process. Follow these steps to start down the road to a healthy mouth:

1. Begin by letting them get used to you lifting up the lips and gently touching the teeth and gums with your finger.

The more matter-of-fact you are about it, the sooner they'll learn to accept it.

2. **When they stop pulling away from your finger, introduce a soft toothbrush, either the smallest one made for dogs or one made for human babies.**

   At first, just touch the teeth with it, but gradually apply a little more pressure. Let them lick beef or poultry baby food (check the label to make sure it doesn't contain onion powder) or other soft treats off the brush to get a taste for it, so to speak.

3. **When they tolerate that, move the brush so it touches the back teeth and gradually add pressure.**

4. **Finally, use a gentle up-and-down brushing motion all around the mouth.** Don't miss the teeth in the back where the cheeks are located (*cheek teeth*).

   It won't be long before you can clean all of their teeth with relative ease.

Pet supply stores sell toothpaste and toothbrushes for dogs in a variety of flavors; you may even find one that makes your pup look forward to their brushings. Some veterinary clinics offer complimentary oral hygiene appointments to help teach the ropes and give tips for success. If your Chihuahua hates all the varieties you try, using plain warm water is better than no brushing at all. You can also use dental wipes, which some dogs prefer to a brush. You can make wipes part of the daily routine; keep them near the sofa and use them while you and your Chi are watching TV or just hanging out.

Never use a toothpaste meant for people on your Chihuahua. At best they can upset your Chi's stomach, and many contain xylitol, which is deadly to dogs. (See "Avoiding Dangerous Foods" in Chapter 6.)

TIP

At least once a year (twice is better), ask your vet to check your Chi for tartar buildup or other early signs of gum disease. A professional cleaning under anesthesia so the vet can treat the area below the gumline may be necessary if teeth have been neglected for years.

Removing retained puppy teeth

Just like people, dogs have two sets of teeth during their lifetimes. The puppy, or *deciduous,* teeth should all be gone by the time your Chi is six or seven months old, replaced by permanent teeth. But that isn't always what happens. Toy dogs often have a problem with deciduous teeth failing to fall out to make room for the emerging permanent teeth. This creates crowding in a dog's mouth. When permanent teeth can't slip into their slots because baby teeth are blocking them, they grow in whatever direction they can. The result is a mouthful of crowded teeth pointing every which way.

Most adult dogs have 42 permanent teeth, but Toy dogs, with their tiny mouths, often have fewer than that.

Now that you're aware of the possibility of a crowded little mouth, don't let it happen to your dog. Just by looking into their mouth, you can tell if a new tooth is trying to emerge before a baby tooth falls out; it will look as if the two teeth are fighting over a single spot in the mouth. Take the pup to your veterinarian to have the retained baby tooth removed so the permanent one can come in strong and straight.

Heeding the symptoms of gum disease

If your Chihuahua was an adult when you got them, they may already have gum disease. The symptoms of gum disease are

>> Bad breath

>> Swollen, bright red, or bleeding gums

>> Tartar against the gum line

>> Loose or infected teeth

Sometimes dogs that appear to be finicky eaters actually are hungry, but they have such sore mouths that they chew only enough to survive. If your pup has any symptoms of gum disease, see your veterinarian right away.

Trimming the Toenails

A Chihuahua's toenails are too long if they make clicking noises on the floor when the dog walks or touch the ground when the dog stands still. Dogs with long nails are forced to walk on the backs of their feet, leading to *splayed* (that's dog lingo for "spread") toes and an awkward gait. Keeping toenails short gives your Chihuahua better traction when they walk, and that's important. When untrimmed for months, toenails and *dewclaws* (an extra toenail higher on the paw that your dog may or may not have) eventually curl under the foot, circling back to puncture the pads.

TECHNICAL STUFF

Are you wondering why wolves, coyotes, and even stray dogs trot along just fine even though no one trims their toenails? In their quest for food, these animals cover enough ground to wear down their nails to a practical length — something that won't occur during your Chi's stroll from the carpet to the tile.

Trim your dog's toenails a minimum of once a month; once every two weeks is better. Our favorite type of toenail clipper for Chihuahuas is the small, guillotine-style implement, although others on the market work just fine. Between trims, teach your dog to use a scratch pad to help keep nails smooth.

TIP

Don't trim your Chi's toenails during the first week you have them. Instead, get them used to having their feet touched first (see Chapter 9).

Some people use a grooming table when trimming nails (see the section "Finding a place to groom" earlier in this chapter); others do the clipping when their Chihuahuas are on their backs in their laps. Pick the place and posture that works best for you and your dog, and then follow these steps:

1. Start the job by lifting your Chi's foot up and forward.

2. Hold the foot firmly but gently in your left hand so your right hand can do the trimming (reverse this if you're left-handed).

3. **Avoid cutting the quick by trimming the nail just outside of the vein.**

You won't be able to see the quick in dark nails, so trim just the tip of the nail, at the point where it starts curling downward. If the nails are white or light, your job is easier because the dark blood vessel inside each nail is easily seen through a light-colored nail.

If possible, have a partner distract your Chi with something special such as tiny bites of hotdog or a textured silicone lick mat or pad smeared with something tasty. That conditions your Chi to equate nail trim time with good things and to look forward to this exciting event.

Trim the nails properly and your Chi will feel nothing more than slight pressure — the same as you feel when trimming your own toenails.

WARNING

If you accidentally cut the quick, the nail hurts and bleeds. Stop the bleeding with a styptic pencil made for people, or you can use the styptic powder sold at pet supply stores. In an emergency, pressing the bleeding nail into a soft bar of soap for a minute or so also will stop the bleeding.

Without a doubt, a dog prefers prevention. Work under good lighting so you can cut nails without a mishap. Your dog may forgive a cut quick if it's a rare occurrence; but if you hurt their toes often, they'll struggle and scream when you try to work on their feet. Wouldn't you?

Chihuahuas that are terrified of having their toenails trimmed morph into monsters at the sight of a toenail clipper. If your Chi is scared, it may take two people to accomplish the nail clip — one to hold the dog and the other to wield the clipper. But remember, regardless of how frustrating the job becomes, no rough stuff. That tiny leg you're holding is breakable. If you can't do the job safely at home, don't hesitate to take your Chi to the veterinarian or a professional groomer for nail trims.

Gazing into Your Chi's Eyes

Oh, those big, beautiful eyes — the mirrors of a Chihuahua's soul. To keep them sparkling, all you have to do (most of you, anyway) is occasionally wipe a bit of "sleep" out of the corners with a clean, damp cloth.

Does your Chi have stains under the eyes that make them look like someone leaving a tearjerker movie with a mascara-streaked face? Those are *tearstains*; but it isn't because your dog just watched *Titanic*. When a Chihuahua has tear ducts that are too small, the overflow trickles down the face. To combat the issue, wipe the area every morning with a soft cloth dipped into distilled water (it becomes a habit, like washing your own face). Avoid using tear stain products that contain antibiotics. Antibiotic resistance—when antibiotics become ineffective because bacteria evolve to resist them—is real in dogs and can mean that one day when your dog has a serious infection, it won't be treatable with antibiotics.

REMEMBER

Although no treatment for tiny tear ducts exists, check with your veterinarian about the issue anyway. Some tearstains may be caused by an infection called *conjunctivitis*; by *entropion*, a genetic condition where the eyelashes turn in and rub the cornea; or by *ectropion*, a condition where the lower eyelid sags and lets in foreign matter. Your vet needs to check out the situation. The good news is that these problems aren't common in the Chihuahua.

If your Chi doesn't have tearstains, the eyes won't need any special care unless they develop a problem (see Chapter 15). Just use common sense in your day-to-day dealings. Don't get shampoo in their eyes (even the tear-free type), never spray insecticide near their head, and don't let them put their curious orbs out of the car window. If a small stone hits them in the face while you're driving, the consequences can be tragic.

Bathing Your Beauty

Your Chihuahua will seldom need a bath if you brush them regularly (see the section "Keeping the Shine in Your Chihuahua's Coat"). But when they need a bath, the following sections let you know what to bring to bath time, how to keep bath time happy for both of you, and how to properly care for your long-coated Chi.

Gathering the equipment

Gather up all your Chihuahua's bathing equipment before you get started so you won't have to turn your eyes away from a soapy-slick dog after you begin. Here's what you need:

>> Old clothes for you

    When your pup shakes, you get wet, too!

>> A tub, preferably with a drain, so your Chi won't have to stand in soapy water

WARNING

Many Toy dog owners use the sink for baths, because it's much easier on the back (and you can use the spray tool). But if you put your dog in the sink, don't take your eyes or hands off them for even an instant. A leap to the floor could be fatal.

>> A rubber bath mat for traction in the tub or part of a rubber mat to line the sink

>> An unbreakable cup for dipping water or a spray hose attachment

>> A pH-balanced dog shampoo or medicated shampoo if necessary

>> Coat conditioner for dogs (this is optional but nice — especially for long coats)

>> Cotton balls

>> A washcloth

>> Mineral oil

>> A nice fluffy, terry-cloth towel (100 percent cotton)

Prepping your Chi for bath time

The following list presents the simple steps for bathing your slick little Chi.

TIP

Wait! Before putting your Chihuahua into the tub or sink, take them for a walk outside and give them time to relieve themselves. Otherwise, the excitement of bath time may make them want to or have to rush outdoors immediately after a bath, which is a bad idea. They need to stay inside until they're thoroughly dry, because Chis become chilled easily.

1. **Begin by placing a cotton ball inside each of your dog's ears (gently; don't push it too far down) to keep water out.**

2. **Spray or pour warm water (temperature test it on the inside of your arm) over their whole body, with the exception of the face and head.**

   Massage them gently as you wet them, helping the water soak into the skin.

3. **Put a few drops of shampoo on their back, spread it around, and massage the lather into their coat.**

   Add a drop or two as needed to soap the legs, underbelly, tail, and neck.

4. **Now you've reached the most important part of the procedure: the rinse.**

   Never rush this step. If shampoo dries in their coat, they'll itch like crazy and you'll rob their hair of its shine.

5. **After the rinse, use coat conditioner (optional), following the label directions and rinsing it out well.**

6. **After their body is rinsed, wet a washcloth in warm water, wring it out well, and wipe the face and head.**

7. **Remove the cotton balls from the ears and clean each ear gently (again, not too far down) with a fresh cotton ball dipped in a tiny bit of mineral oil.**

8. **Wrap them in a towel and dry them thoroughly — from the ear tips to the toes.**

   Pay special attention to their easily chilled chest and underbelly.

Finishing touches for your long coat

After towel drying your long coat, finish the job with a handheld blow dryer. Don't spend much time drying the same spot, and don't hold the dryer too close to their body, because the hot air can burn a Chi's coat and skin. Use the warm (not hot!) or low setting (if your dryer has one) and blow their coat in the direction it grows — starting at the neck and working toward the *plume* (the tail).

When your long-coated Chi is dry, brush them with a natural-bristle brush. Then use a hard rubber comb on the ear fringe, *furnishings* (the long hair on the legs), and plume. Wow! Now they're gorgeous, and they know it! Just watch them strut when you set them down.

TIP

Is the thick hair around your Chi's anus often dirty? Use a pair of sharp scissors and carefully trim away just a little bit of hair from each side of the anus and from just below it. That should keep it from becoming soiled during bowel movements.

Chapter **8**

Chirobics: For Fitness and Fun

Although Chihuahuas are small enough to get a good workout in a one-room apartment, many become obese because their people don't encourage them to be active. They don't know how much fun they're missing! Sure, exercise is essential to your Chi's health, but it can also be a great bonding experience for you both — and tons of fun. Exercise doesn't have to feel like work.

In this chapter, we tell you how to make your Chihuahua's body-building breaks so much fun that you'll find yourself looking forward to them, too. We also include some advice for exercising senior Chis because they need activity, too!

Exercising Your Puppy

Puppies are active, no doubt about it, but it's important to regulate the amount and type of exercise they get. Like all of us, they need to become conditioned to activity over time. And in the case of puppies, their musculoskeletal system is still developing during the first year. Overdoing exercise can cause injury and affect bone growth and development.

That doesn't mean you need to restrict normal play in the house or a grassy yard. We're talking about repetitive exercise on hard surfaces, such as leashed walks on concrete or asphalt. Until your Chihuahua is fully mature physically (usually when they're 9 to 12 months old), limit long walks.

The rule of paw is 5 minutes for every month of the dog's age. So a three-month-old Chi puppy could have one 15-minute walk per day, or you could break it up into three 5-minute walks. A four-month-old puppy could have one 20-minute walk or two 10-minute walks. You do the math for your Chihuahua puppy's age. And it's never a bad idea to break it up into two or three separate walks, always at a moderate pace.

By the time your Chi is a year old, they'll be ready for 30-minute-plus walks at a time — if that's what you want to do. Exercise comes in many forms, which we'll discuss further in this chapter and in Chapter 12.

Making Exercise a Happy Habit

Make exercise a habit for your Chi, even if its form changes from day to day. Otherwise, your puppy may become the pudgy and pooped type. If Chihuahuas were people, you'd find them in the hammock on sunny summer days instead of hiking, canoeing, or swimming. Many Chis become lazy while still young but when encouraged to be active, they take to it with enthusiasm.

Chihuahuas who lead moderately active lives, instead of becoming couch puppies, will look much better *and* live longer. The muscles rippling beneath their coat aren't the only ones that exercise strengthens and tones. Their heart is almost entirely muscle, and even their intestines contain muscle tissue. Regular exercise keeps a healthy supply of blood circulating through these vital muscles. Chances are, if your Chi gets enough exercise, they'll behave better, too. Simply giving a puppy more exercise (and regular naps) cures countless behavior problems!

What's the best way to exercise a Chi? A brisk walk, an indoor game, or playing with another Chihuahua all help keep them fit.

Although your Chihuahua may play with a variety of small dogs, most Chis prefer hanging out with other Chihuahuas.

When it comes to exercise, variety is best. Jackie knows a professional trainer whose motto is, "Never let your body know what you are going to make it do next." If you get on an exercise schedule and stick with it day after boring day, your body gets so used to it that the workout stops being as beneficial as it should be. Vary the regimen so your Chi's body must stay fit to handle an assortment of activities. You may try a walk around the block one day (see Figure 8-1) and an indoor game the next. Organized activities like rally and agility (see Chapter 12) also provide exercise for dogs (and their people).

FIGURE 8-1: When it comes to exercise, nothing beats a brisk walk.

Any form of exercise you and your Chi feel like doing is fine, as long as it keeps them moving and isn't too much for them. When conditions are right, and their bodies are in shape, many

Chihuahuas enjoy long walks and hikes—at their own pace. If you stroll farther than usual, though, or the day is hot and humid, give them a rest in the shade and a drink of water at the halfway point, or simply carry them home.

REMEMBER

Chihuahuas are individuals. A three-pound Chi is typically going to poop out faster than a super-sized eight-pounder.

REMEMBER

Chihuahuas need exercise in some form all their life. That's easy with young dogs but when they're a senior, you may have to initiate play.

Playing Games with Your Chihuahua

The time has come to introduce your sweet Chi to some fun games. Most healthy, well-adjusted puppies learn physical games in a jiffy, but adult dogs who have never played take longer to adjust. If your mature Chihuahua isn't interested in playing games at first, don't give up. First, check your attitude. Perhaps you're trying too hard and making it look like work rather than fun. Next, check your timing. Was your Chi full from dinner or even sleeping when you tried to excite them? A change of attitude or timing may be all it takes to turn them into an avid game player (see Figure 8-2).

TIP

When playing games with your pup, treat them like the healthy animal they are, but don't overwhelm them with your physical superiority. Because food is a reward in many games, play before mealtime so they want to earn a tasty tidbit. Are they a little chunky? Give the pup a smaller supper if they eat several treats during playtime.

The games described in the following sections are fun for Toy dogs of all ages. Show your Chi how to play these games when you're in a good mood, and always stop playing *before* they want to. No matter how much fun a game is, it will feel like work if you keep at it until they're bored or tired. But if you quit while your Chihuahua is still having fun, they'll always be eager for the next round.

WARNING

Tile and other hard, slippery floor surfaces make maneuvering difficult for dogs. Exercise your Chi on flooring with good traction, on a rug, or in the grass. And participate with them. Even if you have a Chihuahua-safe fenced yard, putting your dog outside for an hour or so during nice weather doesn't guarantee a good workout. Chihuahuas don't like to exercise alone any more than most people do. Indoors or out, a Chi won't get active without a companion.

Hide-and-seek

Some physical games are also educational for your Chi. Hide-and-seek is one that may enhance your Chi's memory and scenting ability. Start playing hide-and-seek by following these steps:

1. **Put your pup in another room and close the door.**

2. **Hide a treat in a different room, perhaps beside a table leg or under a chair (the type they can easily walk under).**

3. **Open the door, and when they come into the room, tell them to "Find it" in an excited voice.**

   Of course, they won't know what you mean at first, so keep repeating the words while encouraging them toward the treat.

4. **Help them locate the goodie but let them make the actual find.**

   In other words, they must pick up the treat from the floor, not your hand. When they do, say "Goood Dooog" (dogs love words with stretched out sounds) while they eat it — a double reward!

5. **Put them back in the other room and place another treat exactly where the first one was.**

6. **Open the door, say "Find it," and watch what they do.**

   You'll probably have to help them find the treat a few times before they go straight to it on their own.

7. **When they succeed by themselves, repeat the game one more time and then quit for the day. (No, that wasn't enough action to count as exercise, but later on this game gets lively!)**

8. **Use the same hiding place for the next few days; soon, they'll race to the treat all by themselves on the first try, with you cheering them on, of course.**

9. **When they do, throw them a curve. Put the treat in a new hiding place, farther from the starting point, and start over by helping them find it.**

REMEMBER

   Don't tell them "No!" when they go back to the original spot. They're finding out how to use their memory, and that's good. Instead, have a treat waiting in the old hiding place every so often (once every five to ten times). Eventually, your Chi will remember several rewarding locations (from one end of the house to the other) and will sprint from room to room until they find their treats.

10. **Continue adding new hiding places (after they're familiar with all the old ones) as long as they enjoy the game.**

Chances are, they may start exercising their sense of smell as well as their body and their memory.

Variations of hide-and-seek are easy to create. Adding a second person, perhaps your spouse or child, is one way. Have the person hide behind the drapes or in a closet with the door slightly ajar. Instead of saying "Find it," ask "Where's Tom?" Meanwhile, Tom's waiting to reward the pup with a treat.

Munchkin in the middle

Munchkin in the middle takes two people and a rubber ball that's small enough for your Chihuahua to hold in their mouth but too big to swallow. Use the ball only for playing games together and put it away when fun time is over.

To play the game, the partners sit on the floor facing each other, with about 8 feet separating them. From this position, they roll the ball back and forth. You may want to put on a show to entice your Chi to join in at first, so laugh and act like scooping up the ball is a really big deal. If your partner is a child, remind the youngster to roll the ball gently so your Chi doesn't shy away from it.

Your Chihuahua should get curious about all the fun on the floor and try to intercept the ball. When they capture it, clap and cheer them on for a few seconds while they parade their prize (many dogs strut with pride when they capture a ball). Then say "Out," "Give it," or "Drop it" (whatever cue phrase you choose), take the ball from them by trading it for a treat, and start the game over. Gradually increase the distance between the partners so your Chi must run farther when chasing the ball. Be sure to keep them interested by letting them win sometimes (but not all the time!).

Catch-and-release

Make yourself a Chihuahua fishing rod and bait it to catch your Chi! Use a piece of string about 5 or 6 feet long and tie one end of it to a stick. Bait the other end by tying on a small stuffed animal or a squeaky toy. Now sit down and start fishing. Puppies usually can't resist little twitches but try a variety of "casts" to see what movements attract your dog. If you're not the crafty type, look for one of the many similar cat toys.

TIP Read your dog and make adjustments for their temperament when teaching and playing games. Some Chihuahuas love to hear you clap and cheer and will play all the harder to keep excitement in the air. Others tend to be more timid, and owners who double as pro cheerleaders may spook them into hiding.

Fetching fun

Retrieving games are favorites with some Chihuahuas, but others have no interest in them at all. Any number of objects — from sticks to small balls to miniature flying discs — are suitable for fetching games, as long as their diameters and weights are compatible with a Chihuahua's size.

When rolling or tossing something to play fetch with your pup, seeing it leave your hand is important — especially if they're a rookie. If they chase the object and bring it all the way back to you, give a treat and rejoice — they're a natural! But if the more likely scenario occurs — your Chi chases the object, picks it up, and parades it triumphantly without bringing it back, heck, let them enjoy their triumph. If you want to try to teach them to retrieve, though, after they chase and pick up the object, encourage them in a happy tone to return to you. When they bring the object all the way back to you, trade it for a treat. If they drop it long before they reach you, don't give them anything, but don't be upset, either. Many Chihuahuas don't have a strong retrieving instinct, but that doesn't mean you should give up. Keep trying occasionally, even if they show no desire to retrieve. Chis have been known to change their minds a time or two!

TIP If your Chihuahua loves chasing the object but won't retrieve it, play ball with three or four balls at a time. Roll one in a straight line. Roll the next one sideways so it rebounds off the wall. Toss the next one so it bounces gently. You get the picture. Soon your Chi will run in all directions.

REMEMBER Always roll the object away from (never toward) your Chi. You want to awaken their chasing instinct, not spook them into thinking that a strange object is heading for them. Make your tosses short at first and increase the distance gradually as they catch on.

If retrieving excites your Chi, keep them in that state of mind by limiting the number of times you play to four or five in a row, which is plenty. After that, play something else. If they become a fetching fanatic, add variations to the game by rolling the ball a little faster and a lot farther, rolling it so it rebounds off a wall, or throwing it (not hard) so it bounces (instead of rolls) away from them.

If your Chi learns to fetch well — bringing their ball all the way back to you every time — you'll be able to exercise them the lazy way: right from your recliner!

TECHNICAL STUFF

The word "retriever" is part of some dogs' breed names. The Labrador Retriever, the Golden Retriever, the Chesapeake Bay Retriever, and the Flat-Coated Retriever are just some of the breeds born with the inclination to retrieve. And even they need training to hone their natural talents!

Play-killing a toy

Play-killing a squeaky toy is good exercise, and most Chihuahuas love this type of play. Any toy that squeaks is going to make most Chihuahuas perk up their ears with interest and go investigate. Soft squeaky toys are even better!

If your Chi starts playing this game as a pup, they'll always get excited when you bring out their mousie, hedgehog, or whatever critter they love to "kill." But if you acquired them as an adult and they never learned to play, they may be clueless about what to do with their new toy.

Choose an exciting squeaky toy that their small mouth can easily grip. Play with the toy yourself while they watch. Throw it, catch it, drop it, and chase it.

As they watch you enjoy the toy, occasionally, and only briefly, tease them with it, but don't give it to them. After two or three minutes of fun, "accidentally" drop the toy near them to see if they show interest in it. If they ignore it, put the toy away until another day.

The first time your Chi takes the toy, allow them to play with it without interference for about 20 seconds. Then trade it for a treat and put it away.

Soon, they'll want a longer turn, tossing and pouncing on the toy and shaking it as hard as they can. Bring the toy out only for this special game, because toys with squeakers aren't safe to leave out for everyday use.

Exercising Your Super Senior

One of the wonderful things about dogs is that deep down inside, they'll always be puppies. An old dog may amble rather than trot, but they'll still retain their sense of humor and desire to participate in activities.

The same games puppies play appeal to Chihuahuas of all ages — especially when a treat is involved. Many sassy seniors still play-kill their mousies, and hide-and-seek is a perennial favorite. Watch your golden oldie's weight, though, and reduce the size of their dinner if they already downed several treats.

TIP

Keep your mature Chi interested by varying the routine — a nice, slightly-longer-than-usual walk one day and an indoor game the next. Daily physical activity — even a mild activity such as walking — will help keep your senior's muscles strong and their weight down.

WARNING

If your old dog suddenly ignores their favorite toy, refuses to play the games they've always loved, or doesn't get excited about going for a walk, see your veterinarian (see Chapter 13). Something may be very wrong.

3

Positive Training for Your Petite Pal

Build a bond with your Chihuahua through touch, training, and socialization.

Create confidence and good manners with consistency and positive reinforcement.

Explore the world of trick training, dog sports, and dog shows.

IN THIS CHAPTER

» Bonding with your Chihuahua

» Reading your dog's body language

» Socializing your Chi

» Teaching basic leash manners

» Working with an older Chi

Chapter **9**

Socializing Your Chihuahua

You can raise a puppy only once, so if you're lucky enough to have the opportunity, make the most of it. Socialization is a very important aspect of bringing a dog into your home. It is, simply, the responsible thing to do — for a new puppy or new adult dog.

In this chapter, we tell you how to bond with your Chihuahua, read their body language, and help them gain confidence. You also find out how to teach your Chi to walk on leash and safely introduce them to the world. There's even a section on puppy kindergarten classes. Both of you will have good times as your little Chi learns to share their charm with an admiring public.

Building a Bond with Your Chi

Bonding can be relaxing for both you and your Chi. Chihuahuas love attention and body warmth, so holding your puppy in your lap is one of the better ways to bond with them. And they won't mind if you read or watch television at the same time! While you're holding your dog, you can condition them to be tolerant of touch. If they let you handle every part of their body — from the tip of the nose to the pads of the toes (see Figure 9-1) — it becomes easier to groom and medicate them. Besides, all that touchy-feely stuff lowers your blood pressure (honest, petting dogs does that).

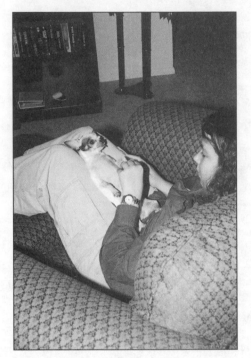

FIGURE 9-1:
Pet your Chi from their ear tips to their toes.

Is your Chi sensitive about having their tootsies (or other parts of their body) touched? You can help them form positive associations with being handled.

Pet your puppy in places they enjoy until they're nearly asleep. As they become limp, continue stroking their body, but include their feet as well. Never force touch. If they tense up, go back to petting only the body until they're sleepy enough that you can try the feet again. After they fall asleep (and they will), gently massage the toes of all four feet. Soon, your puppy will relax and let you touch their toes when they're awake, too, and that makes toenail trimming much easier (see Chapter 7).

If that doesn't work, you can teach your Chi to associate touch with treats. For instance, touch the paw with one hand, give a treat with the other hand, then pull your hands back. Repeat several times. Your Chi will soon start to expect a treat after each touch. Gradually, you can touch for a little longer — just a second. If your Chi moves away, reduce that to half a second. Eventually, you can touch the paw for a longer period, up to ten seconds. Going very slowly, work on picking up the paw, building the amount of time your Chi will let you hold their paw. Touch the paws in different ways, on the toenails or between the pads. These don't have to be long sessions. Once or twice at a time is plenty.

Once your Chi is comfortable with being touched, move on to touching their toenails with the trimmer. (Chapter 7 explains that you should introduce your Chi to grooming tools before using them.) Then pretend to clip the nails so your dog becomes used to the movement and sound of the trimmer. Finally, barely trim the tip of a single nail. Don't forget to reward with tiny treats and happy praise throughout. This can be a boring process, but slow and steady wins the race. You'll be thrilled when your Chi happily presents their paws for nail trims, lets you look at their teeth, and has a great time at the veterinary clinic because they love being handled.

REMEMBER

Be yourself around your new dog and incorporate their schedule into your routine. If your pup is napping and you want to watch TV or play the piano, do it. Your puppy can sleep through normal household noises.

Interpreting Body Language (and Preventing Anxiety)

Dogs may not talk (except on those amusing old Taco Bell commercials and in movies), but if you pay attention to your Chi's body language, you soon find out how to read their needs and even predict their next moves. Your Chi communicates through facial expressions, using ears, eyes, brows, lips, nose, and mouth. They'll also talk through their tail, coat (hackles), and body position, and emit a variety of sounds.

To give your Chi the best care, you need to know them intimately. Sit back and study the differences in body language and facial expressions when they're happy, curious, anxious, proud, and sleepy. Soon you'll be able to *read* your dog.

To start you off, here are some descriptions of general canine body language:

>> **A relaxed dog wags their tail in a methodical, neutral position — the tail isn't high, tucked under, or stiff.** The mouth may be slightly open, and the ears look relaxed (rather than fully alert). The eyes appear soft, without a trace of threat or tension, and weight is evenly distributed on all four legs.

>> **A dog who is aggressive, afraid, or defensive (often all at once) tries to appear larger.** They stand absolutely erect, hold their tail either straight out or up, and raise their hackles (the fur on top of the back). Their mouth usually is closed, and they make eye contact with their adversary.

>> **A dog who is submissive, shy, or frightened tries to look smaller by contracting their body.** They tuck their tail, flatten their ears, avert their eyes, and appear to shrink slightly.

>> **When a dog greets you with their rear end up, front end low, a wagging tail, and lively eyes, they're play-bowing.** This is dog language for "Let's play."

>> **If they flick their tongue up to lick their nose over and over, a dog is uneasy about something.** Maybe they're checking out your new friend or concentrating hard to learn a new trick. In some cases, tongue flicking precedes snapping.

>> **Mounting happens for multiple reasons.** It can definitely be sexual or hormonal, but dogs also mount, or hump, when they're excited (think of it as canine stress relief) or in play. Occasionally dogs hump in response to a medical problem such as a urinary tract infection or a skin allergy that's causing them to be itchy.

The following sections present more behaviors and advice. And remember, although the body language in the previous list is

Chihuahuas love to be loved
and are true companion dogs.
They need affection to thrive
and socialization to cultivate
their character.

Every Chihuahua should
have their own comfy
bed, for when they're
not snuggling with you.

Elegant long-haired Chihuahuas have a beautiful outer coat that can be soft and flat or slightly wavy, and they often have an undercoat, too.

When these puppies grow up, they'll probably be a lot like their parents, which is why it's important to meet the dam (mother) and any other family members the breeder may have on the premises.

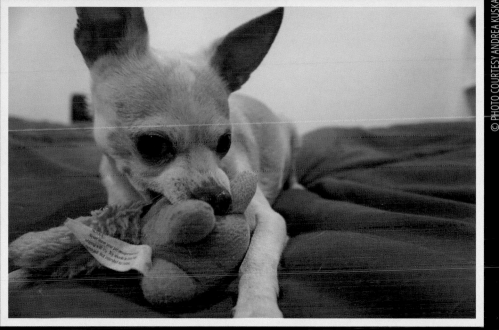

Chihuahuas love to play with toys, from small hard rubber "bones" that they can aggressively chew to soft toys for cuddling, shaking, or tossing in the air.

Although they're too small to stop a thief, Chihuahuas are alert watchdogs. If your Chihuahua's big ears detect a stranger's footsteps, the dog will race to the door, barking a warning.

Dog sports are a fun way to keep your fun-loving Chihuahua active and in shape.

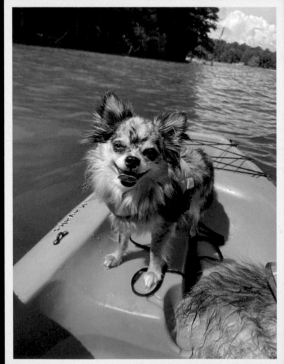

Chihuahuas aren't just house dogs. Plenty of them enjoy outdoor activities such as kayaking and hiking.

Many Chihuahuas are highly athletic. Here, Desmond whips through the weave poles in an agility competition.

Every Chihuahua should know how to walk nicely on leash and respond to basic cues such as sit, down, and come.

A Chihuahua's favorite dog is always going to be another Chihuahua, but they can get along well with larger dogs, other toy breeds, and cats, often ruling the roost.

Agility, nose work, rally, and other dog sports are great for increasing a Chihuahua's confidence and building a bond with them.

A Chihuahua's well-rounded head, often described as "apple-like," embodies the breed's alert, saucy nature.

Chihuahuas are often game for playing dress-up. Clothing is not only cute, it can be functional, accustoming pets to having something on their body in case they must wear a onesie or other protective clothing after surgery, for instance.

Chihuahuas are smart and alert, often having terrier-like qualities.

Chihuahuas come in two coat types—long and short—and many different colors and patterns.

Choose an outgoing puppy and don't neglect socialization. Chihuahuas should grow up to be confident, friendly dogs, never shy or fearful.

Chihuahuas chill easily, indoors and out. A good sweater will keep them warm on a cold winter's day.

© ADOBE STOCK
© ADOBE STOCK
© JEANMFOGLE.COM

universal, your dog will have many unique mannerisms and vocalizations all their own. Have fun learning their language!

Understanding the "jitters"

A dog who is frightened acts jittery. You can recognize this behavior by their tightly tucked tail, contracted body (to appear smaller), and flattened ears. However, sometimes you won't see their body because they'll be hiding behind your legs or the sofa. Chihuahuas often shake all over when they're scared, but shaking alone isn't a good indicator of fear. Chis also may shake from cold or even from extreme happiness or excitement.

Some dogs are born nervous because of poor breeding, but often scaredy-pups act jittery because they weren't socialized at the right time. Dogs who aren't socialized during what's called the "sensitive period" of puppyhood (from 3 weeks to 16 weeks of age) may never become fully confident companions (see the following section). You can understand an unsocialized dog's jitters by looking at the following scenario with a human child.

Imagine how a child (we'll call him Bobby) would react on his first day of school if he had been so overprotected by his parents that it was also his first experience away from home. Bobby's anxiety increases during the walk or drive to school. Traffic sounds startle him, and the sight of so many strange buildings, vehicles, and people confuse him. When he arrives, the big school building intimidates him — especially if he doesn't know how to navigate stairs. In the classroom, Bobby's fear of the strange adult called Teacher keeps him from focusing on the lesson. On the playground, he doesn't know how to respond to his high-spirited classmates. Feeling vulnerable and uncertain, he may back into a corner or become defensive and try to fight off the first child who approaches.

Here's another bad scenario: What if Bobby went on two outings before starting school? Both times, he visited his pediatrician for vaccinations. In his mind, leaving home, entering a strange building, and meeting a stranger all correlate to pain. Now Bobby can't relax or trust his teacher and consequently doesn't learn. A classroom observer who doesn't know Bobby's history probably labels him as shy or stupid — perhaps even stubborn.

Luckily for children, scenarios like that seldom occur because most parents take their kids out often. But puppies — especially Toy breed puppies — don't always have it so good. Some are raised like poor Bobby.

Good breeders socialize their puppies before selling them; the best refuse to sell puppies before they're three months old. Don't worry. Puppies are love sponges and will bond with you in no time. Besides, socialization is ongoing, and plenty of fun stuff is left for you and your puppy to do.

Using the first 16 weeks wisely

The first 16 weeks of your dog's life are critical to their social development. What a puppy discovers during that short time shapes their personality — making them outgoing or shy, happy-go-lucky or cautious.

In an ideal situation, a pup finds out how to behave around dogs during their first two months, which is why a good Chihuahua breeder keeps a litter together until the puppies are at least 8 weeks old and better yet, 12 weeks. By that age, the youngsters are mentally mature enough to leave their canine family and settle into their new human family. From then on, their people shape their personalities.

If you acquire a Chi when they're still a young puppy (under four months old), you can help them establish (or keep) an outgoing attitude. Introduce them to a friendly world and they'll grow up confident —canine clowns who show off for your friends and like learning new things. But if you keep them secluded, they'll begin to fear anything unusual. Here's how to help them blossom.

It's Party Time! Introducing Your Chi to Guests

Socialization has one big dilemma: Your Chi needs to meet plenty of people before they're 12 weeks old, but it's best to keep them away from public places where they could encounter unvaccinated dogs until their series of vaccinations is complete (see Chapter 13), which usually occurs between 12 and 16 weeks. (Puppy kindergarten is the exception because all the puppies in class have had at least one set of vaccinations.) The solution is simple — and fun. Let your dog meet new people right in your home by throwing a few well-organized puppy parties.

Introduce your Chi to men, women, and well-supervised children by inviting a small group of friends over for dessert or a movie. Schedule the get-together before your pup's mealtime. Place a bowl of your pup's dry food on the goodie table so your friends can hand-feed the dog. Show your helpers how to hold a puppy (see Chapter 5) and ask them to take turns holding, feeding, and petting your pup, one at a time so the dog doesn't become overwhelmed. Each time a human gently touches the dog's collar, paw, tail, or other part of the body, they should give a piece of kibble as a reward. You can also suggest that they wear or carry items such as hats, sunglasses, umbrellas, or uniforms so your pup learns that people can have many different looks.

TIP

Going for a short drive every so often keeps your dog from associating riding in the car with receiving a shot. Ask dogless friends or friends with well-behaved, healthy dogs if you and your puppy can stop by for a few minutes or take them through the drive-through lane at the bank or your favorite fast-food place. Investigating new places and meeting new people is wonderful for your Chi, provided there's no chance of contracting a doggie disease. By the time they're vaccinated and ready for real outings, they'll feel secure around strangers and comfortable in the car. In other words, they'll be ready to experience the world!

Leaving Home: Hello, World!

Every time your Chi meets someone new or leaves the house, they're getting socialization. Taking them with you when you visit a friend socializes them. So does meeting someone while out for a walk, playing with another puppy, or examining a beach ball.

The world is your Chi's playground, so they need to get out and enjoy it as soon as they're safely vaccinated (see Chapter 13).

Few people can pass up an adorable Chihuahua, and your pup benefits from these admiring people. They need to meet senior citizens and gentle kids, bearded men and ladies in sun hats, teenagers carrying skateboards, people in wheelchairs or using crutches or a walker, and people pushing strollers. The most important thing is that all of these are positive experiences — nothing scary or hurtful.

WARNING

Never, ever let your Chihuahua run free outside in an unsecured area — not even for a second. Always put a leash on them when they're outside the safety of your home and fenced yard (see the later section "Walking on a Leash"). And no matter how outgoing your Chi is or how well they walk on a leash, always keep them in your arms when riding an elevator. If people rush on without watching where they're going, your pup can get stepped on.

While safely outside (in your arms or on a leash), your Chi gets used to hearing motors, sirens, and the rumble of the garbage truck. Whatever you do, though, don't hold them all the time. They need to walk on grass and pavement and find out how to navigate stairs.

TIP

If your house doesn't have steps, find some elsewhere and show your dog how to manage them. Start by putting them on the third step and encouraging them to come down to you. When they get good at that, place them at the bottom of the stairs, sit on the third or fourth step, and encourage them to climb up to you.

The more people your Chi meets, the more they experience, and the more sights they see before they're four months old, the braver they become. And confident Chihuahuas are the most fun of all. The following sections explain how you can help your pup avoid or overcome fear of the world and how you can take them to class to help with your socialization efforts.

Helping your pup overcome fear

Think of socialization as a game with two rules:

>> Introduce pups to new experiences under calm, controlled, positive conditions.

>> Go slowly and pair new experiences with tasty rewards or interactive play if they prefer that.

Giving your Chihuahua a variety of experiences will help them become friendly and outgoing. Here are some suggestions:

>> Fun visits at veterinary clinics or grooming salons, just to meet the staff

>> Seeing and hearing children playing from a distance

>> Hearing sounds such as construction, lawn equipment, or buses at a distance

>> Playing in water

>> Walking on different surfaces such as gravel, sand, and wood chips

Your Chi may be afraid of things in many different places. The following list gives you some tips for curbing your Chi's fear in different areas:

>> **Objects in your home:** What do you do if your pup is afraid to investigate a new object in your house? Lay a treat trail toward the item so they're encouraged to approach it. End the trail just before the item so they feel as if there's still a safe distance from it. You can also leave them where they are and approach the object yourself. Handle it like it's a winning lottery ticket or sit down beside it. Give your pup time to approach on their own and reward them with praise or a treat if they join you at it. If the object isn't breakable or too large, roll it away from your puppy (never toward them). That may awaken their chasing instinct and entice them to play with the object.

>> **A friendly person:** When your Chi fears a friendly person, follow these steps to make an intro:

1. **Give the person a dog treat and ask them to toss it near your dog and then ignore the dog and chat with you.**

2. **If your pup approaches, tell the person to kneel down so they're near your Chi but not to reach for the dog.**

3. **When the dog gets close, the person holds their hand low, reaching under the puppy's chin to tickle their chest.**

   Reaching over your Chi's head may make them back away in fright.

4. **If your dog doesn't approach the person, don't force them.**

   Like people, some dogs enjoy being touched by or interacting with strangers and some don't. While your Chi must learn to accept handling for care from you, the veterinarian, or a groomer, for instance, it's not necessary for them to love petting from everyone they meet. Be their advocate and let them make the choice to approach someone.

>> **Loud noises:** If loud noises send your Chi behind the sofa, provide positive exposure to recordings of different sounds, going slow and starting at very low volume, maybe even playing the recording in a different room at first. Gradually increase the volume, all the while ensuring that your Chi is staying relaxed and happy.

Dealing with Sudden Fear Syndrome

REMEMBER

Between the age of 8 and 11 weeks, suddenly becoming afraid of anything new isn't unusual, even for happy-go-lucky puppies. Puppies may startle easily or suddenly become afraid of new people or items in the home. That behavior has a name — *Sudden Fear Syndrome.* If your Chi suddenly starts spooking, here's what to do.

Don't force them to face what's scaring them. Let them move away from it if that's what they want to do. If they look at you or at the object, praise and reward them with something extra-special. Do the same if they step toward it or show some other type of curiosity, such as sniffing, but stay at a distance where they're comfortable. If you don't make a big deal about it and let them control the pace, they'll learn that it's not so scary after all.

Puppies may also go through a second fear period between the ages of 6 months and 14 months. This can look like your puppy is forgetting their manners, but they may be afraid or insecure. Continue training with positive-reinforcement techniques and remember not to force them into any situations where they're unsure.

Attending kindergarten for puppies

What's more fun than watching a puppy play? Watching several puppies frolic together and then your Chi being invited to join in. This treat awaits you after your dog has been immunized and can safely attend puppy kindergarten.

Young puppies are soaking up information from their environment and their interactions with people. This is the ideal time for them to attend a puppy kindergarten class, which they can start as soon as they have had at least one set of vaccinations and a deworming. This is the recommendation of the American Veterinary Society of Animal Behavior, whose members are veterinarians with advanced training in behavior.

Puppy kindergarten classes are geared to puppies between 10 and 16 weeks of age (some rules may vary), and usually run once a week for 8 weeks. These classes provide excellent socialization by helping owners introduce their pups to people, places, things, and each other, in an environment where the risk of illness is minimized.

In addition to socialization, puppy kindergarten prepares dogs for further education. Gentle training techniques encourage them to earn praise for a job well done and to learn respect for boundaries you set. Depending on the instructors, pups may also be introduced to basic cues such as Come, Sit, and Down (see Chapter 10), and may learn how to walk on a leash.

REMEMBER

Puppy kindergarten isn't just for puppies; it's for people, too. Instructors give advice on housetraining and answer questions about dog behavior. By the end of the course, you'll know how to solve minor problems before they become major issues.

To find a puppy kindergarten near you, look online for positive-reinforcement trainers who offer puppy programs. You also can check with your veterinarian for recommendations.

TIP

Before enrolling your Chi in any class, talk to the teacher. Find out if they are experienced with Toy dogs and inquire about safety protocols. For example, if the instructor turns puppies loose to play together, you want to make sure your Chi's group is composed only of other small pups.

REMEMBER

Use your head when choosing playmates and play groups. Puppies don't know their own strength (although playing with other puppies helps them learn it). Don't overwhelm your ten-week-old Chihuahua by putting them with an eight-week-old Rottweiler. Instead, try to find other small puppies for them to play with. Sure, most puppies will probably be bigger than your Chi, but Chihuahua puppies can hold their own with other small-breed puppies of similar ages.

Creating happy car rides

To get to puppy kindergarten, the veterinarian, the pet supply store, and wherever you go on vacation, your Chihuahua will need to be comfortable riding in a car. Like anything a dog learns, being comfortable in a car requires practice, practice, practice. You can take several steps to help him stay safe and relaxed during car travel.

>> Start with short trips. Take your pup to the park, the drive-through lane at the bank, or just down the street and back. Gradually increase distance and time.

>> Keep your Chi secure in their carrier. You may have visions of your Chi riding shotgun, head out the window, ears blowing in the breeze, but the safest place is in their carrier in the footwell behind the passenger seat. Think how terrible you would feel if your pup went flying into the windshield if you had to stop suddenly. A crash-tested carrier, crate, or car seat (see chapter 5 for more information on the different types) is the safest way for your Chi to ride.

>> Prepare the carrier so it's cozy. Line it with a soft blanket, and consider spraying the inside with a synthetic canine calming pheromone or a lavender and chamomile calming spray a few minutes before you put your Chi inside. Instead of letting it swing at your side as you walk to the car, hold it in your arms as if it contained something precious — which it does!

>> Enhance the auto environment. The sound of an audiobook — think *A Famous Dog's Life*, not *Old Yeller* — or one of the many recordings of calming music composed specifically for dogs can help your Chi relax.

>> If your Chi shows signs of carsickness such as panting or throwing up, ask your veterinarian about a prescription for a medication called Cerenia, an FDA-approved treatment for motion sickness in pets.

Traveling with your Chi

Once your Chi has mastered car rides and carriers, your pup is ready to go anywhere, including on a plane or staying at a hotel. Because of their size, Chihuahuas make excellent traveling companions; they just need some practice at first. Here's how to get them on the road to being a frequent traveler.

Navigating the airport and plane rides

Is your Chihuahua going to be a member of the jet set? On a plane, they'll be in a comfy carrier, which you have already taught them to love (see Chapter 10), and riding in the cabin with you, not in cargo. But unless you're flying private, there are several steps beforehand that you'll need to master. We also have tips for once you're on the plane together.

REMEMBER

Your Chi's carrier must be small enough to fit beneath the seat in front of you, with enough space inside for your Chi to stand up and turn around. It's handy if the carrier has wheels to make it easy to move through the airport. Prepare it the same way you would for a car ride, with a soft liner and pheromone or other calming spray.

» **Paperwork:** You'll need to have your paperwork at the ready. Although you'll rarely be asked for them, it's a good idea to have a copy of your Chi's rabies certificate and a health certificate signed by your veterinarian saying that your dog is healthy to travel. Have these in hand or readily available on your phone when you check in at the airport.

» **Airport security:** Take your Chi out of the carrier before sending it through the X-ray machine. It's important for the dog to already be wearing a harness and leash before you remove them — you don't want an escapee on your hands. You can walk or carry them through the metal detector.

» **The gate:** Ask if you can board with the people who have children or who need extra assistance so you can have time to get your dog settled. If your budget permits, spring for economy-plus seating so you have a little extra space for your feet and the carrier. Kim prefers a window seat to ensure that her dog doesn't accidentally get kicked or knocked as other passengers and refreshment carts go by. Other people prefer the aisle seat for easy access and a quick exit off the plane.

» **Aboard the plane:** Have water and treats available for your Chi during the flight. You can purchase a pet water bottle that allows you to squeeze water up into a bowl-shaped reservoir for easy drinking. When your Chihuahua has slaked their thirst, any remaining water can be released back into the bottle.

» **Meals:** For long-haul flights that may require your Chi to eat a meal while on board, use a clip to attach a collapsible rubber bowl to your carry-on bag. Have an appropriate amount of your dog's food in an easily accessible zippered plastic bag.

» **Potty needs:** For extra-long flights, it's a good idea to line the carrier with a pee pad to absorb any urine if your Chi needs to potty.

Staying in a hotel

Once you're at your destination, you and your Chi may be staying at a hotel or rental residence. Here's how to ensure your pup is a good guest who will be welcomed back.

>> Have your dog potty before you enter the building — every single time.

>> Introduce your Chi to the staff when you check in so the pup can charm them with their personality and good looks.

>> In the room, set up the crate or carrier before you do anything else so they have a familiar place to rest while you unpack. It's also a good idea to check floors for anything they shouldn't eat and make sure they can't get under the bed.

>> If you need to leave your pup in the room — and if the hotel allows this — take them out to potty beforehand and then leave the TV on so the sound of human voices can keep them company. A kid's channel or an upbeat movie is a good choice.

>> If your dog is trained to use one, you can leave out a pee pad in case they need to go while you're out of the room. And don't forget to pack a bottle of enzymatic cleanser and an old towel or two just in case you have to clean up an accident. Not every dog hits the mark on a pee pad.

Walking on a Leash

If we were asked to list the mistakes Toy-breed owners make most often, waiting too long to teach their dogs how to walk on a leash would be near the top. It's so easy to carry a tiny dog that some people just don't get around to leash training. That never happens with a Great Dane!

If your Chi doesn't know how to walk on leash, and isn't used to wearing a collar or harness, follow these steps:

1. **Put the collar or harness on your dog and play with them.** Is your pup a chowhound? Put the collar or harness

on just before meals and let them wear it a little longer each time. After a few days, they'll ignore it.

2. **When your Chi is accustomed to their collar or harness, attach the leash and let them drag it around.** Keep an eye on them so they don't catch it on something and start struggling.

3. **When they're nonchalant about dragging the leash (or if they're too busy playing with it to drag it), pick up your end and follow your pup wherever they take you.** Reward them for staying close to you. Try moving in different directions — backwards or sideways, for instance — and reward them with praise (a happy "Good" or "Yes") or a treat when they follow you.

When leash-training a Chihuahua puppy, five minutes a day is enough, and more than ten minutes is too much.

4. **When they're comfortable with their collar or harness and leash in the house (this may take a few days), put a few of their favorite treats in your pocket and carry the dog outside wearing the leash, preferably in your fenced yard.** If you live in a crowded city, save leash-training for early on a weekend morning or for whenever the fewest people are out rushing around.

5. **Carry the dog a short distance away, put them down, and walk them home (it'll probably take plenty of verbal encouragement and a few treats).** If they pull and rear like a tiny bucking horse, stand and wait until their behavior subsides, then try again. No jerking, yelling, or pulling!

Keeping the experience positive is important, so ignore the rebellion and praise them when they walk with you (out in front, following behind, or beside you are all okay). Watch your timing. Be sure to give a treat when they're moving with you, not when they're balking. If they pull in a direction you don't want to go, stop and wait. When they notice you're not coming along for the ride, turn and walk in the other direction, encouraging them to follow you.

TIP

Does your Chi scream or resist walking on leash? Stay calm and keep trying. They may be fearful or anxious about this new experience. Whatever you do, don't decide to put off training until they're older. Then they will be more set in their ways and will take longer to learn.

6. **Gradually increase the distance you walk.** Instead of stopping in front of your house, continue past it for a few steps, encouraging them all the way. Show them how to walk both toward and away from home. As they improve, increase the amount of time between rewards. Most important, keep your sessions short and upbeat.

WARNING

Does your Chi cough if they pull against the lead? They may have a collapsing trachea (see Chapter 15). Consult your vet. You can prevent or relieve that problem by having the dog wear a properly fitted harness rather than a collar.

Socializing an Adult Dog

Oh no! People keep telling you how important it is to socialize a dog early, and you didn't even acquire your Chi until they were an adult. Worse yet, you think terrible things may have happened to them before you got them. Is it too late to socialize them? Is your Chihuahua doomed to be insecure for the rest of their life?

No way. Dogs don't have to have ideal puppyhoods to become contented companions. Life may have been unkind to your Chi, but just look how their luck has changed! They have you now, and the rest of their life is ahead of them. Help them make the most of it by giving them positive-reinforcement training and setting kind boundaries. Pity and pampering them might make you feel good, but it prevents the progress they are so capable of making.

To become a well-adjusted family member, your adult Chi needs self-confidence. You can help them find it. How? Show them how to please you. Begin with the basics (see Chapter 10) and then join a positive-reinforcement training class for adult dogs (see Chapter 11). Gradually, they'll gain confidence and start enjoying life.

All of the tips and techniques included in this chapter can work with an adult dog, too, from practice car rides to overcoming fears of new objects to meeting people and traveling. Give them time and patience, and you'll be amazed at how quickly they can learn.

Chapter **10**

Establishing Good Behavior and Manners

Do you know why Toy dogs have a bad reputation for being yappy, hard to housetrain, and possessive? Because so many owners let little pets get away with rudeness. We're sure you're not one of those owners. How do we know? Because you're reading about manners right here! After you train your Chihuahua with the tactics presented in this chapter, your Chi will become a good ambassador for this bright breed.

Dog training methods go in and out of style almost as often as hemlines, but the positive motivation method that's so popular today has always been our favorite. Positive reinforcement, which has been validated by scientific studies not only in animals but also in humans, works because dogs adore attention, and they'll perform encore after encore of any act that elicits your positive interest. Catching your dog doing something right and then praising them for it is the crux of positive training.

See how many good habits you can instill in your Chi through praise, petting, treats, and good timing.

In this chapter, we help you raise your Chi to be a polite pup. You discover how to housetrain — including crate training — introduce them to simple but important cues, and nip problem behavior in the bud. Not only will your dog love the positive attention that comes with training, but a well-behaved nature also will make them welcome in many more places. And going places together is one of the best parts of having a dog.

Making the Crate a Home Base

Besides serving as your pup's private den and their home away from home, your Chi's crate is your best housetraining tool. But before you teach potty manners, you should teach your Chi to love their crate. Here are some simple steps to follow:

1. **Every time you put your dog in the crate, toss a favorite toy or special treat into the crate first.** Feed meals in the crate and randomly leave a favorite toy or treat inside it for them to find. Say "Yes!" or "Good" every time they go in the crate.

2. **Once they're going into the crate on their own, say "Crate" or "Kennel up" as they enter and then gently close the door.**

3. **Now walk away. Don't wait around to see how they respond, because that entices them to react.** If they remain quiet, let them out again after a brief period. Gradually increase the amount of time they stay in the crate with the door closed. Make sure it's a rewarding place, and don't hesitate to hand out some treats while they're inside it.

It won't be long before your Chi learns what "Crate" means and enters their little den on their own.

Your Chi may cry the first few times they're introduced to their crate, but if you leave the room and don't retrieve them until they settle down, they'll soon learn to relax in it. The worst thing you can do is rescue them when they cry, because that teaches them to control you by whining and howling. If they still complain in the crate after a week or two, head to Chapter 11 for help.

At night, make sure your pup potties one last time before you crate them and then put the crate in your bedroom, right beside your bed. No, a young dog won't make it through the night, but they should be okay for three or four hours. If they cry in the crate as soon as the lights go out, sing or whistle soothingly (to let them know that someone is near), but don't take them out of the crate. The first few nights are the hardest on them (and you), because your place won't feel like home yet. A young pup is used to snuggling with their mother and littermates, and misses them most during the wee hours. Be prepared to lose some sleep. Give your pup something comfy to cozy up to.

Eventually, they'll fall asleep and so will you, but expect them to wake you with their cries after a few hours. Like it or not, you must get up quickly and take your puppy outside to eliminate. Carry them so they don't have an opportunity to potty in the house before you get outdoors.

A general rule for calculating the amount of time a puppy can hold urine in the bladder is to take the pup's age in months and add 1 to get the equivalent number of hours. For instance, a 3-month-old can "hold it" for 4 hours, a 4-month-old for 5 hours, and so on.

Dogs don't like to soil their sleeping quarters, which is why a crate is such a good housetraining aid. But if you ignore their plea to go potty, they'll soil the crate. Puppies just don't have much holding power. If crate accidents happen too often, they'll adjust to living with filth instead of maintaining the clean habits they were born with.

Never use the crate to punish your dog, and be careful not to use it too much. Your dog doesn't need to spend the majority of their time in a crate. How do you know if you're doing it right? Watch their reaction as they mature. Eventually, their attitude toward the crate should become neutral. If they either resist going into it or love it so much that it's hard to get them out of it, something is wrong.

TIP

When your Chi matures, you may want to leave a crate in a corner of your living room with the door always open. They may appreciate a private place of their own where they can chew a toy or take a nap when they need one. Let your kids and friends know that when the dog curls up in the crate, they're tired and want to be left alone.

Housetraining: Avoiding Problems

Having accidents in the house is considered one of the biggest behavior problems in the Toy breeds. However, Toy dogs have an undeserved bad reputation when it comes to housetraining. The truth is, Toy dogs are every bit as bright as larger breeds (okay, often brighter), and they can control themselves just as well as big dogs. Thousands of Toys are extremely reliable in the home, and yours can be one of them — if you follow the guidelines in this chapter. Here we show you how to housetrain your Chi from the start and avoid problems.

TIP

Even if you're lucky enough to have some vacation time to acclimate your new pup, you should introduce them to a schedule you can live with and stick to it (see Chapter 5). Don't confuse them by putting them on one schedule during weekends and vacation days and another on workdays.

Common Toy dog misconceptions

Do Toy dogs have poor plumbing systems? Not at all. Toy dogs are considered hard to housetrain because so many owners don't get around to training until their dogs have already developed bad habits. Then they face the enormous job of breaking bad habits rather than the much easier task of establishing good ones. Here's why Toy dog owners let their puppies get away with leaving puddles and poops on the floor:

>> Because the accident is so tiny that it can be cleaned up quickly

>> Because the dog hates to get their feet wet and it's drizzling outside

>> Because no one in the house feels ambitious enough at the time to walk the dog

People love to give those excuses when letting their little dogs do it on the floor just one more time. Bet they wouldn't think that way if a Saint Bernard just did their duty on the floor!

REMEMBER

To clear your head of that kind of thinking, remember the following:

>> The accident may be easy to clean, but you probably don't want to clean up accidents several times a day for the next dozen or more years.

>> Toy dogs are still dogs, and yours needs to learn to relieve themself in the right place, rain or shine. Most dogs learn to potty pronto during bad weather.

>> To housetrain a dog, you must train yourself.

REMEMBER

Just because Chihuahuas are petite creatures with tiny heads, they aren't any less intelligent than bigger dogs. Your dog will understand if you take the time and make the effort to train them.

To help them learn what you want, use a leash to keep your dog close to you until they understand exactly where they're supposed to go potty (see the later section "Keeping to a routine"). It's also your chance to learn their body language when they need to go. And keep in mind that Toy dogs have to relieve themselves a little more often than large dogs.

WARNING

Never train your Chi when you're in a bad mood. Puppies are just learning how to learn, and your earliest teachings color their lifelong attitude toward training.

Keeping to a routine

The keys to housetraining are a regular routine and an alert trainer (that's you!). A housetrained dog is simply a dog with a habit — the happy habit of eliminating outdoors.

Simply put, you need to feed (see Chapter 6), water, exercise (see Chapter 8), groom (see Chapter 7), and take your dog outside to eliminate at the same times every day. Besides being healthier, a routine makes housetraining easier. Dogs are creatures of habit, so sticking to a schedule from day one helps your Chi make sense of their new environment. As they begin to recognize their daily routine, they'll learn to understand your expectations. And because puppies love to please, the habits they form will be good ones.

When housetraining your Chi, take them to the same outdoor area to go potty every time, and repeat the same words — "Go potty," for instance — as they eliminate. Routine is important, so taking the same route to the potty place every time is a good idea (for example, go out the same door and turn the same direction).

If you live on the 20th floor of a building or in a place where the snow drifts as high as a Chihuahua's eye, you can try the litter box method of training. Line the box with several thicknesses of newspaper or use one of the many dog litter products available. Use the same housetraining routines we recommend in this chapter, but when we tell you to take your dog outside, take them to the litter box instead. Soon your Chi will be litter box trained. Pet supply stores also sell chemically treated pads that attract dogs and entice them to squat in the area you choose.

Chihuahuas are naturally clean dogs and don't want to soil their living quarters. When housetraining your Chi and establishing a routine, take advantage of that trait by confining them to a dog crate *every time* you're away or they're left unsupervised. Then as soon as you arrive home, carry them outside and praise them when they potty. If you will be gone for long periods, use an exercise pen, playpen, or small puppy-proofed room with a pee pad laid down for their use.

If they soil their crate, clean up the mess immediately. Besides being dangerous to their health, a wet or dirty crate teaches your Chi to live with their mess — an attitude that hinders the housetraining process.

Training yourself, a.m. to p.m.

Staying on a schedule makes or breaks housetraining, so plan ahead. To adjust to housetraining your Chi, you may need to get up 15 minutes earlier, come home for lunch (or hire a dog walker), and come straight home from work until your pup is a little older. The following sections present a tentative schedule to keep with a young puppy.

Morning

1. First thing in the morning, take your Chi outside for several minutes and praise them when they eliminate.

2. When you bring them in, give them food and water (see Chapter 6 for tips).

3. Take them outside again immediately after they eat breakfast. Young dogs almost always have to relieve themselves soon after eating.

4. Now they can spend time with you to exercise or have the run of a puppy-proofed room if you're at home but unable to supervise. If you're leaving for work, confine them to the crate.

5. Take them outdoors for elimination midmorning if you're at home. Set a timer or have a smart speaker remind you so you don't forget.

Afternoon

1. Take your Chi outside as soon as you get home at lunchtime.

2. Give them lunch and fresh water.

3. Take them outdoors after they finish eating. Confine them again if you can't keep an eye on them or must leave.

Evening

1. When you arrive home, take your Chi outdoors right away and enjoy a nice walk (weather permitting).

2. When you get back, let them watch you fix dinner or join you for the evening news.

3. Feed them for the last time each day between 6 p.m. and 7 p.m.

4. Take them outside after they finish eating. After they relieve themself, enjoy their company for the evening.

5. Take them outside just before you go to bed. Confine them for the night.

Recognizing the signs of need

Sometimes (possibly many times), your Chihuahua must relieve themself more often than what the sample schedule in the previous section suggests. When housetraining, prevention works wonders, so watch them closely. Take your Chi outside immediately if they exhibit the following behavior:

>> Begins walking in circles and sniffing the floor

>> Starts panting when they haven't been exercising

>> Suddenly leaves the room

REMEMBER

Play, activity, and a nice massage act as *on* switches for puppy plumbing. So if you just finished playing with or petting your Chi, it's a good idea to take them outside.

Does it sound like you'll be running in, out, and about the house pretty often? Well, for a while, you will be. But it isn't a life sentence. As your pup gets older, they'll need to eat only twice a day and their holding capacity will increase, so they'll need fewer trips outdoors.

Dealing with accidents

All puppies (and often dogs in new homes) make mistakes. If you get home too late and your Chi had an accident, don't make a big deal out of it. Your puppy won't understand why you're so angry when they were so glad to see you, and that leads to far worse problems. Pointing at the poop while screaming at them won't help. You'll surely scare them, which may lead to anxiety-related problems.

If the dirty deed was done before you got home, take your pup outside anyway. Eventually, they'll learn to expect and to wait for the opportunity to go outside. Have patience and understand that they may still be too young to control themselves for the length of time that you were away. Clean up the soiled spot as soon as you can, using an enzymatic odor neutralizer or a 1:1 mixture of distilled white vinegar and water, plus two teaspoons of baking soda, shaken well.

TIP

Buy a good odor neutralizer and stain remover. Removing the evidence of your dog's mistakes immediately keeps your house looking and smelling like home, not a kennel. An odor-free floor is an important part of housetraining. Dogs tend to eliminate where their noses tell them they went before, so quick cleanups help prevent future accidents.

WARNING

Never use any cleanup product containing ammonia, for the crate or the carpet. The odor of ammonia makes dogs seek out the same spot to go potty again.

If you catch your Chi in the act of an accident, you may be able to stop them mid-squat with a firm "Ah-ah!" or a clap of your hands. Pick them up, hurry them outside to the right spot, and praise them if they finish what they started. Contrary to old wives' tales, swatting a dog with a rolled-up newspaper or putting their nose in their mess won't work. Punishment teaches a dog to eliminate behind the sofa where they think you won't find it, not to go outside and do it proudly in front of you.

TECHNICAL
STUFF

Instead of saying "No!" to your dog when they're doing something you don't like, teach them what to do instead. Then you can say what you want them to do: "Off" or "Sit" if they're jumping on someone or "Wait" if you don't want them to run through an open door, for instance.

Communicating Using a Few Magic Words

Imagine how nice it is living with a dog that always comes when you call, sits and lies down on cue, stays in place when told to, and respects the boundaries you set. Making this happen is easier than you think. We show you how in the sections that follow. Conditioning your Chi to respond to the cues Come, Sit, Down, and Stay can start at any age, but younger is better.

REMEMBER

Conditioning Chihuahua puppies (or adult dogs) requires a trainer with an upbeat attitude — one who gives plenty of praise and *positive reinforcement* (rewarding a behavior you like so your dog is encouraged to repeat it), with absolutely no punishment. If that's you, go ahead and get going! When teaching the meaning of the following cues, praise or reward your Chi every time they give you the correct response, and simply ignore them when they don't. Dogs will do virtually anything for attention, so yours should quickly learn the lingo.

TIP

How often do you and your Chihuahua need to practice simple cues such as Sit, Down, and Come? Every day. But you don't need to set aside a special time for it. Instead, you can use them during daily life: Sit, for the dinner dish. Come, for a treat. Down, for petting. You get the picture.

Coming when called

To teach your Chi what Come means, follow these simple steps:

1. Introduce the word at feeding time by saying their name and then the word "Come" in a happy voice ("Pepe, come!").

2. Show them the dinner dish.

3. Walk backward a few steps while holding it.

4. When your pup follows, praise them and then let them eat.

5. Repeat the process every time you feed them.

When conditioning your Chi to Come, call them only when you know they want to come — not when they're sleepy or busy with food, a toy, or another person. Later, when your Chihuahua is older, you may want to attend training classes (see Chapter 11). There you discover how to teach them to Come no matter what the distraction. In the meantime, practice often. Call them for all the good stuff — dinner, treats, and cuddles — and they'll soon respond happily.

How soon should you start training your puppy to Come? As soon as they settle in. They love the attention, but keep the training sessions short (like puppy attention spans) and always be cheerful and upbeat.

TIP

Puppies love to chase, and chasing games help them learn what Come means. Touch your Chi on the rump playfully, say their name followed by the word "Come," and then run away a few steps while clapping (not too loudly) and talking happily. Let them catch you and then play with them for a few seconds before giving them another playful tap and starting over. Three times is plenty for one session.

WARNING

Never sabotage your training by calling a Chihuahua of any age to give them a pill or chastise them for something. Go to your dog for the upsetting stuff, and keep the Comes carefree. If they're ever at risk, you want them to come to you without hesitation when you call.

Sitting pretty

To teach your Chi what Sit means (see Figure 10-1), follow these simple steps:

1. **Hold a treat in front of their nose, say "Sit," and then move the treat upward and back over their head.**

    When their eyes follow the goodie upward, their head will tilt back and their rear end will lower until it reaches the floor.

2. **Give the treat immediately while they're still sitting and praise them.**

3. **Try it three or four more times, but be sure to quit while they're still having fun.**

TIP

A soft treat, such as a nibble of cheese (provided that your Chi isn't lactose intolerant), makes a good training tool. It's healthy, and a Chihuahua can eat it fast so you can continue training. Tiny pieces of soft, moist dog treats also work well.

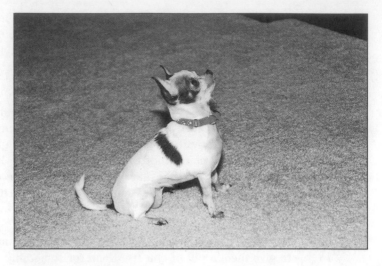

FIGURE 10-1:
Manchita
sits on cue
with eyes
focused on
the reward
to come.

Getting down

To teach the Down cue, start with your Chi in the Sit position (see the preceding section). Now follow these steps:

1. **Hold a tasty treat right in front of their nose and say "Down."**

2. **Make a movement shaped like a capital L by lowering the treat straight down, just in front of their paws, and then slowly pulling it forward at ground level.**

   As they reach for the goodie, the front half of your pup's body should move downward.

3. **If their body doesn't lower completely to the ground, put gentle pressure on their shoulders with your free hand, but don't mash them down.**

4. **The instant their whole body is in the Down position, give them the treat (see Figure 10-2).**

The other way to do this, which always works for Kim, is to wait until you see your puppy or dog lying down (like a sphynx, with paws in front and back legs stretched out behind them) and reward with a treat and the words "Yes!" or "Good!" Repeat every time you see your Chi in a down. Then you can add the verbal cue Down whenever you see them moving into that position, rewarding and praising the instant that belly hits the floor. Soon, you'll be able to say "Down" while your dog is standing and have them drop into position.

Staying put

Your Chi probably bounces up from their Sit right after you give them a treat, but now you'll prolong that process by teaching the Stay cue:

1. **Stand on your Chi's right side, with both of you facing the same way, and hold a treat in your right hand.**

2. **Tell them "Sit," but this time don't give them the treat as soon as their butt touches the floor. Instead, move your left hand sideways, stopping just in front of their nose (palm facing them), and say "Stay" at the same time.**

3. **Let a long second pass before giving them the treat.**

   Gradually — very gradually — work up to a ten-second Stay before presenting the reward. Decide how many seconds each Stay will be before you start, and vary the time. Otherwise, your Chi will soon outguess you.

What should you do if they move before time's up? Absolutely nothing. Don't reward, don't pet, and don't punish. Just try again later and praise your dog when they do it right. After they learn to stay in place in the Sit position, you can use the same procedure to teach them what Down-Stay means.

REMEMBER

Staying in place isn't a puppy's specialty, so when conditioning your young Chi, begin with two- or three-second Stays and don't try to make them remain in place longer than ten seconds (use a timer; you'll be surprised by how long ten seconds actually is). If your ultimate goal is for them to stay in place for several minutes, a training class is your best bet (see Chapter 11).

Redirecting your pup with positivity

Your petite pup may amaze your friends by walking on a leash like an obedience champ and performing Sits and Downs on cue. But if they don't behave when show-off time is over, they aren't the pure pleasure they can be.

That doesn't mean you should spend a lot of time telling them "No!" In fact, you shouldn't say it at all. The word "No" doesn't tell a dog anything. They don't know that it means "Stop doing that right now!" And "No" doesn't tell them what they should be doing instead. All in all, it's just not a useful word when it comes to dog training, so eliminate it from your vocabulary.

Instead, use the same technique that works for parents and pre-school teachers (and great dog trainers) everywhere: distract and redirect. Let's say you see your Chi chewing on the leg of one of your brand-new dining room chairs. Say "Come!" in a happy tone of voice and reward them when they do so. Then give them an acceptable chew toy and praise them for chewing on it.

If they're jumping up on a visitor, call their name and say "Sit!" Then reward them with praise. Maybe your Chihuahua isn't very gracious when visitors arrive and barks at them. Teaching your pup the cue "Go to your bed" gives them an alternative. The goal is to get their attention and give them something different to do.

Preventing Common Problems

Besides housetraining issues, common puppy problems include destructive chewing, persistent barking, jumping, nipping, and possessiveness. Okay, that's the bad news. The good news is that if your Chi is still young, you can prevent most of the typical pitfalls of puppyhood. And prevention is a whole lot easier than correcting problems after they become bad habits. Yes, that's possible, too (see Chapter 11), but why do it the hard way when prevention is so much easier? The following sections help you prevent the common behaviors before they become problems.

WARNING

Never punish your Chi for something they did when you weren't supervising. They won't know why they're being punished, which leads to all sorts of anxiety problems. Always use prevention, not punishment.

Developing appropriate chewing habits

Chewing is a normal and enjoyable behavior for dogs. And chewing is soothing for puppies who are teething. Showing them what's okay to chew isn't always easy, though. This section will help the two of you get through this often-destructive phase.

The first tip is smart management. Put away things you don't want your puppy to chew: your favorite shoes, dirty laundry, the autographed copy of your fave author's latest book. Make it easy for your Chi to succeed.

Offer an assortment of chew toys and make note of the ones they like best. Provide plenty of those but rotate them so they hold your pup's interest. Is there a certain time of day they like to chew? Make sure their favorite toy is ready to go then.

WARNING

Don't give your dog ice cubes to chew. Dogs often like to chew ice, but it can break their teeth. That's painful for them and for your wallet when you have to pay to have the broken tooth extracted or repaired.

Finally, avoid problems by not giving your puppy items to chew that resemble other things you don't want them to chew. They don't know the difference between old, holey sneakers and new shoes, and no amount of lecturing or yelling on your part will change that. Be smart and give only items that are okay for them to gnaw on.

Controlling barking

Chihuahuas make good watchdogs because they have excellent hearing and a loud bark, considering their size. Some barking is a good thing. Most people are glad when their dogs tell them that strangers are approaching their homes. But it's best to be glad quietly, taking your Chi's protective tendencies for granted instead of praising them. For example, the first time they go into a prolonged barking fit at a delivery person, don't act like it's adorable unless you want them to bark long and hard at visitors every time. It isn't barking but rather *excessive barking* that drives people mad. Let your dog know right from the start when they've barked long enough by saying "Enough" and then distracting and redirecting them. Call the dog's name and toss a toy. Ask them to Sit or Down.

The problem is, even if you take your Chi's warning barks for granted and don't bother to praise them for giving you advance notice when a visitor arrives, they usually feel rewarded anyway. That's because every time the meter reader or postal worker leaves (after being barked at, of course), your Chi thinks they chased them away. And that makes them feel macho.

Trying to thwart a Chihuahua's natural tendency to protect their family only frustrates them. Worse yet, they may learn to keep quiet no matter what instead of acting as your early-warning system. Countless Chihuahuas have alerted their families about fires and scared off burglars with their shrill bark. The trick is being able to turn off your live alarm on cue.

REMEMBER

Never punish your Chi after the fact — not even if they have a guilty look. The truth is, dogs don't feel guilt. That's a people thing. Nor do they remember what they did five minutes ago. Sure, there's poop on the rug and your Chi looks worried, but what you're seeing in their eyes is confusion. They sense that you're angry with them, but they don't know why, which makes them apprehensive. Hence, the guilty look. It doesn't mean they know they did something wrong.

Deciding if jumping is okay

Only you can decide if jumping is an okay behavior for your Chihuahua. After all, Chis weigh hardly anything, so the danger of most people being knocked over is nonexistent.

Some people like having their dogs joyfully jump on them. If you're one of those people, nothing is wrong with jumping as long as you enjoy having your Chi jump on you no matter what you're wearing. Your Chi isn't clothes-conscious enough to understand that jumping on you when you're wearing jeans is okay, but it isn't okay when you're dressed to impress. The point is, don't let them do something one day that you don't want them to do another day. Decide right away if jumping is okay or not; if it isn't, read on.

You'll have to change your Chi's method of greeting people when you teach your pup not to jump. For instance, teach them to Sit on cue (see the previous "Sitting pretty" section), and then tell them to sit (in a happy but firm voice) as soon as you open the door. When they do, kneel down to their level and give them plenty of praise. A Chi will want to jump on you for instant attention, but if you withhold your attention until after they're sitting, they'll soon learn to Sit for your praise.

Nipping nipping in the bud

Puppies use their mouths to investigate things, much the same way humans use their hands. They also use their mouths in play and sometimes to vent their high spirits. But needle-sharp teeth hurt, so you must teach your puppy that nipping isn't nice.

WARNING

Resist the urge to jerk your hand away from your puppy when they clamp down on it. That's the canine version of an invitation to play, so pulling away just makes them come back for another nip.

How can you tell your pup that clamping down hurts? Say "Ouch!" Screech it out in a high-pitched voice that lets them know they hurt you. Most pups will lick you in apology. If a week or two of yelping "Ouch!" doesn't make a difference, add a time-out by walking away every time teeth touch skin. Then come back and give them a chance to play nice. The lesson is that fun continues with gentle play but stops when bites happen. As they learn not to bite hard, you can start giving time-outs whenever teeth touch skin until they learn that teeth shouldn't touch people at all.

A last resort (use only on confirmed nippers) is dabbing Bitter Apple (an unpleasant tasting spray that's used as a chewing deterrent) on the part of you your puppy nips. This works especially well on shoelace and sock chasers and can also be used on hands.

REMEMBER

Pay attention to what incites the bite. If you're using hands or feet to play rough with your pup, stop doing that! Use a long chew toy such as a rope bone to put some distance between your hand and your Chihuahua's teeth. Consistently using all these tactics will help your pup get the idea that putting teeth on skin doesn't get rewarded.

Preventing possessiveness

Most puppy possessiveness starts over the food dish. That's because puppies compete with their littermates (brothers and sisters) for food. Sometimes they have to be deprogrammed when they enter a human family. Nothing to it. Here's what to do:

>> As your Chihuahua is eating, casually walk by and toss a high-value treat—a tiny slice of hot dog, a sliver of cheese, or a bit of burger—in their direction. You don't need to approach their bowl.

>> After you do this a few times, they learn that yummy things fall from the sky when you're around.

>> Start to approach more closely until you're standing right by their bowl when you drop the goodie. Gradually, before dropping the treat, add steps such as reaching toward the bowl, touching the bowl, or lifting the bowl.

>> Soon they should be very comfortable with you approaching their bowl. If they show any signs of concern, such as their body stiffening or beginning to eat more quickly, back up to a point where they were unconcerned and continue practicing.

TIP

If you have more than one dog, it can be a good idea to feed them separately, either in their crates or in different rooms. Even if dogs are friends, the possibility that another dog could get their food is stressful. It's also beneficial if one dog is on a weight loss plan or must eat a special diet for health reasons.

IN THIS CHAPTER

» Calming your crier

» Dealing with an excessive barker

» Continuing or correcting your Chi's housetraining

» Addressing behaviors such as humping and possessiveness

» Understanding and combating separation anxiety

Chapter **11**

Being Your Chihuahua's Mentor

You and your Chihuahua are friends and partners in life. And friends and partners don't run roughshod over each other. Even if unspoken, they have rules about how to interact with each other kindly and respectfully. Chihuahuas, however, aren't born knowing the guidelines for interacting with people so we have to help them learn that it's not okay to growl when someone tries to sit in *their* chair, bark as loud and as long as they please, play keepaway with forbidden objects, guard their food, or snap to keep their spot on the bed.

In this chapter, you'll learn how to teach your Chihuahua to channel natural behaviors such as barking or mounting in acceptable ways, curb impulsive reactions to other people or dogs, and understand how to behave in the home you share. The result? They'll go from being a tiny tyrant to a true friend for life.

Calming Your Crier

Puppies often whine and bark the first several times they're confined to rooms or crates. Head that off at the pass by making the crate a desirable place to be (see Chapter 5 and Chapter 10). Place a special treat or a food puzzle inside it when they need to go in so that they're rewarded for being there. The crate should be their happy place.

If your pup still cries, whines, or barks, don't immediately let them out to stop the racket. Doing so makes them feel rewarded for barking nonstop. Instead, wait until they're silent for at least a minute; then you can go let them out.

Some other tactics may also help to quiet your Chihuahua:

>> The first few times you confine your Chi and leave them alone, try to put up with the noise for ten minutes without doing anything. Some dogs quit sounding off when they realize they're dramatizing to an empty theater.

>> Play soft music or an audiobook. Music and the spoken word relax some dogs.

>> Make sure they've had enough exercise. Chihuahuas may be tiny, but they still need activity. If your Chi has had plenty of play and activity before crate time, they should be ready for a nap.

>> Make sure they don't need to potty. You should always take your pup or adult dog out to potty immediately before they go into the crate to make sure they will be comfortable during the time they're in it.

REMEMBER

Your Chihuahua should always have a safe chew toy and something to snuggle under when they're in the crate. This will make them feel safe and may reduce their tendency to whine and cry.

A little bit of whining or crying isn't unusual for pups, but if your Chihuahua is normally quiet in the crate and suddenly begins to cry when inside it or if they never calm down no matter what you do, see your veterinarian to rule out a health issue. If there's nothing physically wrong with them, it's a good idea to seek the help of a veterinary behaviorist, a certified applied animal behaviorist, or a trainer with certification from an organization such as the Association of Professional Dog Trainers (APDT) or Fear Free.

Quieting Your Barker

Some Chihuahuas are noisy little dogs that seem to yip at the slightest provocations and mouth off nonstop when they want attention. Their tendency to vocalize makes them good watchdogs, so smart owners don't want to completely turn off their tiny noisemakers. But frenzied barking for attention or when someone walks near the house gets old fast.

WARNING

You may want to scream when your barking dog drives you to distraction, but resist the urge. If you yell when your Chihuahua barks, they'll think you're joining in. Then the excitement of leading their best friend in a bark-a-long will egg them on all the more. Don't get exasperated and pick them up either. All that does is make them feel even braver. Why? Because in your arms they're taller and protected by you.

The following sections explain what you *can* and *should* do in two specific situations: when your Chi barks at the door and barks for attention.

Mouthing off at the door

This is a common problem, but it's one you can manage with the help of other family members or friends, lots of good treats, and praise.

One of the best ways to cure a Chihuahua that barks like crazy at the door is to set up situations in which friends bearing treats ring the bell. At the sound, put a leash on your dog, open the door, and invite the person in. Say "Sit," and as soon as your dog shuts their mouth and sits, have the visitor give them a treat. This system may take several tries, but eventually your dog will figure out that the doorbell doesn't signal the boogeydog!

Another is to practice having your Chi stay quietly in a particular place when the doorbell rings, following these steps:

1. **Have an accomplice ring the doorbell.** (The person should have their phone or a book handy because this can take some time.)

2. **When your Chi starts barking at the sound of the doorbell, just sit and wait.**

3. **When the dog is quiet, say "Yes!" or "Good!" and give a treat.**

4. **Tell the dog "Sit" or "Down" (whichever they're best at).**

5. **Reward them, say "Wait," then get up and walk toward the door where your friend is patiently waiting.**

6. **If your pup follows you, take them back to where you want them to wait and repeat the Sit or Down, reward, "Wait," and walk toward the door.**

7. **Wait until they're staying quietly in place before opening the door.** If they run over to greet your friend, don't scold them. Have your friend walk outside, and then start over.

Don't do this training more than twice at a time; you'll all get bored. Besides, your Chi can use the down time to think about what you've practiced and begin to internalize it (pros call this latent learning). Continuing practicing once or twice daily and soon your Chi will have it down pat.

TIP

Teach your Chi the cue "Enough" so you can appreciate his warning bark when a stranger comes to the door but turn it off on cue (see Figure 11-1). You can learn how to do that in the next section.

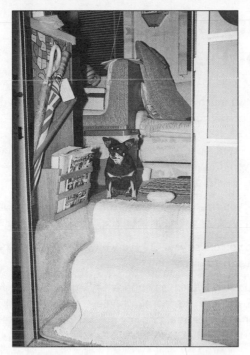

FIGURE 11-1:
Cricket
guards the
entrance to
her motor
home but
quiets down
on cue.

Yapping for attention

If your Chi barks incessantly for attention, don't give in and cuddle them; if you do, they'll discover how to maneuver a petting session whenever they want one. Instead, either ignore them or use the "Enough" cue. Here's how to teach it.

1. Choose a word such as "Enough" or any other word of your choice to be the cue for your Chihuahua to stop barking.

2. When they start barking, say the word and then wait them out.

3. The instant they stop, say "Yes!" or "Good!" and give a treat.

4. Repeat as needed.

Soon you'll be able to say "Enough" and have them respond right away.

Housetraining a Chihuahua Who's Not Getting It

Because so much of housetraining a dog is controlled by the person, let us ask you a few questions:

>> Does the cliché "When all else fails, read the instructions," fit you? Did you set up a routine, as suggested in Chapter 10, and follow it without fail?

>> Did you clean up every *accident* right away (without using ammonia or yelling at your dog)?

>> Did you praise your Chi every time they relieved themselves in the right place?

>> Did you give them an opportunity to go potty as soon as you got up in the morning and every time you arrived home, as well as after every meal, nap, and play session (up to ten times a day when totaled)?

Be honest with yourself. If your routine is haphazard or you're not taking out your dog often enough, it's *you* who are sabotaging housetraining. Get a crate, read Chapter 10, and start over.

Maybe it isn't your fault at all, however. If you did everything right and your Chi still leaves doggy-do on the carpet, keep the routine going but add the following.

>> **When you come home, don't greet your Chi or give them any attention until after you take them out and they eliminate in the proper place.** Then praise the heck out of them.

>> **Figure out your dog's bathroom language.** Most Chihuahuas (and other dogs) circle several times before squatting. If your dog starts circling, pick them up and head for the potty place. Then praise them for going there.

Circling isn't the only body language dogs use to indicate that they need to potty. They might start sniffing for no apparent reason. Some dogs go stand in front of the door or come over and look at you. If your Chi has been napping and gets up and starts moving around, take them out.

Never assume that your Chi is simply seeking attention; more than likely they're doing their best to let you know that they need to go out – now!

>> **Crate your Chi when you go out — even for just a few minutes.**

>> **When you're home, keep your dog with you on lead until they're reliably housetrained.** That way they can't sneak a whiz behind the sofa.

TIP

If you catch them in the act, keep calm, pick them up, and take them outside. Then tell them how wonderful they are for finishing the job in the right place.

The following sections explain different types of accidents.

Marking — it's a communication thing

Dogs, males in particular, have an instinct to mark their territory, for which they use (you guessed it) urine, lifting their legs on trees, fenceposts, or other vertical objects outdoors and occasionally on furniture indoors. It's one of the ways they communicate such messages as "This is mine," "Stay away," or "Hey, ladies, here I am." For male or female dogs, urine marking is natural behavior, but you may feel like bawling when your dog lifts their leg on your favorite piece of furniture or the wooden sculpture at the top of your stairs.

TECHNICAL
STUFF

We tend to think of males as the primary culprits in urine marking, but females can urine mark, too. Usually, they squat and deliver a few drops of urine, but some lift their legs like males.

Urine marking can begin as early as six months of age in Chihuahuas, as they begin to reach sexual maturity. Dogs may also urine mark if they're having conflict with other dogs in the home, if they're anxious about changes in the household, feel the need to mark new objects, or if they're feeling submissive, startled, or scared in response to a certain person's presence or to a frightening event.

Neutering provides the quickest cure. Otherwise, just keep your housetraining routine going, crate your Chi when you're away, and be patient. Housetraining an intact (unneutered) male Chihuahua is possible, but it takes longer.

Dealing with urine marking involves more than training. It's also important to thoroughly clean any areas your Chi has marked, using a good enzymatic cleanser. If your dog keeps returning to the same place, try to prevent him from accessing that area at all.

TIP

Indoors, you can put a belly band on your Chihuahua. This is a wrap that fits around a male dog's waist and covers his penis, preventing urine from reaching his target.

As with any unwanted behavior, prevention is key. If you notice your dog heading to the area where he likes to mark or even catch him starting to lift his leg, distract and redirect. Ask him to do something else and reward him for that. If you suspect that marking is a result of anxiety or changes in the household, do some detective work to see if you can find the root cause and address it. Adding a diffuser that emits a synthetic calming pheromone may help. If all else fails, consider seeking the advice of a veterinary behaviorist, certified applied animal behaviorist, or a trainer with a certification from the Association of Professional Dog Trainers (APDT) or Fear Free.

TIP

Sometimes, just as you relax and congratulate yourself on your housetraining accomplishment, your dog reaches puberty, learns to lift his leg, and must be reminded of his manners. A few weeks of keeping him on lead in the house (so he's always with you) and confining him when you're away is often all it takes to put him back on schedule.

Submissive urination

When you come home, does your dog greet you happily but with a hint of shyness, while squatting and dribbling several drops of urine? That's called *submissive urination*. Though often mistaken for a housetraining problem, this is really an anxiety problem and has nothing to do with housetraining at all. The tendency may be inherited, may be caused by harsh or too-frequent corrections, or even by abuse your Chihuahua experienced before you got them.

Though it happens most often during a greeting, a dribble may also occur when you bend over to pick them up or if you chastise them. The urination is a conditioned reflex, and your Chi isn't doing it on purpose. In fact, they don't know they're doing it at all.

WARNING

Never chastise your Chi for submissive urination, because that only makes it worse.

The easiest way to prevent a host of problems — including submissive urination, whining when confined, separation anxiety, and jumping — is to come and go without making a fuss. Long apologies before leaving and boisterous homecomings over-stimulate many dogs, and excited dogs behave erratically.

Toss a treat for your Chi the instant you arrive home instead of bending over to pick up the dog. After they eat the treat, ignore them until they come to you for attention. When they do, tickle under their chin or rub their chest (with your palm up) instead of reaching over their head or bending over them.

Use a simple cue, such as "Sit," when you greet each other (see Chapter 10). Now you've given them a positive way to express their devotion and earn praise.

REMEMBER

Compliments from you are what eventually break the submissive urination cycle. Being praised for a correct response builds confidence, and confidence is what a Chi needs to conquer submissive urination.

Getting Your Chi to "Drop It"

Chihuahuas are tiny vacuum cleaners with the mouth muscles of Jaws, Jr., and they love what they shouldn't have. How can you get them to release forbidden objects without prying their tiny traps open? Teach a "Drop it" cue (also known as "Trade" or "Swap").

To do this, load up on high-value treats such as small bits of hot dog or cheese — something your Chi really loves — and get practicing. One way is to play with one of your dog's favorite toys, ideally a tug or chew — something they're likely to have in their mouth. At some point, they'll drop it on their own, and when they do, instantly say "Yes!" or "Good!" and give one of those tasty treats. Then toss another treat a few feet away. While they speed off to get it, pick up the toy and start over. Gradually add the words "Drop it" or "Trade," just as they're about to let go of the toy and praise and reward. Eventually you can fade out the treat and simply reward with praise, play, or petting — whatever your Chi likes.

Practice this frequently in lots of different areas, indoors and outdoors, and of course be sure to use it whenever they have something in their mouth that they shouldn't.

REMEMBER

You don't always have to trade for a treat because you're probably not always going to have one handy. Trade for something of similar or higher value that your Chi likes and that's okay for them to have: a soft toy or a squeaky toy, for instance. Practice with those things as well.

WARNING

Never chase your Chi when they have something forbidden. That just makes the game even more fun for them. Get them to chase you instead and they may drop it in the excitement of the chase. And always use a happy tone of voice — not threatening or angry — when you say, "Drop it."

It's also a good idea to teach a different cue — "Leave it" — for those times when your Chi is interested in something you don't want them to have. To do this, place something on the floor that's mildly interesting, such as a piece of kibble. When they approach, say "Leave it." If they continue toward it, cover it with your foot (be sure you're wearing shoes). They may paw at your foot to try to get at it. Ignore them. At some point, they'll look at you or away from the food. When they do, praise and give a high-value reward, such as a small piece of deli turkey or roast chicken. Practice frequently with different food items or toys until it's second nature for your Chihuahua to look at you instead of trying to get at what you want them to leave.

Addressing Humping

Oh no! Your Chihuahua just humped Aunt Amelia's leg during the family reunion. Why does he do these nasty things? Rampaging male hormones are often blamed when your Chi embarrasses you by humping someone's leg or puts on a sex show with a throw pillow. Dogs don't have sexual inhibitions like people do, so they will try to satisfy their needs with whatever is available. Because legs are close enough to the right height and width, many dogs mount them.

REMEMBER

It's important to keep in mind that humping is normal, and it has causes other than sex, sex, sex. Dogs hump, or mount, for such reasons as stress, anxiety, excitement, and canine social interactions. And sometimes they hump because they're trying to relieve a physical itch in the urogenital area. Finally, your Chihuahua may have learned that humping gets your attention, and he definitely likes that, even if maybe it's not positive attention.

If your Chi humps something harmless, such as his stuffed warthog toy, does it really matter? Let him go at it. The times you want to stop him humping are when he's mounting your arm, a guest's leg, another dog who finds it annoying, or your expensive sofa cushions, or if he's embarrassing you by doing it in the presence of others.

Neutering cures many males of mounting and relieves their frustrations, making them better pets in other ways as well. But if the humping is habitual, you may not notice a difference for a month or more after surgery.

Although neutering (see Chapter 13) is the cure of choice, some people may not want to neuter their Chihuahuas because they plan to use them for showing and breeding, so it's helpful to know how to deter the behavior. The most effective method is distract and redirect.

You will soon recognize when your dog's libido is becoming overactive. If he heads for someone's leg with that telltale vacant look in his eye, distract him by using a cue such as "Sit" to stop him in his tracks. You can also block his attempt by moving in front of him and then redirecting him to do something else or to go to his place (see "Mouthing off at the door" earlier in this chapter). Ask "practice" guests to stand up and walk away if your dog attempts to have his way with them. In actual social situations, a time-out in the crate or a safe room stocked with his food, water, and toys is the best solution.

Withhold petting and praise until he works for attention by responding to a cue (such as Sit) or performing a trick (see Chapter 12) and give him more exercise (see Chapter 8).

These techniques also work with females who have a mounting habit.

WARNING

Don't get angry with your dog to teach them who's boss. All that does is teach them aggression.

Setting Boundaries

If your Chihuahua has a tendency to be possessive, their behavior may extend beyond the food dish (see Chapter 10). Some Chihuahuas demand sole ownership of their favorite chairs, their end of the sofa, or even their snuggle spots on the bed. And when anyone tries to sit in *their* spots, the resentful dogs snarl a warning and, in some cases, may even snap.

You may have heard this behavior described as "dominance" but in reality it is fueled by fear, frustration, or anxiety, not your dog's desire to "dominate" you. Aggressive reactions are ways for them to try to feel in control. Punishing this type of behavior is ineffective and can even make it worse. You never want to reward this behavior, of course, but you do want to make it go away. Chihuahuas tend to be sassy, but surly is unacceptable between friends.

When your Chi tries to defend a place, object, or even a person, there are several steps you can take to deal with the situation (see Chapter 10 for more on food aggression).

For something like a toy or other nonessential item, the simplest response can be to remove it from the home. You can also practice the "Give it" or "Trade" exercises (discussed in "Getting Your Chi to Drop It").

Distract and redirect your dog with the suggestion of a walk or play with another toy. Or lure your Chi into another room with a treat or toy. Then close the door and go back to remove the item they were guarding. Don't do this while they can still see you, even if their attention seems to be elsewhere.

A Chihuahua who guards a certain spot on the sofa or bed can be lured by calling them to come and then rewarding them for doing so. Don't risk a bite by trying to force them off. Then prevent them from regaining that sweet spot by setting boxes or books on it. Begin to teach them where they are allowed to go (see "Mouthing off at the door" earlier in this chapter), whether that is the crate or a mat or bed in a certain area, or that they're allowed on the sofa or bed only by invitation. Make their "place" cozy and inviting with a comfy bed, treats that you toss in that spot for them to find, and maybe a spritz of synthetic canine calming pheromone (not while they're on it).

If your Chi barks and growls when a person or animal approaches you, don't pick them up. You're rewarding them for responding with aggression in a misguided attempt to protect you.

Don't respond when your Chihuahua demands petting, attention, or treats by pawing at you, nudging you with their nose, or trying to get between you and someone else. Walk away. They're not your canine chaperone! Do have your significant other, family members, roommates, or frequent guests become important to your Chi by feeding them, tossing treats, taking them for a walk, or playing with them.

TIP

If possessiveness is becoming a problem, encourage other members of your household to have your Chi earn rewards by responding to cues the dog knows. Otherwise, they may learn that they don't have to respond to anyone else in the family.

Coaching a possessive pup

The same techniques both prevent and manage possessiveness (but prevention is always best). Teach your Chihuahua to exchange behaviors for food and privileges. If you haven't taught them the basic cues in Chapter 10, start now. If you did teach them, you're ahead of the game. Use them in everyday life. Say "Sit" when your Chi wants food, "Down" when your dog wants petting and "Come" when they want a treat. Have your dog sit and "Stay" before you invite them up on the sofa. Say "Enough" when you need to stop petting them and they paw you for more. You get the picture. At the first hint of possessiveness (see Figure 11-2), make these acts privileges, not rights.

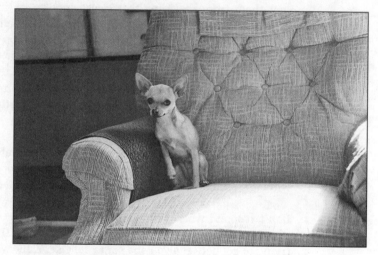

FIGURE 11-2: Possessive dogs defend "their" chairs, but Tiko hopes her owner will join her.

It's okay to have rules about when your Chihuahua can or cannot be on the furniture. Establish what's expected by inviting your Chi to sit beside you by saying "Up" and patting the sofa when you say it. Lift them up beside you if necessary. At the same time, teach "Off" by giving that cue while pointing at the floor. They'll figure out the signal if you place them on the floor every time you say it. Eventually, they'll jump up and get down on cue under their own steam. If you don't want them on the furniture at all — although we can't imagine that — then never let it become a habit. You can't say "Oh, just this once," because in a dog's mind, that's forever permission to get on the furniture.

WARNING

Young puppies can't jump up on the sofa themselves and shouldn't be allowed to jump down because they can damage their legs or shoulders. Using the cues "Up" and "Off" before your puppy matures is a good idea but place them on the furniture and always lift them down while they're young or teach them to use steps to get on and off furniture.

Finally, it's always a good idea to get your Chi checked out by your veterinarian for a physical problem if they're acting out. That may be the only way they have to let you know something's wrong. If they get a good bill of health, seek the advice of a skilled veterinary behaviorist, certified applied animal behaviorist, or trainer with a certification from APDT or Fear Free.

Dealing with hard cases

If your Chi has serious possessiveness or biting issues, don't try to deal with them yourself. Chihuahuas may be small, but they can still do damage — especially if they snap at your face. Ask your veterinarian to recommend a professional trainer or behaviorist who uses positive-reinforcement methods. The investment you make is worth it. A good pro puts your relationship back on the right track and teaches you how to maintain it.

If you ask your Chi to do something they know how to do and they don't respond, don't assume they're being defiant. They may be distracted (Look! A squirrel!), afraid, unmotivated, or confused. Think about your own job. Do you always work at the highest level every day, no matter what? Of course not. Sometimes it's Monday or you've had a fight with your spouse, or you're not feeling well. Dogs have off days, too. Your Chi may need more practice in different locations or situations, or you may need to up their "pay" by providing better rewards.

Feeling Frantic when Home Alone

Most mature dogs catch a nap when their people leave the house, but some anxious dogs experience fear, anxiety, or stress if they're left home alone. In an attempt to cope, they may chew on the carpet, shred toilet paper, urinate, bark nonstop, or unleash any combination of destructive behaviors. They sometimes drool, pace, lick, or refuse to eat or drink. These dogs are miserable because they have a problem called *separation anxiety*.

REMEMBER

Destructive behavior, excessive vocalizations, and housetraining accidents aren't always related to separation anxiety. Sometimes it's normal puppy behavior (which you can prevent with training and management). Sometimes barking is a dog's attempt to get attention. And sometimes housetraining accidents are because your dog hasn't been fully trained or has a medical or cognitive problem that is causing them to pee or poop in the house. A veterinary exam can help to get at the root of the problem.

To better understand separation anxiety in dogs, consider the phobias people have. Some people are afraid of heights, tight places, or spiders, for instance. Dogs are social creatures, and some of them are afraid of being alone. They panic, pure and simple, and then make noise or destroy stuff to release pent-up nervous energy.

The following sections provide some tips for alleviating your dog's nerves.

Adjusting your exits and entrances

Some dogs seem to be born with tendencies toward separation anxiety. Others develop it after a major change — the owner's divorce or being given up for adoption. But a surprising number of dogs "catch" the problem from their owners. It goes something like this:

"Oh, poor, poor Carina. I'm leaving now. Are you gonna miss me? Are you? I'm gonna miss you. Poor sweetums. You'll be all alone (kiss, kiss). Now you'll be a good girl, won't you? Give mama a kiss. That's my girl. Poor baby. I'll be back soon. I promise (kiss, kiss)."

And then the owner leaves.

Now, Carina just got a lot of attention and sympathy and then her human left. No wonder she feels anxious!

The best way to prevent separation anxiety is to make your comings and goings low key. Ignore your Chihuahua for ten minutes before you leave and be matter-of-fact when you return.

REMEMBER

While dogs certainly have emotions, they aren't capable of complex ones such as spite. They don't tear up the house because they're mad at you for leaving them alone. Your Chi needs help, not punishment.

The following section details what you can do for a dog that already suffers from the problem.

Alleviating the anxiety

The first step toward alleviating your Chi's anxiety while you're gone is to practice leaving the house frequently for short periods. Eventually, they learn that comings and goings are unimportant because you always return. Here's how to set up your scenarios:

1. Take your Chi outside to eliminate about ten minutes before you leave.

2. Play some soft pop, reggae (both are canine faves), or an audiobook and leave out two of their favorite toys. A food-stuffed puzzle toy is a good choice for one of them.

3. Leave your dog's crate in its normal place with the door open so they can go inside if they want to.

4. Don't say goodbye or use a lot of soothing baby talk. Just before you leave, have them go to their mat, bed, or crate and then calmly give a favorite treat. (We guarantee that it won't be long before you find them there waiting for their treat with anticipatory relish. Kim's dogs practically pushed her out the door they were so eager for their treats.)

5. Leave, close the door behind you, and count to ten. Open the door, go inside, and ignore your Chi for a minute or two. Then say "Sit" and praise them when they do (see Chapter 10).

6. **Gradually increase the amount of time before you come back in. Progress slowly at first. It's okay to take two weeks to go from ten seconds to ten minutes.**

7. **If you find a puddle or the beginning of any destruction, don't scold your dog but make a mental note of how long you were gone. Decrease the amount of time you stay away, then gradually work your way back up.**

WARNING

Now that you know what to do, here's what you shouldn't do: If your Chihuahua becomes a demolition demon when home alone, the worst — yes, the absolute worst — thing you can do is punish them when you get back. This simply causes additional anxiety. Instead of being scared only when you leave, they'll be terrified of your return, too. That means double trouble.

With practice (and patience), you may be able to work your way up to spending a few hours away from home without your Chi having an anxiety attack. Unfortunately, this doesn't work with every dog. If your dog doesn't learn to accept separations, they may need professional help, which you should seek sooner rather than later. Ask your vet for referral to a behaviorist (if you're lucky, there may be a board-certified veterinary behaviorist in your area).

The solution will include desensitization work and may include a temporary prescription of a medication to help keep your dog calm as they complete the desensitization program. Medication isn't a quick fix, and it can't solve the problem on its own, but it's a useful adjunct to behavior modification.

IN THIS CHAPTER

» Enhancing your dog's natural ability with training

» Earning the Canine Good Citizen certificate

» Introducing dog sports

» Spreading the love with a therapy dog

» Turning your Chihuahua into a trickster

» Reviewing the ins and outs of showing your Chihuahua

Chapter **12**

Teaching Your Chi Tricks, Canine Sports, and Ringside Skills

D o you want to show the world your wonderful Chihuahua? Would you like to partner with your dog to bring a little light into someone else's life? Does competition bring out the best in you? If so, this chapter contains plenty of ideas to help you and your Chihuahua find sports and hobbies you can participate in together.

Some Chihuahua owners enjoy making the most of their dogs' intelligence and dexterity by participating in dog sports like agility, nose work, obedience, and more. Others like to show off their dogs' beauty in the world of dog shows. Chihuahuas can also earn Canine Good Citizen titles, serve as therapy dogs, and even earn titles for the tricks they can do.

In this chapter, we tell you about some activities you and your Chihuahua can participate in as partners — activities that will benefit your Chihuahua and make them a better companion. We also give you a short course in trick training, for fun and functionality.

REMEMBER

Chihuahua mixes or purebreds without papers can still participate in every event in this chapter with the exception of dog shows. The American Kennel Club (AKC) will grant a Purebred Alternative Listing to Chihuahuas or Chihuahua-looking dogs to allow them to compete in such sports as obedience and agility. (See Chapter 17 for more on the AKC.) Chihuahua mixes can get a Canine Partners number that allows them to compete in dog sports. The UKC also welcomes spayed/neutered, unregistered purebreds, and mixed breeds to their dog sport competitions. Therapy dogs and Canine Good Citizens may be any breed or mix.

Beginning Training

We like to call this *companion dog training,* because it teaches the dog how to be a happy and responsive partner and you how to train, understand, communicate with, and enjoy your dog. During classes, your Chi discovers how to work with you despite distractions like strangers and other dogs. The result is enhanced companionship. Some simply call it teamwork. Whatever you call it, training provides a great background for any other activity you may want to do with your dog.

WARNING

If a dog trainer suggests a training method or correction that doesn't feel right to you, don't do it. This is your dog, and you have the final say in their training. Advocate for your Chi!

Years ago, common knowledge said that dogs shouldn't attend training classes until they were at least six months old. Back then, obedience exercises (such as the long sit; see Figure 12-1) were tools people practiced on the training field once a week and for a few minutes a day at home. Today, training schools are modernized. Contemporary classes concentrate on practical training, and up-to-date instructors teach students how to incorporate training into everyday life. Modern instructors also promote positive reinforcement rather than punishment so dogs learn without becoming stressed. We also know that four months is an ideal age to enter your Chi into a beginner, or novice, class (the next step after puppy kindergarten), although dogs benefit from training at any age.

Reviewing training basics

In puppy kindergarten and beginner classes, a Chihuahua learns to

>> Walk nicely on and off leash

>> Sit on cue or when you stop

>> Lie down on cue

>> Come when called

>> Remain in both the "Sit" and "Down" positions amid distractions from other dogs or people

>> Understand cues like "Leave it" or "Stay"

>> Touch or target an item with nose or paw

>> Become used to having their body handled or touched for examination

>> Perform cooperative care behaviors such as a chin rest or giving a paw, which are useful for veterinary visits, giving medication, or trimming nails

>> Go to a specific place, such as a bed, mat, or crate

In the same class, you, the handler, will learn

>> Socialization skills

>> Housetraining skills

>> Crate training skills

>> How to deal with play biting, jumping up, and other unwanted behaviors

>> How to recognize and respond to your dog's fear, anxiety, and stress

>> How to understand what your dog is trying to communicate through body language and vocalizations

Best of all, if the training is positive and upbeat (don't stick around if it isn't), you and your Chi gain considerable confidence from the classes.

Dog clubs and private instructors offer obedience classes. Your veterinarian may have info about nearby classes or be able to recommend a positive-reinforcement trainer.

TIP

Although the ultimate goal of training is a happy partnership with your dog, the various dog sports are a great way to build a bond and have fun with your Chi.

Choosing a trainer

Whether you're starting with basic training or wanting to get started in a dog sport, shopping around is a good idea when it comes to dog training — not for a bargain but for the best school for you and your Chihuahua. Your Chi needs an instructor who has experience with dogs of all sizes — especially tiny ones.

You'll recognize a first-rate teacher even though you don't know much about dog training yet. How? By your powers of observation. Watch a session or two of each beginner class offered in your area before signing up for one. Top-notch teachers have several attributes in common. Look for the following traits:

>> **Good instructors are safety conscious**. They demand that all dogs be vaccinated (see Chapter 13). They don't crowd too many student teams into too small a space, and they provide a training area with sufficient traction and no hidden obstructions.

>> **Good instructors are masters of positive motivation.** They show their students how to use praise, petting, and toys to encourage correct responses.

>> **Good instructors are flexible.** They adapt their methods to fit the needs of their students, both human and canine.

>> **Good instructors are approachable, friendly, and helpful.** They have upbeat attitudes.

>> **Good instructors are creative.** They incorporate games into training so handlers and dogs have a good time while learning.

>> **Good instructors are attentive to all their students.** They work well with handlers and dogs of all sizes, shapes, ages, and genders, and they aren't prejudiced against any breed or mix.

>> **Good instructors have lesson plans.** They discuss training goals and explain how to work each new cue into everyday life. Their classes are never chaotic.

>> **Good instructors keep the class moving.** They don't allow one student to monopolize the lesson.

>> **Good instructors respect their students and have empathy.** They're aware that everyone in the class has feelings — including the dogs.

FIGURE 12-1: Maxie and Ginny demonstrate an obedience exercise called the long sit.

TIP

One of the really cool things you discover in training class is that dogs, because they're closer to the ground, see things differently than humans do. When a student's dog seems leery about something, a good instructor will tell the student to get down and look at it from the pet's perspective. Try it sometime.

Passing the Canine Good Citizen Test

According to the AKC, "A Canine Good Citizen is a dog that makes its owner happy without making someone else unhappy." That means Canine Good Citizens behave at home, are good neighbors, and are polite in public.

The Canine Good Citizen (CGC) test is pass-fail and noncompetitive. During the test, dogs are evaluated on how they behave during everyday situations, like being touched by a friendly stranger, walking on a crowded street, meeting another dog while out for a stroll, and coming when called. They are also graded on their reaction to distractions and their attitude when you're out of sight (they shouldn't show separation anxiety). In addition, they must respond to simple cues such as "Sit" and "Down" (see Chapter 10).

All CGC tests are performed on leash. Chihuahuas who pass the ten-part test earn the title Canine Good Citizen. Additional CGC titles include AKC Community Canine, where dogs are tested in a real-world environment, and AKC Urban CGC, which tests dogs in an active city or town setting. In Canada, dogs can earn the Canine Good Neighbour title from the Canadian Kennel Club.

Why go for the CGC or CGN? While preparing for the test, owners find out how to train their dogs, and their dogs become better companions. Many dog clubs and private obedience schools offer short courses for these tests, and some of them give the test as their graduation exercise. In addition, the AKC offers free info to help people train for the test.

TIP

For training material and information on how to find a test site near you, visit the website of the American Kennel Club or the Canadian Kennel Club.

Getting Active in Agility

How much fun can you handle? If you're thinking "a whole lot," agility may be the sport for you and your Chi. Thousands of dog owners swear that agility is the most fun you can have with a dog.

At agility trials, dogs are timed as they navigate a course that resembles a colorful playground. They soar over hurdles, weave through poles, stride across balance beams, sprint up A-frames, play seesaw, and crawl through tunnels. Meanwhile, their handlers point out the next obstacle in the path (dogs must take obstacles in the correct order) and direct them through the course. Audiences at agility trials are always encouraging, but when the crowd sees a Chihuahua, the applause always amplifies!

TIP

Sporting events for dogs may occur indoors or outside in all kinds of weather. Be aware that your Chihuahua won't be allowed to wear a sweater during competition. Your Chi won't do their best when chilled, so plan to attend dog events during the warm months unless the trials take place indoors.

Many owners do agility training with their dogs just for fun, but plenty of titles await you and your Chi if competition is your thing. Few people want to landscape their yards with agility equipment (at least not at first), so most agility enthusiasts attend a private instructor's classes or join an agility club. Besides having the attributes of a good dog trainer (see "Choosing a trainer" earlier in this chapter), a good agility teacher also

>> Provides sturdy obstacles with neither rough edges nor a hint of a wobble

>> Goes slow and keeps the obstacles low, making sure every dog and handler in the class has a firm foundation

>> Provides new challenges by building on that foundation

Other sports you and your Chi might want to try include

>> Flyball (Active Chihuahuas who love tennis balls are MVPs on flyball teams because their small size lowers the jump heights for the rest of the dogs on the team — hurdles are set to the height appropriate for the shortest dog.)

- Barn Hunt (finding rats in a box — don't worry; no animals are harmed)

- Freestyle (dancing with dogs)

- Nose work (sniffing out specific scents)

- Obedience (performing specific skills with precision)

- Rally (a more free-form style of obedience)

- Tracking (following a human scent)

TECHNICAL STUFF

DOG SPORT ORGANIZATIONS

To try out any or all of the sports you and your Chihuahua might enjoy, contact the following organizations, open to all breeds and mixes, for information about training, rules, and entries:

- Agility: American Kennel Club, akc.org; Canadian Kennel Club, ckc.ca; Canine Performance Events, k9cpe.com; United States Dog Agility Association, usdaa.com; United Kennel Club, ukc.org; North American Dog Agility Council, nadac.com; Teacup Dogs Agility Association, k9tdaa.com; and Australian Shepherd Club of America (not just for Australian Shepherds!), asca.org

- Barn Hunt: Barn Hunt Association, barnhunt.com

- Flyball: North American Flyball Association, flyball.org

- Freestyle: World Canine Freestyle Organization, worldcaninefreestyle.org; Canine Freestyle Federation, canine-freestyle.org

- Nose work: National Association of Canine Scent Work, nacsw. net; United States Canine Scent Sports, uscaninescentsports. com; AKC; CKC; UKC

- Obedience: AKC; UKC; CKC; ASCA

- Rally: AKC; World Cynosport Rally, rallydogs.com; UKC; CKC

- Tracking: AKC; ASCA; CKC

Helping Kids, Seniors, and Hospital Patients with Therapy Dogs

Many scientific studies have found that interacting with friendly animals is therapeutic for people. As a result, trained pets are welcomed at hospitals, schools, and nursing homes.

Well-socialized Chihuahuas make top-notch therapy dogs because they're world-class lap-sitters and trick performers. But becoming qualified to perform animal-assisted therapy visits isn't easy. This special service calls for a pet that keeps their cool in an institutional setting.

REMEMBER

Therapy dogs must have dependable dispositions and impeccable manners. Although a Chi's main assignment is lap-sitting, they still need plenty of confidence to remain relaxed in an institution. After all, they'll be sitting on strange laps amid the distractions of hospital equipment (like wheelchairs and walkers), institutional odors, crowds, and noise.

DIFFERENT KINDS OF CANINE HELPERS

Service dogs, therapy dogs, and emotional support animals are not the same. *Service dogs* are trained to perform specific tasks, and *therapy dogs* undergo training to make sure they are calm, friendly, and well-mannered in the facilities where they visit, but *emotional support animals* (ESA) simply provide comfort through their presence and are not required to have any training.

Businesses and facilities must permit access to service dogs, but they don't have to allow therapy or emotional support animals. However, no-pet housing is required to allow service dogs or ESAs, although they may require people with ESAs to provide a letter from a physician stating that the animal is necessary for the person's mental health.

HELPING THE HEARING IMPAIRED

Chihuahuas can and do help people who are hearing impaired through *hearing dog programs*. After a training regimen to learn to alert their handler to the doorbell, telephone, alarm clock, smoke alarm, oven timer, or baby crying, the dog is paired with a deaf person. The two practice communicating with each other, and the handler learns how to care for the dog. They then go home together and the dog serves as the person's ears. Because they're so small that they fit anywhere and so smart that they easily take to the training, Chihuahuas are popular hearing dogs.

Hundreds of organizations across the United States are dedicated to pet-assisted therapy. These groups prepare their members through classes and tests. At least two national organizations — Pet Partners (www.petpartners.org) and Therapy Dogs International (www.tdi-dog.org) — have local clubs or certified instructors in many cities. Pet Partners also operates in Canada and other countries around the world, including Argentina, Australia, Colombia, India, Japan, South Korea, Spain, Switzerland, and Uruguay. These organizations are eager to help people prepare their pets for therapy work. Your local dog club also may have a volunteer training program.

TECHNICAL STUFF

The test used most frequently to certify dogs for therapy work is the AKC's Canine Good Citizen Test (see the section "Passing the Canine Good Citizen Test"). Some organizations modify the test to include institutional equipment. A health certificate from your veterinarian may also be mandatory (see Chapter 13).

Requirements vary among organizations and institutions, but the rewards remain the same: Bored eyes light up and tired faces break into smiles at the sight of your Chihuahua. And the warm feeling remains with you and those you help for hours. But don't take our word for it. Give it a try!

Teaching Your Dog a Trick or Two

Close your eyes and visualize your Chihuahua greeting people with a paw shake, waving hello and goodbye, asking for a cookie (or make that a taco?), even dancing on hind legs while you whistle. Does that image make you smile? Good. Chihuahuas love showing off, and it will surprise you how fast your Chi will learn tricks when you start teaching them. Put some treats in your pocket and call your Chi, because in this section we teach enough tricks to tickle your family and friends.

REMEMBER

The tricks in this section build on each other, so you should start with the first one and move on only after your Chihuahua can reliably perform the trick.

Seeing the benefits of trick training

Chihuahuas like learning tricks. After all, during training, they have what they want most — your full attention, plus praise and treats. Chis think trick training was created just to make them feel special, but you reap rewards, too. Besides giving you a chance to have fun and impress your friends, teaching tricks enhances your Chi's vocabulary, encourages closer bonding, and leads to better behavior and mental enrichment.

Another advantage to trick training is that it makes your Chi an impressive ambassador for the breed. Many people believe tiny dogs are brainless and lack character, but a Chi that waves and barks on cue changes that thinking in a hurry.

Besides, after a shy Chi learns how to pull off a trick or two, they'll have something other than fear to focus on in social situations. And making people laugh improves their confidence.

Pushing your dog's performance buttons

When it comes to motivation, the happier your Chi is about learning a new move, the faster they'll perfect it. So, if you're a good motivator, your dog can be a terrific performer in no time.

What's the key to effective motivation? Praise. But praising your Chi works only when your tone is sincere and maybe a little silly — okay, mighty silly with some dogs. Praising your pet in a drab monotone won't get them excited. It'll sound like elevator music.

How can you make the praise so powerful that your Chi wants more? Give it with gusto. Give your Chi a big smile when you say, "Good job, sweetie!" If your Chi is a little lethargic, accentuate your praise with a little applause. Use joyful words that come naturally to you, and say them in an excited voice. Don't become boring by using the same praise words and treats every time. You can surprise your Chi with new words: "Way to go!" "All right!" "Yes, Yes!" Scratch their back. Give a taste of cheese, a sliver of hot dog, or a bite of burger, or toss a toy.

TIP

Read your Chihuahua's reactions to rewards. Praise should make your dog eager to continue the lesson. Don't make it so shrill that it's scary or so invigorating that it's distracting.

Soon, you'll discover which phrases inspire your Chi to try harder, which treats are most tempting, and whether chasing a squeaky toy or getting a back rub is preferred. In other words, you'll identify your Chi's buttons. Pushing those buttons makes Chis happy, and when they're happy, they're willing to try the trick again.

Putting your Chi in the mood

Because treats are an important part of trick training, try to train when your Chihuahua is hungry — before, not after, meals. Before beginning a training session, take your dog outdoors to potty. When you get back inside, your Chi can watch you prepare and pocket some treats. When you have their undivided attention, start with something they know. Have them Sit for a tidbit (see Chapter 10). That sets the tone and puts them in a cooperative mood to learn their first trick.

REMEMBER

Don't try trick training until your Chi can sit on cue. Sitting is a prerequisite to most tricks.

Using praise and treats wisely

When teaching tricks, use praise and treats/toys to motivate your Chi, and don't bark out "No!" when they make a wrong move. When they do something right, reward them. When they do something wrong or do nothing at all, don't reward them. It's as simple as that. Neither force nor punishment should ever be involved.

TIP

Reward every correct move, no matter how tiny or tentative, when your dog is learning something new. Rewards let your dog know that they are on the right path.

Shaking Hands or Gimme Five

If the Sit cue is second nature to your Chi (see Chapter 10), you can teach Shake Hands or Gimme Five (see Figure 12-2).

Just follow these simple steps:

1. **Ask your Chi to sit, then kneel down and say the cue word you choose, such as "Shake!"**

   Be creative. It doesn't matter what verbal cue you use as long as you use the same one every time.

2. **Lift up a foreleg from underneath, then gently release it.**

   Praise as soon as you drop the leg, and give a tiny treat.

3. **Repeat the process five times and then try it again later or the next day.**

4. **After your Chi is comfortable with you picking up the leg, gently move it up and down before releasing it.**

   The big breakthrough comes one day when your Chi lifts their leg as soon as you say the cue word. When that happens, let your Chi know how happy you are!

Gradually wean your Chi away from expecting a treat every time, but always give praise. And even after they perform reliably for praise, surprise them with a treat occasionally. After your Chi has this trick down pat, you can let family and friends practice it, too (but not more than five tries at a time—you don't want your Chi to become bored or tired).

FIGURE 12-2:
Glad to
meet you,
Manchita!

Waving hi and bye

When your Chihuahua is able to shake hands as easily as a state
senator, you can start teaching Wave. Use these simple steps:

1. **Use your cue words and ask your Chi to shake hands
    (see the previous section).**

2. **Just as your Chi lifts a paw, pull your hand away while
    repeating your cue words in a happy voice.**

    Most dogs wave their paws in the air in an effort to make
    contact with their humans' hands.

3. **The instant your Chi waves even a little, say "Wave" and
    give a treat.**

    Keep at it, having your Chi wave just a bit longer each time
    before giving a reward. When your dog starts to master the
    wave (see Figure 12-3 for an example of a master waver),
    you can eliminate asking for the handshake by going
    directly from Sit to Wave. Finally, you can wean your Chi off
    the treat by giving it only once every few times. But continue
    praising for every wave.

It's also fun to hold your Chihuahua at chest level in both hands
and ask them to wave at someone. You can teach this trick the
same way, except that you need a helper. Hold your Chi while
your helper walks up; the person should ask your dog to shake

hands and then pull the hand away to elicit a wave. Some Chis will wave with both front legs when they're being held.

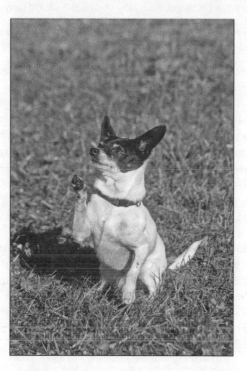

FIGURE 12-3:
This well-trained Chi waves at a friend.

TIP

Use the cue Wave rather than the more obvious "Hi" or "Bye" because it's more versatile. You can cue your Chihuahua to wave hi and wave bye, and you can personalize the trick by saying, for instance, "Wave to Aunt Amelia."

Speaking and shushing

Time to get silly! Here's your chance to teach your Chi how to speak with the following steps:

1. **Start by showing your Chihuahua a favorite treat.**

   Wiggle it right in front of them but don't let them take it.

2. **Get your Chi all wound up by teasing them with the treat.**

3. **As they prance around, say "Speak" excitedly, over and over.**

   The object is to get your dog to make a sound (any sound).

4. **When you get a sound (even if it's a wimpy squeak), give the treat and plenty of praise.**

   After your Chi eats the treat, try again. Stop after five tries no matter how much fun you're both having.

It won't be long before your Chi makes the connection and barks loudly when you say Speak and show the treat. That's a good start. Continue using the treat until you have to say Speak only once. Gradually wean your dog off the treat.

The real fun begins when you get creative. "Speak to me." "If you want a cookie, Speak." "Speak to Aunt Amelia!"

Some Chihuahuas anticipate this trick and begin barking before you can say the cue word. Every time your Chi tries that, say "Shhhh" and don't give the cue (or the treat) until your dog quiets down and stays quiet for several seconds. After repeating this process, they'll learn that "Shhhh" means hush — a bonus trick that can come in handy if your dog is a problem barker (see Chapter 11).

Teaching your Chi to cha-cha

Chihuahuas make marvelous dancers, with moves that are the envy of larger breeds. To teach your Chi the cha-cha (or the tango, waltz, jitterbug, two-step, or mambo), turn on your favorite tune or hum a few notes. Hold a treat several inches above their head and say, "Let's dance!" The object is to get them to walk a few steps on their hind legs, so move the treat forward slightly after they rear up.

If you see your Chi standing on their hind legs on their own, praise and reward ASAP! That can be the beginning of a new trick: Sit Pretty.

When they realize what you want, it still may take several weeks until their leg and back muscles are developed enough to let them dance on their hind legs for several seconds. As soon as they can balance well on their hind legs, start moving the treat in a circle above their head to teach them to turn. Soon, they'll be pirouetting in either direction!

What do you do with a dancing dog? Join in, of course! As your Chihuahua swings and sways on their hind legs, start moving to the music along with them. Having a partner encourages them to make up steps of their own. They may soon add hops, skips, and jumps to their dancing repertoire.

Touring the Dog Show Circuit

Dog shows are similar around the world. Wherever you live, if you want to see more than a hundred breeds of gorgeous dogs gathered in one place, treat yourself to a dog show. Besides seeing beautifully groomed and trained representatives of all your favorite breeds, you become acquainted with rare breeds that few people ever get to see. Agility and obedience trials often are held in the same venues as dog shows, too. Dog shows are interesting regardless of whether you understand the judging procedure, but a little knowledge will make your first experience more rewarding.

In this section, we explain the basics of dog judging so you understand what the exhibitors and judges are doing, the upside and downside of the "dog game," and how to get started if you want to become a player.

TIP

Dogs not entered in competition aren't allowed at dog shows, so leave your Chi at home when you go to a show just to check it out. Rather than a dog, put a notebook on your lap and jot down your impressions of why certain dogs won. Later, if you get into the dog game, dig out that notebook and read what you wrote. Your first impressions may help your handling.

To be eligible to show in conformation, your Chihuahua must be

>> At least six months old

>> Registered with the AKC (see Chapter 4), UKC, CKC
(Canada), KC (Britain), or FCI (Europe), or registered with
the club sponsoring the event

>> Unaltered (spayed or neutered dogs aren't eligible to show)

TECHNICAL
STUFF

When exhibitors compete at dog shows, they say they're show-ing their dogs in *breed* or *conformation.*

The judging process and other show basics

Dogs look their finest when competing at a dog show, and with so many gorgeous creatures to choose from, your first reaction may be to pity the poor judge. But a dog show judge has help in the form of guidelines, called the *breed standard* (see the Chihuahua standard in Chapter 2). The standard describes an ideal specimen of the breed. The judge's job is to select as the winner the dog that most closely conforms to this written description of physical perfection.

TIP

In other words, no matter how many different dog breeds com-pete in the show ring, the winner should be the dog that most closely resembles the ideal dog described in that breed's stan-dard. Second place goes to the next closest dog, and so on.

When watching a show, you see dogs of the same breed judged together early in the day. But later, you see the winning dogs of each breed competing against each other. That's when novices really get confused. After all, how can a judge choose between an animated Chihuahua and an elegant Maltese? Well, the judge isn't comparing the Chihuahua to the Maltese. Instead, they are comparing how close the Chihuahua matches their breed stan-dard with how close the Maltese matches their standard.

The following sections explain the order of the dog show classes and what it takes to get that coveted Champion title for your Chihuahua.

TIP

When you arrive at a dog show, buy a show catalog right away. Then you can match each dog's catalog number with the handler's armband number, thus finding out who's who.

Winning or losing — it's the judge's call

Your first experience with subjective dog show judging may leave you confused. Most sports are judged objectively. During games of baseball, basketball, football, golf, or tennis, you always know the score. But it's different at dog shows, where winning or losing depends on the judge's opinion. You may see a dog get a "Best of" prize one day and not even place in their class the next.

The more you discover about canine conformation and the Chihuahua standard (see Chapter 2), the better you'll understand how judges pick their winners. One judge may be a stickler for movement. A superior head may sway another. Because judges interpret the standards in their own unique ways, different dogs may win under different judges. And that's a good thing because it lets many excellent dogs have their days in the sun.

Getting through an elimination contest

Shows where dogs are judged on their conformation are *elimination contests*. The process of an elimination contest has many steps, listed here:

1. All the dogs of a single breed (or variety of a breed) compete with others of their sex in one of the regular classes — Puppy, 12-to-18-Month, Novice, Bred-by-Exhibitor, American-bred, or Open.

2. First-place winners of the same sex from each of the classes compete against each other for Winners Dog and Winners Bitch.

3. These two winners are awarded points toward their championship (see the section "Becoming a champion" later in this chapter) and return to the ring for Best of Breed (or Variety) competition.

Dogs that are already champions are called *Specials,* and they also compete for Best of Breed or Variety.

4. **Three awards are presented in the final elimination contest at the breed level:**

   - The top dog is awarded Best of Breed or Variety.

   - The best dog of the opposite sex than the Best of Breed is presented with the Best of Opposite Sex (BOS) ribbon.

   - The best of the two class winners is named Best of Winners (BOW).

   Sometimes, a class dog (a dog that isn't a champion yet) goes to the top and takes Best of Breed or Variety, as well as Best of Winners.

5. **When Chihuahua judging is complete, all but the Best of Variety winners are finished for the day. The Best of Variety Chihuahuas are now eligible to compete in the Toy group. (Remember, Chihuahuas have two varieties— shorthaired and longhaired—which is why you see two Chihuahuas competing in the Toy Group.)**

   The Toy group is where all the Toy dogs that won Best of Breed or Variety compete for group placements.

6. **Following a group judging and elimination, only seven dogs — the first-place winners from each group — are left in the show. They compete for Best in Show (BIS).**

   When the show is over, only one undefeated dog remains — but a couple of hundred dogs may have earned points toward their championships, and many others thrilled their owners by placing high in their classes.

Becoming a champion

REMEMBER

To become an *AKC champion* on the dog show circuit, your Chihuahua must win 15 points, including points from at least two major wins (*majors* are shows where three or more points are awarded). The two majors must be awarded by different judges, and at least one of the remaining points must be won under a third judge.

GROUP CLASSIFICATIONS

For purposes of showing, the American Kennel Club (AKC) divides dogs into seven groups as follows:

- Group 1: Sporting Dogs
- Group 2: Hounds
- Group 3: Working Dogs
- Group 4: Terriers
- Group 5: Toys
- Group 6: Non-Sporting Dogs
- Group 7: Herding Dogs

The most points ever available at a show is five, and the fewest available is one. Your Chi must win points at a minimum of three shows to earn a championship. Five-point majors are few and far between and competition is keen, so most Chihuahuas are shown several times before becoming champions.

When a dog *finishes a championship*, they're permanently recorded as a champion of record and entitled to the word "Champion" before their name. The AKC abbreviation is *Ch*, as in "Ch Manchita." With an additional three major wins (25 points total), a dog can become a Grand Champion (GCH).

The ups and downs of showing dogs

All hobbies have good points and bad points. In the sections that follow, we list some of the things, both positive (upside) and negative (downside), you may want to consider before deciding you want to show your dog.

The upside of showing dogs

Here are the many benefits that come with competing in dog shows:

>> Competing with your dog is fun and exciting.

>> You can make new friends with people who have similar interests, and you may be invited to join dog clubs.

>> You and your Chihuahua can both make new friends in conformation classes.

>> Depending on your goals and budget, it can be a casual or an absorbing avocation.

>> Showing dogs is educational. If you go in with an open mind, you'll discover something new every time you attend a show.

>> You get to meet the top Chihuahua breeders.

>> Becoming seriously involved means you may become a breeder (at least occasionally).

>> Training your Chihuahua for the show ring strengthens your bond.

>> Showing involves traveling. Hello world!

>> You get the opportunity to learn from your losses to make you a better competitor.

>> Winning feels wonderful!

The downside of showing dogs

Although showing your dog can be a wonderful experience, there are certainly some challenges you should consider before signing up.

Here's the other side of the coin — the disadvantages of joining the dog show circuit:

>> Winning at dog shows means you'll need a dog with superior conformation.

>> Showing dogs is expensive and requires some special equipment.

>> The alternative to training and showing your own dog is hiring a professional handler, which is expensive.

>> Training your Chihuahua for the show ring is time consuming.

>> Showing can be stressful to dogs and their owners.

>> Showing involves traveling. You may miss your own bed or have a job that doesn't allow for travel.

>> When you become seriously involved, breeding dogs becomes a probability (at least occasionally).

>> The sport can take over your life. Between conformation classes, club meetings, dog shows, and breeding, showing dogs can become all-encompassing.

>> Losing usually feels lousy.

Getting started in showing

WARNING

We hate to be bearers of bad news, but no matter how handsome you and your friends think your Chihuahua is, if you didn't buy yours as a potential show dog, chances are they won't win at dog shows. Some dogs are rare exceptions, of course, but your Chi is probably tops at exactly what you bought them for — companionship.

Eventually, you'll need another Chi if you want to take up showing, but in the meantime, make your companion Chi your compadre for learning the ropes. Take them to conformation class and discover how to train and handle them in the ring. They'll love the attention, and you can get the hang of showing in a relaxed way. This way, you become a better handler for your next pup — the one you buy with showing in mind.

REMEMBER

Take your time purchasing a show-potential Chihuahua. Study the breed standard (see Chapter 2) and attend some shows. (You can also find breed and group judging videos online.) Watching the judging helps you develop an eye for a show-quality dog. Soon, you'll find out which attributes are more important to you, and which breeders' dogs are strong in those traits. Then talk to the breeders whose dogs you most admire and check out their available show-potential pups. But don't expect to get one right away. You may have to put your name on a waiting list and fork over a deposit (money alert!).

Preparing for what show dogs do

Assuming your Chihuahua is show quality and has full AKC registration — a requirement for showing — what's next?

Besides possessing physical beauty and a steady temperament, show Chis must take travel, crowds, noise, and strange dogs in stride. They also must

>> Stand still for grooming

>> Pose in a line with their competitors

>> Stand on a table for the judge's examination

>> Be willing to have their mouth examined

>> Circle the ring at a smooth trot in a line with their competitors

>> Trot on leash with the handler in the designated pattern

>> Keep cool from the first burst of applause through the hush that settles over the arena just before the judge points to the winner

Yikes! You know what to expect after watching a show or two, but how will you and your Chi get used to all that? Easy. You take lessons together. Dog clubs and private instructors offer *conformation classes* where you become familiar with the finer points of handling. At the same time, your dog gets used to stacking (posing) and trotting (gaiting) around other dogs and people.

TIP

When you attend conformation classes, you find out when matches take place in your area. *Matches* are practice dog shows — much like the real thing except they're informal and no championship points are awarded. Matches are great for honing your handling skills and getting your dog used to the show atmosphere.

Of course, many people hire professional handlers (*agents*) to show their dogs. If you decide to hire a handler, choose one who has an excellent reputation for taking care of and winning with Toy dogs.

Your dog's breeder may be happy to help you locate and choose a handler.

If your Chihuahua is ready to show, enter well ahead of the closing date so you aren't disappointed. Late entries are not accepted.

Speaking dog show lingo

Every sport has its unique terminology, and dog showing is no exception. When studying the breed standard (see Chapter 2) or evaluating dogs with other fanciers, certain words always come up. Knowing and understanding these terms early in the game is a good idea. The following sections present many common terms that float around whenever dog showing is the topic du jour.

Type

Type is what sets one breed of dog apart from every other breed. The concept of breed type is easiest to understand if you remember that each breed has only one correct type. It's type that makes you instantly recognize the features that combine to make up a Chihuahua. Type enables people to differentiate your dog from a Papillon, Miniature Pinscher, or any other breed.

And in the show ring, the most *typey* dog is the one that comes closest to matching the characteristics described in the breed standard.

Soundness

Soundness refers to a dog's ability to function well, and it includes physical and behavioral characteristics such as a correct skeleton, proper musculature, and a stable temperament. Also, no physical impediments, temporary or permanent, should inhibit the dog from using these attributes. A dog that's deaf, blind, lame, overly aggressive, missing a testicle, or painfully shy is *unsound*. If a sound dog steps on a smoldering cigarette and limps because their burned pad hurts, they're *temporarily unsound* and can't be shown. But as soon as they heal enough to move normally, they become sound again.

REMEMBER

Not all faults in a dog are considered unsound. For example, your Chi's ears may be on the small side (the standard specifies large) yet function just fine. Because having smallish ears doesn't interfere with the ability to hear, the characteristic doesn't make a Chi unsound. (Pun not intended.) However, small ears are uncharacteristic of the Chi breed, so this dog lacks type.

Balance

Balance means that all parts of the dog fit each other without exaggeration of any single part. The size of the head corresponds with the size of the body, and height, width, and weight are proportionate. If people look at your Chihuahua and say, "My, what long legs she has," or "Doesn't she have a big head for her size?" chances are the dog lacks balance.

Don't fret over balance too soon. Puppies often go through an awkward stage when they're temporarily out of *proportion*, another word for balance. When your Chi is young, their head may look too big for their body. They may have a well-developed front and a wimpy rear, or they may seem to be walking downhill because their back legs grew faster than their front legs. However, by the time they mature into a good show dog, all their parts must be balanced.

Condition

When it comes to condition, the ball is in your court. You can't control whether your Chihuahua matures typey or balanced, but their condition depends on you. A Chi is in *condition* when they carry the right amount of weight for their size (see Chapter 2) and have an immaculate coat with a healthy sheen, good muscle tone, clean ears, and clear eyes (see Chapter 7).

Style and showmanship

Style and *showmanship* are similar terms with respect to the show ring, but they're not quite identical. *Stylish* is the dog-show term used to describe dogs that carry themselves elegantly and with pride; a *good showman* indicates a dog with a pleasantly bold attitude that performs well during the judging. It's not unusual for a judge to say that the dog who placed first "asked for the win."

MANCHITA'S SHOWY STORY

Show breeders sell their top-quality puppies as *show-potential pups*. That means the pups appear to have all the attributes necessary to become champions. But potential is only potential. As a dog matures, things may change. That's what happened to Jackie's dog, Manchita, a show-potential puppy. At six months, she looked mighty fine, so they entered a show. Manchita won the Puppy class and then beat the other class winners for Winners Bitch. That day, Manchita was awarded her first (and last) championship points. During the next few weeks, her bite changed, and she matured with a wry mouth and the habit of letting the tip of her tongue dangle. So much for showing!

Manchita's breeders guaranteed her for show potential, as many top breeders do. When her mouth went awry, the breeders were prepared to trade for a different pup and place Manchita in a pet home. But Jackie wanted to keep her (and the timing wasn't right for raising a second pup), so she never asked them to honor the guarantee.

Chihuahuas who have showmanship and style show off their breed characteristics, making the most of their typeyness. Judges recognize a dog like that easily. These dogs step out with pride — neck arched, head up, aspect bold, happy, and eager — yet remain under control. A good showman that lacks style may still be appealing because of their saucy, outgoing manner, but they'll never fool a knowledgeable judge.

REMEMBER

At a dog show, style often separates the superior from the good and the winners from the losers — especially when all other points are nearly equal. Style or elegance is a quality you can't give your Chi. They are either born with it or they aren't. They may be typey, sound, well balanced, and in fine condition, yet still lack style. That doesn't mean they won't win, because correct dogs — especially ones with showmanship — win their share of champion points. However, what it does mean is that when competing against an equally correct dog that's also stylish, your Chi will come in second.

Unlike style, which you can't instill into a dog through training, you can help your Chi grow into the best show dog they can be:

» Give plenty of socialization to bolster confidence (see Chapter 9).

» Leash-train with praise and patience (see Chapter 9).

» Keep training periods upbeat and brief so they don't become bored.

Follow this advice and you'll elicit your dog's best attitude.

4

Chihuahua Care and Concerns

IN THIS PART . . .

Select a skilled and caring veterinarian to help keep your Chihuahua healthy.

Fight creepy parasites that can invade your Chihuahua's body — inside and out!

Recognize signs of illness and injury and respond to emergencies.

Cope with aging and pet loss.

Chapter **13**

Visiting the Vet

It takes two to save a sick dog — one to diagnose the illness and prescribe the treatment (the vet), and the other to follow up at home (that's you). Choosing a vet and making responsible health decisions is one of the most important parts of having a dog. We're here to help you find a veterinarian you can trust with your Chihuahua's life and help you become the kind of client every caring veterinarian wants.

In this chapter, we tell you be a great canine caretaker by to preventing problems whenever possible, seeing the signs of sickness before they become severe, keeping calm, remembering the vet's instructions, and carrying them out exactly as prescribed. Finally, we cover other important health topics, from your dog's first exam and all-important vaccinations to altering your Chi and providing ID.

Choosing Your Chihuahua's Veterinarian

By now you know that all dogs aren't the same. Toy breeds like Chihuahuas have special needs, and sometimes specific problems. Therefore, you need a veterinarian who likes and understands Toy dogs. Depending on where you live, you may have several excellent choices right in town, or you may have to drive 50 miles to visit the vet most of the Toy owners in your community trust.

Near or far, picking your dog's vet is a major decision. Someday, your Chi's life may depend on the doctor's diagnostic ability. Here are some ways to find a good veterinarian:

>> Ask your Chi's breeder. If the breeder lives within a reasonable distance, try their vet first. Even if the breeder lives far away, they may have sold pups to other people in your area and can tell you how to contact them for referrals.

>> When you see people walking Toy dogs in your neighborhood, ask them who they use and if they're satisfied with the quality of care.

>> Contact the state or province veterinary association (you can find them online) and look for a directory, usually listed under Resources or Public.

>> Look for a veterinary hospital with AAHA (American Animal Hospital Association) accreditation. AAHA may also accredit animal hospitals in Canada. In the UK, the Royal College of Veterinary Surgeons accredits the hospitals. Accredited hospitals voluntarily meet a high standard set by the accrediting organization and undergo regular inspections to make sure they maintain standards. In the U.S. and Canada, check out www.aahanet.org for help finding a local hospital that goes this extra step. When you find a candidate, ask for a tour of the hospital. If the staff is friendly and happy to show you around, this is a good sign. If not, stay away.

>> Look for a veterinarian or practice with Fear Free certification. This certification indicates that they are specially trained to handle animals in a way that reduces, fear, anxiety, and stress. You can also look for practices or practitioners with certification in Low Stress Handling.

Humans have health insurance to help cover the cost of expensive surgeries or unexpected illness, and it's available for dogs, too, from a number of companies. A good pet insurance plan allows you to say yes to lab tests and other diagnostics, dental cleanings, surgeries, and emergency care, to name just a few. We think pet health insurance is a must if you never want to face the choice between your money and your Chihuahua's life.

After you choose a vet with an awesome reputation and make the first appointment for your Chihuahua, you must decide whether you're satisfied with your choice. Many clinics have several vets on staff, so if you don't click with the first one, you may be able to change to one you feel more comfortable with in the same office. Or you may be required to go with whoever's available. If that's not your style, find another clinic where your needs are accommodated. The right veterinarian will do or have the following. (If the vet you visit doesn't do or have these things, you may opt to discuss your dissatisfaction with the vet or simply change veterinarians.)

>> **Handle your Chihuahua with professional proficiency.** Whether your dog is everybody's pal or shy with strangers, your vet should know how to get on your Chihuahua's good side. A complete physical examination should be performed carefully but with practiced ease (see Figure 13-1). Steer clear of any vet who seems rushed or harsh or says or does anything that leads you to believe they may not like Chihuahuas.

>> **Weigh them and take a complete history.** This should include where you got your Chi, how long you've had them, age, diet, vaccinations, dewormings, activity level, appetite, and previous illnesses.

>> **Explain the examination and discuss the results with you.** A caring vet may give you tips on how to improve your Chi's condition or keep them healthy over the long term.

>> **Answer your questions thoroughly in language you understand.** Any vet who purposely talks over your head or has an arrogant attitude doesn't need you for a client. Good vets answer their clients' questions in everyday language without talking down to them.

>> **Make provisions for emergency care during weekends, holidays, and the middle of the night.** Some veterinarians handle emergencies themselves; others refer their clients to services that specialize in emergencies. If your vet opts for the service, make sure a vet knowledgeable about Toy dogs is always available.

>> **Have a pleasant receptionist and staff, a clean, odor-free waiting room, and an organized and well-equipped facility.**

>> **Discuss fees.** Although most clinics expect you to pay for regular office visits right away, you may want to ask about their policies for unexpected, expensive emergencies.

>> **Be caring.** If you sense coldness or indifference in the vet or staff, your pup is in the wrong place.

FIGURE 13-1: Your Chihuahua needs a vet who likes and understands small dogs.

Being the Best Kind of Client

If your Chi becomes ill or injured, it takes more than an excellent vet to cure them. It also takes you — a conscientious and composed client. A dog does best if veterinarian and owner work together during a crisis. The following list explains how you can be the type of client veterinarians are glad to have on their team:

>> Call and make appointments for routine visits such as annual exams.

>> Arrive at appointments on time.

>> Don't assume your vet can diagnose your dog over the telephone.

TECHNICAL STUFF

Why no phone diagnosis? Because a variety of canine illnesses display similar signs. It generally takes a hands-on examination, and possibly some tests, to find out what's causing the problem and to decide on the best method of treatment. However, telemedicine has become more widespread in the wake of the COVID-19 pandemic, and veterinarians may use it both for mild conditions and for triage—determining whether the condition is an emergency that requires immediate care. Sometimes recheck exams can be done as telemedicine, too, by sending a photo or video to the clinic before the phone appointment.

>> Have an understanding attitude when the vet runs late because they had to drop everything to take care of an emergency.

>> Know your dog's normal behavior and call the clinic immediately if something doesn't seem right.

TIP

Write down your dog's normal vital signs and keep them handy. Yes, your vet should keep a record, but your Chi may get sick while you're traveling, and knowing what's normal for your dog helps an emergency vet make a better diagnosis.

>> Bring along a written list of recent behavior changes, if any exist (for example: excessive thirst, loss of appetite, change in activity level, unexplained fear or aggression, and so on).

>> Bring the health and vaccination records the breeder gave you (for your first visit; see the following section).

>> Keep your dog on leash on your lap or in the crate in the waiting room. Don't let them play on the floor or sniff strange dogs. It's easy for pups to pick up germs.

>> Be honest. When your vet asks if your Chihuahua has been on any medication, don't be ashamed to admit that you tried an over-the-counter medication from the pet shop. Admitting a mistake may make you feel like a dummy, but your vet has to know exactly what your dog has ingested to make a correct diagnosis. Not only that, but mixing medications can be fatal. Also, if your Chi seemed slightly sick for several days and you kept hoping they'd get better on their own, admit that, too. Don't try to make yourself look better at your dog's expense.

>> Make a list of your dog-care questions and bring it along. Your vet should be glad to answer appropriate questions about feeding, grooming, toenail trimming, and anything else related to your Chihuahua's health; however, the vet doesn't have time to listen to you ramble on about how Grandma Mildred thinks your Chihuahua should be a television star.

>> Take notes when the vet gives you instructions.

>> Follow all instructions exactly. You must give medications at the right time and in the correct dosage or they won't work. If you don't understand how to administer a medication, ask. Your vet can explain or demonstrate.

WARNING

Never increase the dosage of a medication (not even a little) in the hopes of making your Chihuahua feel better faster. Medication doesn't work that way. In fact, what cures at the proper dosage can kill when overdosed.

>> Stay as composed as possible, even during an emergency. The more serious the injury or illness, the more your vet needs you as a clear-thinking partner in your Chihuahua's treatment.

REMEMBER

No matter how frightening the emergency and how fast you want to get your dog to the vet, you need to secure the crate for the trip so it doesn't roll or slide while you drive. The last thing a sick or hurt Chihuahua needs is a terrifying tumble.

>> Don't be argumentative or belligerent. Most vets care about their clients and understand how deeply people love their dogs. But vets aren't magicians; they can't guarantee that a badly injured or gravely ill dog will recover, no matter how skillful the care. If you lose confidence in your vet, the best thing to do is change clinics.

>> Pay your bills according to clinic policy.

Your efforts to work with your veterinarian in these ways will help the two of you become true partners in your Chihuahua's care.

Preparing for the First Exam

REMEMBER

The best time for a Chihuahua and veterinarian to meet is within 48 hours after you acquire your pup. In fact, breeder contracts usually spell out how soon the initial exam must take place; ignoring contractual requirements voids the guarantees. Although most puppies purchased from reliable breeders are healthy (see Chapter 4), a timely first examination is especially important for three reasons:

>> Your veterinarian either confirms that your dog is healthy or gives you bad news (we're talking major problems here, not a minor infestation of worms or a loose baby tooth that needs attention). If something is seriously wrong, finding out while you can still return the Chihuahua is better than falling hopelessly in love with a puppy so sick that they can never live a normal life.

>> The clinic can establish a permanent record of what's normal for your dog (assuming there are no problems). If your Chi ever shows signs of sickness, tests can quickly disclose deviations. Besides, why not get to know your vet when your Chi is healthy instead of entrusting your dog to a total stranger during an emergency?

>> Your new dog probably needs vaccinations, a checkup for internal and external parasites, and medicine to prevent heartworm. We tell you more about preventive medicine later in this chapter and in Chapter 14.

Unfortunately, we don't always get to decide when to visit the veterinarian. In case of an emergency, take your dog to the vet ASAP. Speedy treatment often is the difference between death and complete recovery. Call the clinic first and explain what happened so the staff can prepare.

Here's to hoping your first visit will be routine and painless. The following sections dig deeper into the visit details.

Getting organized

Here's a checklist of what to do before your pup's first visit to the veterinarian:

» Spray the carrier with synthetic canine pheromones about an hour beforehand to help your Chi have a relaxed ride.

» Withhold food beforehand to help prevent an upset stomach and so your Chi will be more interested in any treats offered by the veterinarian or staff.

» Put a roll of paper towels and a container of wet wipes in your vehicle in case a quick cleanup is necessary.

» Bring a copy of your dog's health record, which you should have from the breeder if your Chi is a new pup.

» Collect a recent stool sample. You can use a resealable plastic bag. (Some vets want you to bring one along for the first exam. Be sure to ask about that when making the appointment.)

» Transport your dog in a crate or soft carrier. Carry it to the car in your arms, holding it as if it were a precious parcel (which it is!). Secure the crate to make sure it doesn't take a tumble if you have to swerve or make a quick stop. The safest place for a soft carrier is in the footwell behind the passenger seat.

» Bring cash, credit card, or checkbook. Vets get paid at the time of treatment.

Making the most of your first visit

Surely you have questions about dog care before your first visit. The initial visit is the time to ask. Write your questions down at home as you think of them so you don't forget anything. To get you started, here are a few questions new Chihuahua owners often ask:

>> When is it safe to start taking my dog to public places?

>> What do normal bowel movements look like?

>> How often should my dog have a bowel movement?

>> What's a good balanced diet for my Chihuahua?

>> How often can my Chi have treats, and what makes a good treat?

>> Does my dog need a vitamin and mineral supplement?

TIP

If you want to buy health insurance for your Chihuahua, pet health insurance is readily available. Discuss this option with your veterinarian or search for pet health insurance on the internet. You'll find many options. Before buying a policy, be sure you know what it does and doesn't cover, what percentage it pays, and how to make claims. For example, some pet policies are for emergency care only; others offer wellness plans that cover annual examinations, prescriptions, and more.

Keeping the visit fun

Dogs aren't born fearing the vet. They learn to be afraid because of what they experience. For a puppy, their first visit is the perfect time to learn that the vet clinic is a great place to be, with people who give petting and treats and speak kindly and calmly.

Even if the thought of your dog getting their first shot makes you cringe, don't let them know that. Be friendly with the veterinarian, not nervous, or your dog will feel your tension and get scared. The ideal attitude for the first visit (and those thereafter) is patient but matter-of-fact. Your dog takes their cues from you, so if they sense that you're relaxed and like the vet, they'll relax and like the vet, too.

Sometimes dogs fear the vet because of their previous experiences, but things may have changed since the last time you took a pet to the vet. Most clinics these days cover the slick exam table with a nonskid mat to provide good footing and may prep the room with calming canine pheromones or essential oils. Heck, you may feel as if you've accidentally wandered into a spa.

The vet or technician may talk to you first to give your Chi time to relax and get used to their presence. They may offer treats during the exam to distract your dog or perform the examination on the floor if your tiny dog seems more comfortable there than way up on the exam table. Other good techniques include letting the dog check out instruments such as stethoscopes or otoscopes before they're put to use. For vaccinations and blood draws, small-gauge needles offer a more comfortable experience — something we've noticed ourselves when we go to the doctor.

Processing your first visit and practicing for the next

What if you and your dog visited your vet for the first time, and now you're home again, filled with new information — some of it different from what you've read in this book? What should you do? Who should you believe?

Trust your veterinarian. This book is a general reference, meaning that it contains good, solid information about Chihuahuas in general. But your dog is an individual that just had a thorough examination, and now you have personalized instructions. Follow them. They're meant especially for your pup.

The next step is to prepare for the next vet visit. (Yes, already!) That's because veterinary visits aren't going to be a daily or even monthly experience for your Chi — at least we hope not! So it's a good idea to practice at home so your Chi isn't surprised or scared during the next one, So how do you practice for the vet? Handle your dog's paws and ears regularly, lift the lip to look at teeth, run your hands over the entire body, including the tail, and gently touch the neck or leg with a ballpoint pen to simulate a needle poke. Get your dog used to these sensations. Then they won't bat an eye when the vet reaches to touch the ears or check their teeth.

Understanding Those Vital Vaccinations

For your Chihuahua's sake, you must know the worst conditions your pup can contract — and how to prevent them. The good news is that modern dog lovers are lucky. They don't have to worry about losing their pets to the host of deadly diseases that wiped out dogs by the thousands just a few canine generations ago. Today, the main focus of dog care is preventive medicine. The vaccinations your vet schedules are the best safeguards to keep your Chi from contracting a variety of potentially fatal diseases.

Dog vaccines are divided into core and non-core. *Core vaccines* are the ones recommended for all dogs. *Non-core vaccines* give dogs additional protection in special circumstances. This section breaks down all the vaccination knowledge you need.

WARNING

No canine vaccine is 100 percent effective or gives permanent immunity, which is why dogs should get booster shots throughout their adult lives. However, most boosters are no longer annual, the exceptions being vaccinations for Bordetella, canine influenza, leptospirosis, and Lyme disease. National and international veterinary associations and veterinary schools recommend triennial (every three years) boosters. You can also have your Chi's titers tested to see if previous vaccinations are still protective. Bear in mind, however, that if you're planning to travel internationally with your Chihuahua, a titer won't meet the requirements for travel documentation. In that case, only a vaccination will do. When in doubt, ask your vet.

Taking extra precautions for Toy puppies

Don't be surprised if your Chihuahua's vaccination schedule is different from the plan your friend follows for her Doberman Pinscher puppy. Chihuahuas and other Toy dogs tend to be at higher risk of vaccine reactions when they receive many vaccines at the same time. Your Chihuahua's veterinarian may separate the shots and give tiny dogs their rabies shots alone rather than in combination with other vaccines.

In the past, the leptospirosis vaccination (which is non-core) has been an issue with Toy dogs, but new vaccines for lepto, as it's nicknamed, are highly purified, reducing the risk of reactions. It used to be believed that big dogs living in the country were most prone to leptospirosis, but studies show small city dogs are most at risk, so talk to your veterinarian about the pros and cons of this vaccination for your Chihuahua.

TECHNICAL STUFF

Leptospirosis is spread by contact with urine from carrier animals: think rodents and urban wildlife such as raccoons, deer, and skunks. Even walking on a sidewalk can lead to exposure.

Your puppy's vaccinations must never be closer than two weeks apart. Three to four weeks apart is ideal. Your vet will recommend the proper schedule for your pup.

TIP

If your dog is allergic to a vaccine, a reaction (swelling around the muzzle, difficulty breathing, or even collapse) usually occurs between 20 and 30 minutes after the shot. If you live far from your clinic, don't drive home immediately after your dog is vaccinated. Instead, stick around for about an hour (read a book or listen to music in your vehicle with your dog on your lap). That way, immediate help is just seconds away.

TECHNICAL STUFF

An allergic reaction to an injection is called *anaphylaxis* or *anaphylactic shock.* The sooner treatment to counteract the reaction begins, the better the chances of survival. Discuss allergic reactions with your vet during the first visit. Serious allergic reactions are rare, so don't let fear of them prevent you from protecting your Chihuahua from deadly diseases such as parvo and distemper.

Breaking down DAPP

Although your Chihuahua may not get the whole combination in one shot, the core vaccines given to dogs are called *DAPP.* The following sections break down what the letters mean.

D is for distemper

Distemper is a highly contagious disease that is airborne or transmitted through shared food or water bowls. Its victims usually are puppies, although older dogs may come down with it, too. Because distemper manifests in various forms, it can be difficult even for experienced vets to diagnose. Signs may include diarrhea, vomiting, reduced appetite, cough, nasal discharge, inflamed eyes, fever, convulsions, exhaustion, and lack of interest in toys, games, or attention. Although dogs with distemper occasionally recover, they may suffer permanent damage to the brain or nervous system. Dogs that receive treatment immediately have the best chance of survival.

A is for adenovirus, types 1 and 2 (aka infectious hepatitis)

Adenovirus in dogs affects the liver just as it does in humans, but humans don't catch the canine form. In dogs, it spreads through contact with an infected dog's stool, saliva, or urine. Intense thirst is one specific symptom, but all the other symptoms are similar to those of distemper. Adenovirus progresses rapidly and often is fatal, so prompt veterinary treatment is critical.

P is for parvovirus

Parvovirus (or *parvo*) attacks the stomach lining, lining of the small intestine, bone marrow, and lymph nodes, and in young puppies, even the heart. It's highly contagious and spreads through contaminated stools. Your dog may encounter the stools via their paws or your shoes. Beginning with depression or exhaustion and a loss of appetite, symptoms soon progress to vomiting, diarrhea (sometimes bloody), and fever. Puppies with infected hearts (*myocardial parvovirus*) often die suddenly or within a day or two of contracting the disease. Those few that recover may suffer chronic heart problems. How severely adult dogs are affected depends on the individual. Some dogs become extremely ill, and others just lose their appetites and lower their activity levels for a day or two.

P also is for parainfluenza

Parainfluenza, also known as *infectious canine tracheobronchitis* and most commonly called *kennel cough*, spreads rapidly from dog to dog. It's caused by several different viruses, as well as a bacterium. Symptoms are a frequent, dry, hacking cough and sometimes a nasal discharge. Other than that, the dog appears to feel fine; many dogs infected with parainfluenza don't even miss a meal. Dogs vaccinated against parainfluenza sometimes get the condition anyway, but they usually have milder symptoms than unvaccinated dogs.

Although the disease usually runs its course, it's more dangerous to puppies than it is to mature dogs. Puppies should be kept in a warm, humid room while recovering. No matter how old your Chi is, though, your vet probably will prescribe antibiotics to prevent complications and medication to control the cough.

REMEMBER

Whether they're nine weeks or nine years old, your dog needs to see your vet right away if they start coughing frequently. It could be a sign of something serious, including choking, heart disease, or pneumonia.

Preventing Rabies

Rabies is always fatal to dogs. And a dog with rabies is a danger to humans and other animals, which is why the law mandates rabies vaccinations. *Rabies* is a virus that can infect dogs that come in contact with cats, raccoons, skunks, foxes, or other warm-blooded animals that already have the virus. It affects the nervous system and is generally passed from animal to animal or animal to human through infected saliva — usually from a bite. Rabies also can infect a victim through cuts or scratches that come in contact with saliva from a rabid animal.

One of the first signs of rabies is a difference in disposition. A gentle dog may start to act aggressively, or an independent dog may suddenly crave affection. Soon, the dog's pupils may become dilated and light may seem to cause him pain. Eventually, the dog won't want any attention and may develop stomach trouble and a fever.

As the disease progresses its symptoms can include bared teeth, random biting, lack of coordination, twitching facial muscles, and loss of control of the facial muscles, resulting in an open mouth with the tongue hanging out. The dog's voice may change, and it may drool, paw at its mouth, and cough. Finally, it will slip into a coma and die. All warm-blooded animals are susceptible to the disease, so anyone bitten by a dog (or any other animal) needs to see a doctor right away for a series of post-exposure vaccinations.

Rabies vaccine prevents this dreaded disease. Your vet will give the rabies shot to your Chi separately, not in combination with other vaccines. Some rabies vaccinations are labeled for one year and some for three years, so be sure to ask your vet when your dog's shot should be renewed.

Avoiding other deadly diseases

If it has been a while since you had a new puppy, you may think all vaccination programs are similar. They used to be, but now they are personalized for your dog. Besides the diseases you read about in the previous sections, depending on where you live, your vet may also recommend vaccinations against leptospirosis, Lyme disease, Bordetella, and canine influenza, depending on where you live and your Chihuahua's lifestyle. They are known as non-core vaccines, meaning that not all of them are right for every dog:

>> *Leptospirosis* is caused by a spirochete — a microorganism often carried by rats. A dog that comes in contact with a rat can become infected, as can one that eats or drinks something contaminated by rats. The result is a bacterial infection capable of causing permanent kidney damage or in severe cases, death. Because of increased incidence, experts are starting to think that the leptospirosis vaccine should be given to all dogs but it is not yet considered a core vaccine.

>> *Lyme disease* (spread by the blacklegged tick, sometimes known as the deer tick) attacks nerve tissue, joints, the heart, and, occasionally, the kidneys. Its symptoms include lameness due to joint pain, loss of appetite, and fever. Lyme disease is more of a danger in some areas than in others. Not only that, but veterinarians aren't in agreement about how well the vaccine works. Discuss Lyme disease with your vet and trust him or her to make an educated decision about whether your Chihuahua should be vaccinated.

>> *Bordetella* is a contagious and potentially serious respiratory disease that breaks out most often during the summer months when many dogs spend a week or so at the boarding kennel.

>> *Canine influenza* is a highly contagious and potentially serious viral respiratory disease that can occur when dogs visit crowded areas such as parks, dog shows, boarding kennels, or grooming salons.

These days, your Chi can be vaccinated against all these diseases. But just because a vaccine exists doesn't mean your dog needs it, so discuss it with your veterinarian and make the decision together. (In addition to your vet's vaccination schedule, your Chihuahua needs to be on a regular program that prevents heartworm. We tell you more about this in Chapter 14.)

WARNING

If you plan to travel a great deal with your dog, tell your vet because exposure to strange dogs and new places may require extra precautions. Don't take your Chi on any outings (except to puppy kindergarten with other vaccinated puppies) until the puppy series of inoculations is complete, usually by 18 to 20 weeks.

Administering Medicine the Correct Way

Lots of us like to give pills hidden in food, Kim and Jackie included. If that works, it's the easiest medicating method. But it's not always effective. Lots of Chihuahuas are talented at eating around the treat and then dropping the pill on the floor. Also, your dog may begin to associate their favorite treat or mealtime with medicine. This may cause your dog to avoid food and treats.

If you're looking for another way to administer medicine, we've got you covered. Here are some methods to try in case just hiding it in food doesn't work or the medication can't be given that way.

>> **Use the three-card monte method.** Give your Chi something delicious. Then give him a second piece, with the pill hidden inside. Finally, give a third pill-free goodie.

>> **Use psychology.** If you know your Chi will cut and run if they think you have a pill or ear medication, call over another pet and give them loads of tasty treats and petting.

Trust us, your Chi will be standing there wanting in on the action. Release the first dog, ply your Chi with treats and attention and, during the process, give the medication, following up with more goodies. We call this the Mary Poppins "spoonful of sugar helps the medicine go down" technique.

» **Send it down the hatch.** If your Chi doesn't fall for these methods, place your hand on top of the muzzle and gently squeeze just behind the canine teeth (fangs). Your Chi will open their mouth a bit at the pressure and you can use your other hand to gently lower the jaw further. Place the pill on the tongue as far back as you can reach and then close the mouth. Stroke your Chi's throat to encourage a swallowing reflex. Always follow the pill with a treat or a sip of water to make sure it goes down and doesn't get stuck, irritating the esophagus.

TIP

If you get your puppy used to having their mouth handled from the first day you bring them home, giving pills and liquid medications later in life will be much easier on both of you.

Use an eyedropper to give your Chi liquid medication. Lift the lips slightly and place the eyedropper in the back corner of the mouth, where the upper and lower lips form a pocket. Hold the head up and the lips shut and squeeze the eyedropper. Keep holding the muzzle, tilting it slightly upward until you're sure the medicine went down the throat.

TIP

If you get your Chi used to taking delicious liquid from an eyedropper, administering liquid medication becomes a cinch. Occasionally, melt a teaspoon of vanilla ice cream (or another tasty liquid that is safe for your dog), put it in an eyedropper, and give it to your Chi just as if it were medicine.

Spaying or Neutering for a Happier, Healthier Dog

If showing in conformation (see Chapter 12) isn't your game, the nicest thing you can do for yourself and your Chihuahua is to have your dog spayed or neutered. The following sections explain why.

REMEMBER

The age at which your Chihuahua should be spayed or neutered should be determined on a case-by-case basis, in consultation with your veterinarian. There are many factors to consider.

You may decide it's best to spay or neuter your dog at 6 months, when they are still young and likely will recover quickly. But some Chis are still awfully tiny at six months and you may prefer to wait until they're older and closer to their adult size. If you plan to do dog sports with your Chi, you might prefer to wait until 14 months old. By that time, *growth plates* (soft areas of developing cartilage at the ends of bones, which gradually harden with maturity) have closed. That's also when your dog is likely past the second fear period, which can occur between 6 and 14 months of age. A surgical experience during the first or second fear period can plant an ingrained fear of going back to the hospital or increased fear of new experiences.

Spaying

Spayed females are at much less risk of developing breast cancer than unspayed females. And because spaying removes the female's reproductive organs, spayed females never suffer cancers or infections of the ovaries or uterus. In addition, they don't have unwanted pregnancies and won't drip blood all over your carpet and furniture for several days twice a year!

Spayed females also are nicer to live with. Her sexy scent won't entice males to serenade in chorus on your front lawn, and she won't suddenly develop a desire to roam. Spaying helps to keep a female's disposition consistent and lets her participate in competitive events such as obedience and agility without taking three weeks off every six months (because females in season are banned from performance events). In short, spaying your Chi when she's young gives her a healthier life, presents you with fewer hassles, lessens the risk of a big dog mounting her, and doesn't add to the pet overpopulation problem.

WARNING

Please don't breed your female Chihuahua so you can get back your initial investment or so your children can witness the miracle of birth. A beloved female may need an emergency Caesarean section or even die giving birth, leaving you with traumatized children and orphan puppies. And as far as your investment goes, any emergency will result in big vet bills, and raising even healthy puppies is an expensive endeavor.

DEBUNKING MYTHS AND OLD WIVES' TALES ABOUT ALTERING

Several myths and old wives tales about spaying and neutering began circulating long ago, and every one of them is wrong. Here's the real story:

- Spaying or neutering does not make a dog fat and lazy. Overfeeding and lack of exercise do that. The truth is, altered pets are often the top performers in competitive events. Neutered males can keep their minds on their work, and spayed females can compete throughout the year without losing several weeks because of being in season. In fact, almost all service dogs (hearing dogs, guide dogs for the blind, and dogs that help the physically handicapped) are spayed or neutered.

- Spaying or neutering does not prevent a dog from being an alert watchdog. Neutered males concentrate on their homes better than males that have the scent of sex on their minds. And spayed females alert to strange sights and sounds every bit as quickly as unspayed females.

- Male dogs don't get sad or resentful about being "castrated." Dogs don't have human feelings about romantic love and sex. Males never miss the hormones that made them feel frustrated and constantly steered them toward trouble, and females don't feel unfulfilled because they didn't have litters. In fact, altered dogs usually become closer to their human families, which is where dogs really want to be.

Plus, even if all goes well with the whelping, it's common for one or more seemingly healthy puppies to die one day to four weeks after birth. This also can be very traumatic to children.

Neutering

Neutering your male dog makes him easier to live with. Male hormones make dogs desire every female in season whose scent wafts by on the wind, and some of the males perform Houdiniesque feats to escape and find the female. Male hormones also may contribute to housetraining problems, such as scent marking (when the male urinates on objects inside the home to stake out his territory).

Frustration (also caused by male hormones) is what may make a dog embarrass you by making love to Aunt Amelia's leg during Thanksgiving dinner. Although neutering won't immediately cure a frustrated escape artist with a housetraining problem, it will eliminate the production of male hormones, which almost always will start your dog on the road to improvement.

Tagging Your Dog

The traditional form of doggie identification is a tag inscribed with the owner's name and telephone number attached to the dog's collar. Perhaps this would be enough for the nice family down the block to see whom your Chi belongs to if they ever wander out the door unseen. But collars can come off and tags can get lost, so this section presents an additional ID method to discuss with your veterinarian, which ensures that your Chi carries identification all the time.

The best method of permanently identifying dogs is the *microchip.* This tiny device (about the size of an uncooked kernel of rice) is encoded with your pet's identification information and implanted under the skin (usually at the juncture of the neck and the withers) by your veterinarian. The procedure is similar to receiving a vaccination.

If your Chi becomes lost and ends up in a shelter, a device called a scanner reads the microchip and identifies him. Or a person who finds the dog can take them to a veterinary clinic to be scanned. Most shelters and vet hospitals have scanners these days that can read all microchips.

Chihuahuas who have been microchipped need to be registered with a national registry (database) to ensure that the finder can contact you. Excellent registries include the following:

>> **AKC CAR (Companion Animal Recovery):** www.akc.org/lostfound; 800-252-7894.

>> **AllPaws Pet Microchip Registry:** www.allpawsregistry.com.

>> **Home: Found Animals Microchip Registry:** www.found.org.

>> **HomeAgain Pet Recovery:** www.homeagain.com.

>> **The National Dog Registry:** www.nationaldogregistry.com; 800-NDR-DOGS.

TIP

To be on the safe side, have your dog microchipped and use a buckle collar and tag. A collar and tag ensure that someone who finds your dog will have your contact information immediately. But if the collar and tag are missing, they can take your Chi to a veterinarian or shelter to be scanned for a microchip. If you've registered the microchip, the registry will be alerted that your dog has been found. As long as they have your current phone number or email, they will contact you with the good news.

Chapter **14**

Debugging the Dog

The dictionary defines a *parasite* as an organism that relies on another living thing for survival but contributes nothing to the host organism. That's true as far as it goes, but many parasites do contribute something in a negative sense — they hand their hosts an array of afflictions.

A host of creepy-crawlies is looking for a free lunch and a cozy condo, compliments of your Chihuahua. Some prefer camping under a tent of hair; others want to set up housekeeping indoors and homestead in the intestines, bowels, ears, and even (horrors!) the heart. In this chapter, we unmask these intruders and tell you how to protect your dog from parasitic invasions, both internal and external.

TECHNICAL STUFF

Parasites that live inside their hosts are called *internal or intestinal parasites.* Those found on the skin are called *external parasites.* For example, worms are internal parasites, and fleas are external parasites.

Kicking Worms and Other Internal Bugs to the Curb

Don't be embarrassed if your Chi gets intestinal worms. No matter how carefully you look after your pup, they can still become infected with them. Heartworms, however, are a different story. These deadly dependents are preventable, so if your dog is unlucky enough to be diagnosed with them, someone made a big mistake. Here's the skinny on the nasty critters that may try to move in on your Chi.

Heartworms

Heartworms are transmitted by mosquito bites. As the worms mature inside the dog (a process that takes about six months), they migrate to the large blood vessels of the lungs and eventually to the heart, where they reproduce, blocking blood flow. The results can be severe lung disease, heart failure, and organ damage. Heartworms grow so big that as few as two can kill a Chihuahua. A single heartworm can grow up to 14 inches long.

WARNING

Heartworms used to be limited to hot, humid areas where mosquitoes thrive, but now they have been diagnosed in all 50 states. In 2019, the states with the highest heartworm infection rates were Mississippi, Louisiana, South Carolina, Arkansas, and Alabama. In Canada, high-risk areas include southern Ontario, southern Quebec, Manitoba, and the Okanagan in British Columbia. Other areas with a high prevalence of heartworms are South America, Japan, Australia, and Italy. Any area that is tropical or temperate can harbor heartworms.

Many dogs die without showing symptoms. Prevention is the only defense, and it must start as soon as you get your Chi and continue for life, even if they spend most of their time indoors. If you acquire your Chihuahua as a puppy, ask your veterinarian to put them on a heartworm prevention program and then stick to it without fail.

REMEMBER

Even after starting preventive medication, your Chi still needs an annual blood test for heartworms. Why? Because prevention is the best thing going, but it isn't 100 percent perfect (and neither are we, the people who have to remember to give our dogs pills).

If you slip up and don't give your dog their heartworm medication appropriately, you should have your Chi tested before resuming their monthly prevention program. That's because if a dog already has heartworms and takes preventive medication, the combination can be fatal. If you acquire your Chi as an adult dog, your vet will require a heartworm test before prescribing preventive medication.

What if you acquired your Chi as an adult and they test positive for heartworms? On the plus side, treatment is available but it needs to start immediately. Unfortunately, the treatment to rid a dog of heartworms is a series of painful injections that can cause soreness and swelling at the injection site. Be sure to go to a veterinarian who provides effective pain management for your Chi. The medications used today have fewer side effects, which makes the procedure less hazardous to a Chi's health than it used to be. You can also ask your veterinarian about a "slow kill" treatment technique. It has pros and cons, which your veterinarian can explain to you.

Roundworms, hookworms, whipworms, tapeworms — yuck!

Many puppies are born with roundworms, and some get hookworms and/or roundworms from their mothers' milk. Your Chi can pick up one of several species of worms, including hookworms and whipworms, when simply out for a walk or at the dog park. Fleas play host to tapeworms, so your dog may ingest one while nipping at a flea that suddenly sprang from the grass and landed on their well-groomed back. So what's a dog owner to do?

The best preventive steps are maintaining clean quarters and quick removal of internal parasites. Prevention works best if started as soon as you get your puppy. In addition to vaccinating your Chi (see Chapter 13) and starting a heartworm prevention program, your vet also needs to perform a fecal exam to check for intestinal parasites. After your Chihuahua checks out negative for worms, take a stool sample to your vet at least twice a year (three times the first year). That way, if one comes up positive, you'll get rid of the new worms before they become overwhelming and endanger the dog's health.

The symptoms of roundworms, whipworms, tapeworms, and hookworms are similar:

>> Dull eyes

>> A rough, dry coat

>> Weakness

>> Weight loss despite an enormous appetite

>> Coughing

>> Vomiting

>> Diarrhea (sometimes bloody)

>> A big belly (all the time, not just right after eating)

Most dogs have only two or three symptoms; others totally lose their appetites when harboring worms. Occasionally, a dog may show no symptoms at all but then suddenly become severely anemic from a heavy infestation. Hookworms, for example, are bloodsuckers and can kill a dog as tiny as a Chihuahua puppy within weeks.

WARNING

Don't try to diagnose and deworm your Chihuahua by using over-the-counter medications. Many symptoms of worms are also signs of other serious illnesses. Not only that, but different worms require different treatments. The amount of medication is determined by your dog's weight; it can be dangerous if you give too much, and ineffective if you give too little. Always take your dog to the vet to get a clear diagnosis and the right medications.

On the bright side, getting rid of intestinal worms is a routine veterinary procedure. If your vet discovers that any of these worms are living inside your Chi, he or she may give the dog a shot or prescribe medication and schedule a follow-up treatment. Don't overlook or reschedule the follow-up visit, because timing is important.

Giardia

Giardia are found in lakes, ponds, and other outdoor water sources. Chihuahuas seldom contact Giardia because the *protozoans* (one-celled microscopic organisms, not worms, bacteria, or viruses) are most often ingested by thirsty hunting dogs and dogs accompanying backpackers — not comfort-loving critters like Chis. However, your Chihuahua can ingest Giardia by an act as simple as lapping water from a puddle, so it's good to be aware of it.

After a dog ingests them, Giardia attach to the intestinal wall and feed on the inner lining of the small intestine. Naturally, this creates irritation, which is accompanied by the following:

>> Inflammation

>> Stools coated with mucous

>> Weight loss

>> Diarrhea

>> Bloating

If you travel with your dog, Giardia should convince you to carry water from home. But dogs can pick up the protozoa from licking an affected dog's stool (yes, sometimes dogs do yucky stuff like that). If your Chi gets diarrhea after eliminating at a highway rest stop or the dog park, let your vet know that Giardia is one possibility. Prompt treatment is important.

Coccidia

Coccidia, another protozoan, lay eggs in animals' stools. And dogs sometimes get up close and personal with poop. After they get inside your Chi, coccidia line the intestinal tract, causing

>> Watery stools and bloating

>> Straining during elimination

>> Vomiting

>> Weight loss

>> Streaks of blood in the stool

Is there any good news? Yes. Coccidia are easily diagnosed by your vet and quickly eliminated when treated early.

TIP

It is best to pick up all feces as soon as your puppy goes to help prevent your yard from becoming contaminated and a constant source of reinfection for your dog.

Controlling External Pests: Fleas, Ticks, and Mites

Fleas, ticks, and mites are the most common external parasites that annoy and endanger dogs. In the following sections, we explain what you need to know to keep your Chihuahua safe from a variety of bloodthirsty bugs.

Defeating the terrible tick

Here's the good news. If you walk your Chihuahua in the sunshine during the warm months and keep them away from tall grass and profuse plants, chances are they won't pick up any ticks. Why? Because like Dracula, these bloodsuckers prefer darker areas — especially the woods. But occasionally ticks appear in unexpected places, and because the diseases they can transmit are so dangerous, your best bet is to check your Chi's body for them daily if they've been outdoors. It used to be that ticks were seasonal menaces but with milder winters ticks can now be found year-round. It takes at least 24 to 36 hours for ticks to do their dirty work, so if you remove them quickly, your dog probably won't come down with any of the dire diseases ticks can transmit.

WARNING

Tick-borne diseases can affect humans, too, and some are deadly, so if your Chihuahua has a tick, you should check yourself carefully too.

REMEMBER

Dogs seldom get all, or even half, the symptoms that a particular tick-borne disease can cause. If you've found a tick on your dog within the last two weeks, just one or two symptoms of a tick-related illness warrant an immediate trip to the veterinarian.

Scanning for and removing ticks

When checking for ticks, pay special attention to your dog's head, face, neck, and the inside of the ears. Those are a tick's favorite lunch counters. Another choice spot is between the toes. But a tick can cling to any part of a Chi's body, so run your fingertips everywhere — up and down the legs, under the pits, and down the back, sides, belly, and tail. It sounds like a big job, but you can easily complete the whole exam in a minute. Now aren't you glad you chose a Chihuahua?

TIP

If you find an attached tick, don't try to pull it off by hand. Use a pair of tweezers with pointy tips or, if you live in tick country, get a special tool called a tick twister, available from veterinarians and pet supply stores. It's the preferred method for tick removal, because it is less likely to squeeze the tick too hard, which can accelerate bacterial transmission.

Grab your tick-removal device and follow these steps:

1. **Separate your Chi's hair so you can see where the tick is embedded in the skin.**

   The embedded part is the tick's head.

2. **If you have rubbing alcohol handy, put a drop of it right on the tick.**

   That makes some ticks release their hold.

3. **Use tick twister or tweezers to clamp down as close to the head as possible and pull it out slowly.**

   Ideally, you'll remove the entire tick, head and all.

4. **Put a dab of alcohol on your Chi's skin where the tick had been.**

Uh oh. You did everything right, but the tick's head broke off and stayed under your pup's skin. If that happens, play it safe and call your veterinarian for further instructions.

TECHNICAL
STUFF

If the tick's head remains embedded beneath your dog's skin, it can develop into an infection. Poking and prying at it with tweezers can make things worse. Your vet may advise you to apply antibiotic ointment to the area and recommend that you bring your dog in if a rash develops.

If you're sure you removed the tick within 24 hours of when it attached, your dog is probably home free. But it can't hurt to keep the tick in a small jar of alcohol for a couple of weeks. If your dog shows any signs of sickness, you can have the vet test the tick (for a cost) to see if it was carrying any diseases that affect dogs.

Go to the vet if anything seems wrong. The following sections tell you what signs to watch out for, and all the many miseries ticks carry.

Tick Paralysis

The American dog tick (which carries the scientific name *Dermacentor variabilis* and is sometimes called the Eastern wood tick), the Lone Star tick (*Amblyomma americanum*), and the Western Mountain or Rocky Mountain wood tick (*Dermacentor andersoni*) all inject toxins into their hosts through their saliva. Early signs of sickness are weakness, fever, a loss of or change in the dog's voice, vomiting, dilated pupils, and lack of coordination. The clinical signs usually disappear gradually after you remove the tick. But if the tick remains undetected, paralysis, difficulty breathing, and death may follow these symptoms.

Rocky Mountain Spotted Fever

Rocky Mountain Spotted Fever is a deadly disease brought to your dog by the same ticks that can cause paralysis. It occurs when a carrier tick injects a particular bacterium beneath the skin. Signs of this disease are a high fever, a tender abdomen, water retention (look for swollen legs and feet), blood in the urine or stools, nosebleeds, difficulty breathing, and general weakness. Symptoms may not show up until two weeks after the tick bite.

Lyme disease

Transmitted by the deer tick (*Ixodes scapularis*), *Lyme disease* occurs when a carrier tick transmits a particular bacterium into a dog (or person) through its saliva. Depending on your location, up to 50 percent of deer ticks are carriers. These ticks are also more difficult to find on your dog because they're so small. The good news is that generally they must be attached for nearly two days before infection can occur.

You may have heard that dogs don't get Lyme disease. That's not true. However, only 5 to 10 percent of dogs diagnosed with Lyme disease are symptomatic. But it's still not something you want to risk.

A dog with Lyme disease may become lame, depressed, weak, and feverish; suffer painful joints; and be reluctant to move. If you live in a rural area known for having a large population of deer ticks, your veterinarian may suggest vaccinating your Chihuahua against Lyme disease.

Lyme disease has been diagnosed in dogs in all 50 states and in Canada. It is found in Europe and parts of Asia, too.

Fleas are no circus

We wish we could offer you a quick and easy method for getting rid of fleas, but unfortunately, eliminating fleas isn't easy . . . not even with all the new formulas marketed every year. Sooner or later, fleas become resistant or adapt to insecticides. That's why new flea preventive products appear at veterinary clinics and on pet supply store shelves regularly. It's an ongoing battle.

With a dog as small as a Chihuahua, using any over-the-counter flea remedies is a bad idea due to the risk of overdose. Instead, discuss your Chihuahua's lifestyle with your veterinarian, and he or she will prescribe a safe and effective program to keep fleas from moving in on your Chi.

With fleas, prevention is key and earlier is better. Those bad little buggers are capable of producing another generation every 21 days, and one female flea can produce thousands of eggs in her lifetime. Not only that, but flea bites itch something awful, often cause an allergic reaction that turns into an oozing *hot spot,* and fleas can carry tapeworms. A dog with a fleabite allergy is miserable with just one or two fleas on them. Chances are, Chihuahuas will let you know when they have fleas. Most Chihuahuas scratch themselves silly when fleas bite them.

The only way to control fleas is to eliminate them not only from your dog, but also from inside and outside your home . . . and from your vehicle if your dog travels with you.

TECHNICAL STUFF

Fleas don't live on dogs all the time — they just feed on them and ride around for a while. Then they hop off and camp in the carpet, dog bed, or grass until they get hungry and want to hitch a canine ride again.

The best way to terminate fleas is with an oral or topical preventive product prescribed by your veterinarian.

Flea preventive products and insecticides for the home and yard must be used with great care — especially when you own the smallest of all breeds. Don't try to come up with a flea management program on your own. The use of more than one product often is necessary, and your vet knows which ones can be safely used at the same time and which products become toxic when combined. If you prefer natural products, ask your vet to recommend some effective environmental treatments but know that you will have to work harder to keep fleas at bay.

TIP

Some medications are dual purpose, preventing heartworms and fighting fleas. Ask the vet about what's right for your Chi.

TIP

Your vacuum cleaner is your best friend when fighting fleas. Besides inhaling the adults, it also sucks the eggs and larva right out of the carpet and upholstery. Vacuum every room often when fighting fleas. Pay attention to baseboards and cracks as fleas like to hide from light. Make sure you seal the vacuum bag well and throw it away when you finish.

CAPTURE THE FLEA

Finding out if your home has fleas is easy. Fill a large, shallow pan with water and add some liquid dish soap. Before retiring for the night, put the pan on the floor and place a desk lamp right next to it with the light cocked over the water. After you go to bed, and the lamp is the only light on in the house, fleas will jump at it, fall in the water, and sink immediately, because dish soap makes the water soft, or slippery. If you find drowned fleas in the pan the next morning, you know your home has been invaded. Some people set this flea trap every night during the summer and say it's a big help in controlling fleas.

Managing mites

A myriad of microscopic mites, including one commonly called *walking dandruff*, feed on the skin, blood, and even hair of a dog. Your Chihuahua may never be bothered by any of them, but it's smart to be familiar with the symptoms. Chances are your dog doc will do a skin scraping (it's painless) to find out what kind of mite is making your Chihuahua miserable. Don't try to diagnose and treat skin problems yourself. Some of them have such similar symptoms that even your vet won't be sure how to proceed without a test, and each mite requires different medication.

Sarcoptic mange

Sarcoptic mange, sometimes called *scabies,* is caused by crab-shaped mites that literally get under your dog's skin. After burrowing in, they sip your Chi's blood, mate, and lay eggs. These mange mites make your dog itch. Symptoms are relentless scratching, tiny red bumps, and patchy crusted areas, especially on the ears and feet. Visit your veterinarian before your pup suffers hair loss or a bacterial infection. Scabies responds to medication.

Follicular or demodectic mange

Commonly called *red mange,* follicular or *demodectic mange* is caused by a different type of mite. Because itching is a symptom in some dogs but not in others, look for small, circular patches that look moth-eaten. They're usually found on the head, or along the back, sides, and neck.

In young dogs, red mange often is stress-related. Anything that produces anxiety — such as going through the hormonal changes of adolescence or staying in a boarding kennel for the first time — can trigger a minor outbreak. So, do mites crawl around with miniature blood pressure cuffs so they can tell when a dog is stressed out? Not exactly. The truth is that most dogs have some of these mites on them all the time and never have a problem. But when they're under stress, their defenses break down and the result is a small patch of demodectic mange (sometimes called *juvenile mange*) — easily treated by your veterinarian.

Generalized outbreaks of red mange are another story. If your Chihuahua ever gets a case of mange that covers much of her body, have her spayed or neutered (if she isn't already). Never breed a dog with a generalized case of mange — the disease and its misery can be passed on to the puppies. Talk to your veterinarian about the best treatment for your dog. Isoxazolines, available only by prescription, are now considered the therapy of choice for sarcoptic and demodectic mange. Unless your pet has a history of seizures, these products have minimal risk and cure cases of mange within a few weeks.

Ear mites

Does your dog continuously scratch their ears or shake their head? They may have ear mites (*Otodectes cynotis*). You may have heard that only cats get ear mites, but that's a myth. These critters move into the ear canal and proceed to nibble on the outer layer. Wipe gently inside the ear with a cotton ball. If it comes out with rusty-brown or blackish goop on it, your Chi has mites. These bugs are easily treatable when caught early, so go see your veterinarian.

Walking dandruff

This mite's scientific name is *Cheyletiella* but you can just call it walking dandruff. If your Chi tries to turn their body into a circle so they can nip and nibble along their spine, lies on the rug upside down and wiggles around in an effort to scratch their back, or you notice an abnormal amount of flaking when you groom them, those signs all point to walking dandruff, a mite that devours the skin along a dog's spine (and sometimes other places, too). Your veterinarian can get rid of these itchy critters, but it may take several treatments. You'll have to clean all your dog's bedding and favorite rugs, too.

IN THIS CHAPTER

» Watching for signs of sickness or injury

» Dealing with emergencies and transportation

» Administering meds

» Understanding ailments specific to Chihuahuas

» Maintaining your old dog's comfort

» Facing the facts of life and death

Chapter **15**

Dealing with Sickness, Injury, and Other Considerations

Although prevention is always the best plan when it comes to health care, being perceptive and prepared run a close second and third. The sooner you seek help for a sick dog, the better their chance of recovery.

This chapter helps you recognize the earliest signs of sickness or injury. It also describes some hereditary ailments that occasionally afflict Toy dogs and shows you the first-aid basics so you can act in an emergency until professional help is available.

Finally, we discuss the most painful fact of life: death. Losing a precious pet is heartbreaking enough without having to make sudden decisions, so we discuss options such as euthanasia and different methods of caring for the body. We also include some information on the stages of grief and healing.

Yes — this chapter covers some of the more difficult and upsetting parts of having a Chihuahua. But with luck, the chapter has more info than you'll ever need. We hope you never have to use it, but it's here for you just in case.

Recognizing Signs of Sickness

REMEMBER

Many signs of sickness in Chihuahuas, although subtle at first, are symptoms that you may sense rather than actually see — the way a mother instinctively knows when something is troubling her child. So if something seems wrong but you can't figure out what it is, don't chalk it up to an overactive imagination. It may actually be an early warning, which is the best kind. Prompt treatment, before your Chihuahua weakens, has the greatest chance of success.

If something doesn't seem right, even if that *something* doesn't appear in this chapter, trust your intuition and take your Chihuahua to the vet for a checkup. The following sections present a tiered approach to recognizing signs and taking action.

When you should wait and see (but not very long)

Some problems go away on their own, but your Chi needs medical attention if any issue continues longer than 24 hours. If your Chihuahua has any of the following symptoms, pay attention:

>> Refusing to eat anything at all but having no other signs of sickness

>> Limping, or refusing to put weight on one leg, yet eating normally and showing no obvious signs of a fracture or other pain or sickness

A LITTLE LESS HOP IN THEIR STEP? CALL THE VET

Years ago, when Jackie showed American Staffordshire Terriers, she had a female named Frankie who bounded over obedience jumps with several inches to spare. One day, at a Chicago show, Frankie seemed a little less spirited than usual during breed judging, but she still started the morning on a high note by winning Best of Breed. Later on, she also earned a qualifying score in open obedience competition; however, Jackie noticed that she just cleared the jumps with no room to spare. She wanted to attribute Frankie's sedate attitude to a muggy Midwest afternoon, but it nagged at her on the drive home.

The next morning, she called the vet for an appointment, telling him only that something about Frankie didn't seem quite right. It turned out that Frankie had a uterine infection. Because Jackie caught it early, it was easily cured, but if she had waited for more evidence of illness, the problem might have become serious. What's the moral of the story? No one knows your dog better than you do.

>> Changing personality or activity level but exhibiting no other signs of pain or sickness

>> Mild diarrhea

Loose stool but not liquid, with no blood in it; no signs of straining or stomach pain

>> Vomiting two or three times but showing no other signs of sickness (Plenty of perfectly healthy dogs vomit after eating grass.)

>> Scratching or nipping an itchy spot or two but not hard enough to break the skin

>> Drinking and urinating more than usual but showing no other signs of sickness

If your dog seems ill, you might want to check their temperature. To take your Chi's temperature, use a rectal thermometer with a rounded end. Shake it down below 100 degrees Fahrenheit, smear it with petroleum jelly, and insert it carefully into the rectum between ½ and 1 inch. Talk soothingly while holding the dog firmly in a standing position for two minutes (don't let them sit). Remove the thermometer and check the reading. Disinfect the thermometer with rubbing alcohol before putting it away.

The average dog's temperature isn't like a human's at 98.6°F (37°C). Your dog's temperature should be between 100.0°F and 102.5°F (39.2°C). If it's higher than 102.5°F, you know your pup isn't feeling well.

TECHNICAL STUFF

Dogs have a pulse rate between 80 and 120 beats per minute and typically take 20 breaths per minute.

When you need to call your vet immediately

If your little Chihuahua has any of the following problems, call your vet immediately and explain the symptoms in detail. You'll probably need a same-day appointment:

>> Refusing to eat and seeming depressed or lethargic. They may be suffering from stomach pain.

>> Suffering an eye problem. This includes excessive tearing, an eye swollen shut or partially shut, or an eye that looks cloudy or off-color.

>> Breathing that's labored or fast and shallow. May or may not be in combination with a cough.

>> Vomiting frequently, combined with depression or exhaustion.

>> Incessant diarrhea. A liquid stool, combined with a terrible odor and possibly pain and straining.

>> Swallowing an object without choking. A swallowed object can turn into a life-threatening problem if your Chi can't pass it. The sooner your vet assesses the situation, the better.

>> Swelling on any part of the body. It may feel hard and hot to the touch or be infected and oozing.

>> Scratching and/or biting at itchy skin until it's inflamed, with possible hair loss brought on by intense scratching.

>> Suffering an injury, like a deep puncture that can become infected, a cut that needs to be stitched, or severe lameness with no indication of a fracture.

What to do in an emergency

A real emergency is a situation so scary that your Chihuahua needs the attention of your vet or veterinary hospital immediately — no matter if it's Sunday, New Year's Eve, or three o'clock in the morning. The following lists outline the many emergency situations you may encounter; for more on handling these issues, see the following section.

Emergencies resulting from accidents include

>> Broken bones

>> Heavy bleeding

>> Severe trauma (possibility of internal bleeding and/or shock)

>> Burns from fire, scalding, or chemicals

>> Poisoning

Emergency illnesses include

>> Seizures

>> Staggering and/or falling down

>> Uncontrollable diarrhea (sometimes bloody)

>> Frequent vomiting

>> Breathing problems

>> Allergic reactions

>> Obstruction in the throat (choking)

>> Obstruction in the intestine or urinary tract (straining to eliminate)

>> Paralysis

>> Heatstroke

>> Bloat (extremely rare in Chihuahuas)

Handling Serious Issues: First Aid and Transportation

Emergency situations demand the service of a veterinarian ASAP. In the meantime, handling your Chihuahua properly until they're in the hands of a pro is important. Keeping calm is the hardest part. If a wave of panic doesn't rush over you when you first see your sick or injured pet, you're stronger than we are. But panic won't help, so take a deep breath and resolve to stay calm and think straight. Then get to work.

If your Chihuahua has an emergency, call your veterinary clinic (or its emergency number) immediately and tell the receptionist (or whoever answers the phone) what happened. That way, the clinic can prepare for your dog's arrival. Then give first aid and get to the clinic immediately. The following sections address this process with various emergency situations.

REMEMBER

Unless the clinic gives you other instructions for transporting your Chihuahua, put them in a crate with a lot of clean, soft bedding, secure the crate in your vehicle so it won't slide or roll, and drive to the clinic.

WARNING

Be careful when handling a dog who is in pain or panicking. They will bite.

If you suspect that your Chihuahua has been poisoned by ingesting or inhaling poison, absorbing a toxic substance through the skin, or by injection (snake, scorpion, or spider bite), get professional help immediately. If you're far from a vet, call the ASPCA Animal Poison Control Center hotline at 888-426-4435 or Pet Poison Helpline at 800-213-6680. Both can be called from the U.S., Canada, or the Caribbean. Be prepared with a credit card to pay the fee. In the United Kingdom, there is the Animal

PoisonLine (www.animalpoisonline.co.uk). Australia has Animal Poisons Helpline (https://animalpoisons.com.au/), a free service for pet owners.

Heavy bleeding

Use a pressure bandage (not a tourniquet) to control heavy bleeding or blood spurting from any part of your dog's body. It's best if you have a helper so one person can keep the pressure bandage on your Chi while the other drives to the clinic.

If you have two people, follow these steps:

1. With clean hands, apply direct pressure to the wound by holding a gauze pad firmly against it for 30 seconds.

2. If bleeding continues, apply a second gauze pad on top of the first and continue applying pressure.

3. Wrap your Chi in a clean towel, and with one person holding them and keeping the gauze pad(s) in place, go to the veterinary clinic.

If you don't have a helper, follow these steps:

1. Wrap a wide adhesive bandage around the wound and the gauze pad.

2. Put your Chi in a crate with a towel or blanket.

3. Secure the crate in your vehicle so it won't slide or roll and head for the clinic.

If the clinic is many miles away and the adhesive bandage is around one of the legs, stop and check the foot below the bandage after half an hour. If it's swollen or cold, loosen the bandage but leave the gauze pad in place.

WARNING

Resist the urge to clean or wipe a wound while it's still bleeding. Stopping the bleeding is your first priority, and cleaning the wound often makes it bleed more heavily.

Choking

If your Chihuahua paws at their mouth, drools, seems unable to close their mouth, coughs, tries to vomit, strains for breath by stretching their head and neck, or appears frantic, they may be choking.

If they're getting enough air to sustain themselves, put them in the crate and take them to the clinic immediately. If they appear on the verge of passing out or if their tongue is turning blue, follow these steps:

1. Wedge something (the handle of a small screwdriver works well) between the top and bottom molars on one side of the mouth to keep it open.

2. Use a flashlight or put them under good lighting and look into the mouth and down the throat.

3. Pull the tongue straight (careful, they may try to bite) to see if the offending object is on top of it.

4. If you find the problem, remove it with your fingers, using a sweeping motion so you don't miss anything, or a pair of long-nosed pliers. If you use pliers, be careful because they could damage soft tissue in the oral cavity. Try to only touch and pull the object that's causing the problem—which can be difficult if your hands are shaking from stress.

5. If all else fails (you can see the wedged object but your Chi can't catch their breath), hold them upside down by the hind legs and shake the dog (or pat them on the back if you have a helper to hold them).

With luck, that will dislodge the object so they can breathe again. Then get to the vet right away. Your Chihuahua just suffered a major trauma. (If you can't see the object, follow the instruction in the next section.)

Trouble breathing is not necessarily the same as choking. It can have many different causes, including viral or bacterial pneumonia, collapsing trachea, internal bleeding, pain, heart disease, and trauma, such as a fall or being hit by a blunt object, whether that's running head-on into a piece of furniture or being hit by a car.

Signs of labored breathing include persistent coughing, stretching the neck out in an attempt to get more air, a rapid respiratory rate (more than 35 breaths per minute at rest), restlessness or pacing, panting that doesn't stop, and tongue or gums that appear blue. Your dog may look fearful or panicked, just as you would if you were having trouble breathing. These are all signs that your Chihuahua needs to get to the vet—fast!

But if the dog isn't breathing, start mouth-to-nose resuscitation right away. Here's how:

1. **First try the methods recommended in the preceding "Choking" section.**

2. **If they're still not breathing, lay them on their right side on a table. Close their mouth and tilt their head back.**

3. **Keeping their mouth closed, place your open mouth over the dog's nose (you can do it through a handkerchief if you prefer) and breathe five or six shallow (short) breaths into it.**

   Of course you're terrified, but try to control your breathing. Your dog is small, so they don't have much lung capacity. If they start breathing, you've saved their life. Now take them to the vet for observation or further treatment.

4. **If they're still not breathing, keep giving mouth-to-nose resuscitation. Try to give approximately 20 shallow breaths per minute.**

Keep trying for a full ten minutes. When they start breathing by themselves, go to the clinic. If breathing doesn't resume by then, they're probably dead, but at least you know you did everything possible to help.

Broken leg

When treating and transporting a dog with a broken leg (or any broken bone), your job is to get them to the clinic without making the injury worse on the way. Steady the limb (without pulling on it) by wrapping absorbent cotton around the entire leg. Then use gauze bandage, held in place with adhesive, to keep the leg from moving during transport.

Heatstroke

Symptoms of heatstroke include rapid or heavy breathing, a bright red mouth and tongue, thick saliva, unsteadiness (possibly falling over), diarrhea, vomiting, a hot and dry nose with legs and ears hot to the touch, and complete collapse — often combined with glassy eyes and gray lips.

REMEMBER

Dogs don't sweat. The only way they can regulate their body temperature is by panting.

To save your Chihuahua during a case of heatstroke, you must start cooling them immediately — even before you call the clinic:

1. **Take the dog to a shady or air-conditioned place.**

2. **Soak a towel in cool (not ice) water, wring it out, and apply cold compresses to their belly and groin. You can also apply rubbing alcohol on paw pads, groin, and armpits to help with cooling.**

3. **Lay the cool towel on their back and gently wet their head with it.**

4. **Let them drink a small amount of cool water at intervals — not all they want at one time.**

   If they're too weak to drink, wipe the inside of their mouth with the water.

5. **Call the clinic, put the cold, wet towel in the bottom of the crate, and take them to the vet.**

WARNING

Although most emergencies are the result of bad luck rather than bad management, heatstroke is absolutely preventable. Don't overexert your Chi on a muggy day or leave them alone inside your vehicle. The temperature inside a car or truck, even one parked in the shade, usually is 25 degrees hotter than outside the vehicle. Every year, hundreds of pets die from being left alone in parked vehicles for just a few minutes.

Familiarizing Yourself with Chihuahua Conditions

Although Chihuahuas have fewer genetic defects than many breeds (maybe because so many breeders try hard to eliminate problems), no breed is perfect. In the following sections, we present some idiosyncrasies — a few serious issues but most not — that are sometimes seen in Chihuahuas and other Toy breeds.

Subluxation of the patella

Subluxation of the patella, or *luxating patella*, is a relatively common problem in small breeds and some large ones as well. In dog lingo, this defect is called "slipped stifles" or "loose kneecaps." When it occurs, the kneecap (we're talking about the rear legs) slips out of its groove — sometimes often and sometimes rarely, depending on the severity of the problem. If your dog is unlucky enough to have their kneecaps slip often, surgery may be the solution. A dog with a mild case can live a normal life, kind of like a person with a trick knee.

Hypoglycemia

Hypoglycemia refers to low blood sugar and is a common problem in young Toy puppies. Most of them grow out of it before they're old enough to leave the breeder's home, but for a few, it's a danger throughout their lives.

Symptoms of low blood sugar include a staggering gait, glassy eyes, and sometimes limpness or rigidity. If the dog doesn't receive immediate help when the symptoms show, they can suffer seizures, unconsciousness, and, finally, death. Treatment involves putting some sugar in your dog's mouth, calling your veterinarian, and heading for the clinic.

TIP

When you know that your dog has a tendency to develop hypoglycemia, you can prevent future attacks by changing the feeding schedule. Give small amounts of food several times a day and avoid sugary treats (check the ingredients before buying dog treats). Too much sugar can put your Chi on a roller-coaster ride of sugar highs and lows instead of keeping blood sugar nice and level. (For more on diet, head to Chapter 6.)

Collapsing trachea

Collapsing trachea is a problem for Toy dogs of many breeds — mostly in dogs older than five years, but occasionally a puppy has it from birth. The symptoms include coughing, shortness of breath, and exhaustion. To understand the condition, think of the trachea as a straw made of cartilage that carries air from the neck to the chest. When the cartilage collapses, breathing becomes difficult — kind of like sipping soda through a flattened straw.

WARNING

Your vet can treat the condition with medication, but if you smoke, your Chihuahua's prognosis may be poor. Secondhand smoke is a proven contributing factor to the problem, and smoke tends to settle low, where a little dog's nose is.

Heart murmur

Heart murmurs are relatively uncommon in Chihuahuas. Thankfully, even those that have one usually have the functional type. As in people, that means they can be as active and athletic as they want and live long, normal lives. If your Chihuahua is unlucky enough to develop a severe murmur, your vet may detect it during the annual exam. Further tests, such as an ultrasound and an EKG, performed by a veterinary cardiologist, may be recommended. The specialist can discuss treatment options with you.

Molera

The Chihuahua's *molera* (or *fontanel*) is considered a breed characteristic and not a condition or defect. Most Chihuahuas (80 to 90 percent) have a molera — a soft spot on the top of the head similar to a human baby's soft spot. But unlike babies, most Chihuahuas don't outgrow it. It usually shrinks as the dog matures and ends up nickel- or dime-sized. Your Chi's molera won't be a problem as long as you're gentle when petting or handling their head. In rare cases, the molera remains quite large and can sometimes (but not always) be a sign of a life-threatening problem called *hydrocephalus.* The following section tells you more about this rare but frightening condition.

Hydrocephalus

A dog with hydrocephalus (also called "water on the brain") may have an unusually large head caused by swelling. Other signs of this condition are frequent falling, seizures, a lot of white showing in the eyes, an unsteady gait, and east-west eyes (the opposite of crossed eyes). Depending on whether the condition is congenital, meaning the dog is born with it, or acquired, which may happen if the dog has a brain tumor or brain infection, it may be treatable with medication, surgery, or radiation therapy. In severe cases, however, humane euthanasia (a kind, vet-assisted death) may be the only solution.

Going under anesthesia

The possibility that your dog may someday need anesthesia is one main reason why you need to choose a veterinarian who's experienced in treating Toy dogs (see Chapter 13). Although deaths from anesthesia are rare, its use has potential risks. Your vet uses anesthesia only when necessary (before surgery, for example).

Prevention is the best course of action. Be sure to read about how to clean your Chihuahua's teeth (see Chapter 7) so that cleaning them under anesthesia won't be necessary as frequently. And when your dog *has* to go under anesthesia (during spaying or neutering, for example), ask your vet if any necessary dental work (such as pulling impacted baby teeth) can be done at the same time.

Ask your veterinarian about anesthesia safety procedures, such as bloodwork beforehand to identify underlying health problems; monitoring by a specially trained technician; intravenous fluids for hydration and blood pressure maintenance; and warming protocols before, during, and after the procedure.

Be sure your vet uses modern anesthesia techniques, which combine intravenous and gas anesthesia, plus use of anti-nausea and sedative drugs. Your Chihuahua should never be "masked down" or "boxed down," which involves placing a mask over the face or putting the pet in a box and adding anesthetic gas until they are unconscious. It's a dangerous, stressful, old-fashioned technique.

Watching those eyes

Because Chihuahuas have big eyes and live close to the floor, they're prone to eye injuries. Put several drops of saline solution in your dog's eye if an injury seems minor. That's often all it takes to flush out a foreign object that was accidentally kicked up by someone's shoe. If that doesn't relieve the problem or if the injury appears more serious (your dog is squinting, pawing at the eye, blinking rapidly, or producing excessive tears), take your Chihuahua to the vet right away.

Keeping Your Senior Sassy

We hope you have to use this section. It's about taking care of a golden oldster. All pet owners hate seeing the signs of aging in themselves or their pets. Yet, as the cliché goes, getting old is a whole lot better than the alternative. So don't let a little gray on your dog's muzzle depress you. Your sassy senior can enjoy a high quality of life for many years, and this section helps you keep them in super shape.

One day, you may notice that your Chihuahua is getting gray hairs. Even though they're healthy, rambunctious, and still in their prime, seeing the first signs of aging is scary. But it doesn't have to be. Keeping your oldster healthy and happy isn't hard. If you're lucky enough to share your life with a golden oldie, you can help them stay feisty by keeping their infirmities in mind.

There is good scientific evidence behind the use of acupuncture for relieving many disorders — especially arthritis. You can learn more about it at `https://pets.webmd.com/features/acupuncture-for-your-pets`

Noticing the initial signs of aging

Dogs age much like humans do. Even if your Chi has led a worry-free life, one of the first signs that they're becoming a senior is sprouting gray or white hairs. They appear first on the face, encircling the eyes and giving the muzzle a grizzled look. Don't let them spook you. Chances are your Chihuahua will have gray hairs for several years before feeling the first creaky joint of old age.

Other signs of aging include dental problems, including the loss of teeth. Eventually, your Chi may no longer be able to crunch kibble (dry food) as well as in younger years. One solution is to soften it by soaking it in warm water for several minutes and mixing it with canned meat. If a Chihuahua develops kidney disease (or other organic or allergic problems), your veterinarian can prescribe a therapeutic food that can help. (Check out Chapter 6 for more on feeding your senior Chi.)

TIP

While recovering from an accident or illness or when suffering the dental problems that may come with old age, your Chihuahua may welcome baby food. You can find boxes of rice cereal and jars of strained meats in the baby-food section of the supermarket. A combination of rice cereal and strained meat (warmed slightly) may entice your dog to eat when nothing else works. Avoid baby food that contains garlic or onion powder. Your veterinarian may prescribe a canned gastrointestinal diet that is complete and balanced to help with recovery, but sometimes with little dogs, baby foods are just more enticing.

REMEMBER

Older dogs often are less tolerant of cold than even puppies are, so be sure that

>> Your senior Chi has a warm sweater for outings.

>> You keep them away from drafts.

>> You put an extra baby blanket in their bed.

And speaking of their bed, they may start spending more time in it, preferring an afternoon nap to a brisk walk. I'm sure you've heard the saying "use it or lose it," and that advice applies to dogs as well as people. An older Chi still needs their exercise, although you shouldn't expect them to take part in strenuous activities. Let your Chi set the pace, and be willing to make your walks together leisurely rather than lively. When playing indoor exercise games (see Chapters 10 and 12), don't be surprised if they shuffle rather than speed through the house!

No matter what speed your Chi chooses, playing helps them stay mentally sharp and keeps their joints and muscles oiled, too. Not only that, but exercise helps them avoid obesity — a serious health problem in older dogs.

Dealing with other signs of aging

Arthritis often attacks older dogs, and although nothing cures it, your veterinarian may be able to provide relief. Many good medications and *nutraceuticals* (foodstuff that provides health benefits in addition to its basic nutritional value) are available to help treat those achy joints. Don't assume there's nothing that can be done. For instance, Librela, a new monthly injectable pain reliever, has shown good results.

You can also make changes at home to ease mobility difficulties. If your Chi can't jump on and off the sofa anymore, lift them up and down. Same with walking up and down the stairs. And if they can't reach the traditional easy chair they sit in when they're home alone, make sure they have a place to nap and stay warm while you're away. Either build (or buy) a ramp so they can reach their favorite spot or place a doggie bed by it for comfort.

WARNING

Changes in behavior are common signs of pain in dogs. If your Chihuahua is less active, suddenly doesn't enjoy being petted, doesn't get up to greet you, seems grumpy, moves more slowly or stiffly, frequently licks a specific area, pants when it's not hot, or hunches their back, take them to your veterinarian for a pain exam. Many options are available to help them find comfort.

If your Chihuahua were an older human, they would need bifocals and a hearing aid. The problem is this equipment isn't made for dogs. So if your Chi always came when you called them but suddenly starts to ignore you, chances are they have a hearing (not a behavior) problem. And if they were on the same elimination schedule for a dozen years and then start waking you up at 4 a.m. to go outside, they're not just looking for attention.

Your Chihuahua may become a crotchety old codger, too, detesting even minor changes and unwilling to make new friends (perhaps because of failing senses or twinges of arthritis). Report sudden changes in routine and disposition to your vet. Many problems can be relieved. Others can't, and some of them probably bother you more than they bother your Chi. After all, dogs don't agonize over the signs of aging like people do. As long as your Chihuahua still enjoys life and isn't suffering severe pain, they'll be happy as long as you love them.

The branch of medicine called *geriatrics* treats problems specific to aging; *gerontology* is the study of aging in people or their pets.

Coping with the Death of a Pet

Owners often know in advance when death is threatening their pets, but sometimes dogs die without warning, leaving owners saddened and shocked. Complicating the process are the decisions you may have to make concerning euthanasia and a final resting place. Understanding your options in advance may make things a little easier. We hope this section will help you with your planning and grief.

Well-being for life

For years, you live with and love your Chihuahua. As you watch them age and then move from being a senior to the geriatric stage of life, you may start to wonder about their quality of life. What does that mean? It's defined as the degree to which an animal or person is healthy, comfortable, and able to enjoy or participate in life. There are scales that can help you to measure your Chihuahua's quality of life by evaluating such factors as appetite, water intake, mobility, pain management, and physical and emotional comfort. PetMD and Lap of Love have some great resources available.

Considering euthanasia

Euthanasia is the most humane ending if your Chihuahua is in severe and constant pain with no hope of recovery. It consists of a lethal dose of a strong anesthetic, humanely administered by your vet. The injection puts your dog to sleep instantly and stops their heart. Often, especially if they have Fear Free or Low Stress Handling certification, veterinarians may prescribe a gentle sedative for you to give at home before bringing your pet in for the procedure. The sedative will reduce any anxiety your pet may feel about going to the veterinary clinic. If your vet doesn't suggest this treatment, feel free to ask them about it.

Only you can decide when the time is right. You may not want to say goodbye but taking your dog's quality of life into account will help you make the decision that is best for your Chihuahua. Trust your instincts and what your dog is showing you. These factors tell you when letting your dog go is the most merciful thing you can do for them.

TIP

You can choose to have the procedure performed at your veterinary clinic or by a house-call veterinarian at your home or a favorite place such as a park. This can be a good alternative if your Chihuahua is fearful at the veterinary clinic or you simply want them to be in a familiar spot surrounded by family. You can find a veterinarian who performs at-home euthanasia through organizations such as Lap of Love (www.lapoflove.com) or with an online search. If your veterinarian doesn't provide that service, they may be able to refer you to a colleague who does.

After you make that painful decision and make your final trip to the vet, the receptionist will ask if you want to leave your dog or stay with them during the procedure. Staying may be hard on you in the short run, but it's best for your dog in the moment, and for you in the long run. You will be grateful that you spent those last minutes together, sharing how much you love them.

TIP

Take care of all the paperwork first so you won't have to handle it through your tears. Then hold your Chi in your loving arms while the vet administers the injection. That way you'll know for sure that your dog didn't suffer, and they'll die peacefully, nestled against your chest.

Do you ever get over it? Well, no. You'll probably always miss your Chihuahua. But someday you'll be able to talk about their antics without a tear in your eye or a catch in your throat. Instead, you'll smile as you relate some of your favorite Chihuahua stories. And you'll know that the good times you had together will never be gone. They'll always remain in your mental bank of happy memories.

Handling your dog's body

Many people choose to leave their departed pets' bodies at the veterinary clinic. Usually the clinic notifies a service, which picks up the body and cremates it. Several dogs usually are cremated at the same time, and the *cremains* (ashes) are buried in the earth. Don't be shy about asking how your vet will dispose of the body. Veterinarians will often offer to make a pawprint keepsake for you or trim some of their hair for you to have as a remembrance.

Private cremation is an option you can request at the time of euthanasia. It may take place at a pet cemetery or private pet crematorium. Afterward, your Chihuahua's ashes will be returned to you, usually in a keepsake wooden box. You can keep your pet's ashes in a beautiful urn, bury them, scatter them in a place that is special to you and your pet, or have a piece of jewelry made from the cremains.

Some people prefer to bury their dogs in their own yards. You can mark the spot with a beautiful perennial plant or with a stone marker. This is an excellent option, provided that it's legal in your area. If not, pet cemeteries offer burials, which can be as simple or as elegant as you choose (and can afford).

TIP

Because not all pet cemeteries are created equal, look for one that's neat, clean, and has been around for a long time.

Helping Yourself and Your Family Heal

Shock, disbelief, anger, alienation, denial, guilt, and depression are all stages of grief. Most people go through every one of them, although not always in that order. To help yourself through these painful stages, you need to

>> **Understand that mourning the loss of a beloved pet is natural.** Your Chi wasn't "just a dog." They were *your* dog and you loved them. You had a strong bond, and broken bonds cause broken hearts.

>> **Take time to mourn.** Don't tell yourself to "get over it" and then bury your grief so deep that it eats you up from the inside. Everyone works through the stages of grief differently. Some people need more time to mourn than others. There's nothing wrong with that.

>> **Make a few changes in your habits and decor.** Put your Chi's bed, bowls, crate, and toys out of sight. Take the treats out of the cookie jar and the leash off the hat rack. Because walking them was probably one of the first things you did each morning, create a new morning routine.

>> **Talk about your feelings.** Find an understanding ear — someone who also adored your Chihuahua or who loves their own dog deeply — and share your feelings of loss. Many pet-related organizations and veterinary schools have support groups that help people through the pain of losing a pet. Ask your vet for a recommendation.

In the days that follow your Chi's death, don't be afraid to say that you miss them in front of your family. Encourage your kids to talk about their feelings, too. Look at pictures of your dog together and recount their hilarious escapades. Tell the kids (more than once) that the dog will always be part of them, because the good memories they have are theirs forever.

TIP

Sometimes sadness may sweep over you at work, and your co-workers may notice. If they ask you what's wrong and you don't want to talk about it, or you aren't sure how they feel about pets, just tell them that you recently lost a good friend. After all, it's the absolute truth.

>> **Read a book about pet loss.**

>> **Give your other pets extra attention.**

>> **Consider getting another dog.** No, not a replacement. It's impossible to replace your Chihuahua because they were an individual and no other dog will be just like them. But you *can* love other dogs, as long as you don't expect them to act like your previous Chihuahua. If you think you'll have a problem with that, you might choose a different color Chihuahua or a different breed entirely. That will help you learn to love your new dog's unique personality.

Also, be sure to tell your children that your Chihuahua can't be replaced, but that learning to love another dog is okay. In fact, some say the greatest honor you can give your dog is to love another one.

REMEMBER

If your Chihuahua's death was preventable, forgive yourself but learn from the experience. Maybe you didn't feel up to walking them one morning, so you turned them loose "just that one time" and they ran in front of a car. Or maybe you lost track of when their booster vaccination was due and they caught a deadly disease. If you contributed to their death, you're probably beating yourself up with guilt. But that won't bring them back. Instead, face what you did, learn from it, and go on. Give their death meaning by resolving never to make that mistake again. After all, no one is a perfect pet owner. Pet owners are just people who love their dogs but like anyone else are occasionally prone to poor judgment. Forgive yourself. It's one of the best lessons we can take from dogs.

Helping your spouse and your children cope with the loss of a pet can be soothing to you at the same time. One of the ways families come to terms with the finality of their situations (and then go on) is by combining their efforts and creating memorial ceremonies for pets who have died. You can hold a ceremony regardless of whether you have remains to scatter or a body to bury, and you can perform the ceremony indoors if you don't have a yard.

Explain the ceremony to your family as a celebration of your Chihuahua's life and all the joy they brought to your family. Ask each family member to think of why they loved your dog or something funny that the dog did so they can tell it during the ceremony. Before the ceremony, the family may want to go out together and choose a plant to grow in your Chi's memory.

5

The Part of Tens

Find out the top ten questions to ask breeders before buying a Chihuahua from them.

Bone up on ten fun facts about Chihuahuas, from their interesting history to their long lifespan.

Get to know celebrity Chihuahuas and discover what they're famous for.

Chapter **16**

Ten Questions to Ask Chihuahua Breeders

The best place to buy a healthy Chihuahua is from a breeder. Beware of puppies being sold by intermediaries or brokers. For example, no matter how clean the pet shop seems, that appealing pup in the window may have been born in a puppy mill (an overcrowded and filthy facility that breeds and sells hundreds of puppies of various breeds) or in a large commercial facility where they don't receive the attention and handling young puppies need. The combination of poor breeding practices and lack of human attention during the formative weeks can cause lifelong complications. We concede that may not always be the case, because the pet store could be getting its pups from caring breeders. But you may not be able to tell for sure. Most caring breeders don't sell their pups through other sources.

So, buyer beware — and be sure to get answers. This chapter walks you through all the questions you should ask the breeder to ensure that the seller is reputable, cares about the breed, and that their puppies are healthy. You should feel free to ask as many (appropriate) questions as you like, but there are several that should be at the top of your list.

REMEMBER

When dealing with a rescue organization, chances are employees won't know where the dog originated, but the person fostering the dog can tell you the circumstances of the rescue and everything that's known about the dog's health and temperament. Chapter 4 goes into much more detail about buying from breeders and adopting from other organizations.

How Many Litters a Year Do You Breed?

Okay, you've found some potential Chihuahua breeders. But how do you recognize a good one? For one, the best breeders specialize in only one or two breeds, and they never breed more puppies than they have time to care for. And that means plenty of individual attention. Good breeders adore their pups, give prospective owners the third degree, and may exhibit their best dogs at dog shows. Their facilities are clean, their puppy play areas contain toys, and their dogs enjoy being handled.

REMEMBER

When a breeder houses more puppies than they have time for, it usually shows. Two of the surest signs are spooked, unsocialized puppies and dogs living in unclean quarters.

Can You Tell Me All about This Dog's Personality?

Some breeders are more talkative than others, so if the seller you visit needs some help getting started, ask about a prospective pup's position in the litter or how they've been socialized. Good breeders know all about each and every one of their pups, and most of them will be happy to fill you in on a particular puppy's antics and personality. Beware if the breeder hesitates when asked if the pup is dominant or submissive with littermates, or hems and haws about how they were socialized. Caring breeders can tell plenty of stories about puppies no more than a few weeks old because they're observant when the puppies play and nurse together and make time to give each one individual attention.

May I See the Pup's Family?

After you've found a puppy or adult dog that twangs your heartstrings, it's time to meet your prospective pet's family. Expect to see at least the *dam* (that's mom in dog lingo) and the pup's littermates (siblings). With luck, you may also see an aunt or uncle, and maybe even a granddam or an adult brother or sister from an earlier litter. Don't be disappointed if you don't see the *sire* (papa). He may live far away, but his picture, pedigree, and videos of him will probably be available. There may not be any aunts, uncles, or older sibs on the premises, but buyer beware if you don't at least meet the puppy's dam.

What Were the Pup's Temperament Test Results?

A temperament test helps breeders evaluate each puppy's personality and potential in such areas as food motivation, problem-solving, resource guarding, and toy drive, to name just a few.

In combination with the breeder's overall observations, what they learn helps them place each puppy with the right family. It's good information for you to have, too. The breeder might say something like "Duke has the most bombproof, easygoing temperament of the boys. He's never had a bad day except when he isn't fed fast enough. He has a couple of minor disqualifying faults that rule him out from being a show dog."

TIP

If you're choosing a puppy from a distance, ask the breeder to send videos of temperament testing and early socialization experiences or a copy of temperament test results. The results may simply be the breeder's handwritten observations of each pup's behavior, or they may fill out a form from a particular organization such as Volhard Puppy Aptitude Testing.

Do You Provide a Copy of the Puppy's Feeding Schedule and Health Records?

Most breeders give new owners a copy of the puppy's feeding schedule and health record. If the breeder only offers to tell it to you verbally, write down all the information, but it's better to have an actual copy so nothing is misconstrued. Making sudden changes to a dog's diet can lead to digestive upset (see Chapter 6). Also, your veterinarian needs to know what vaccinations your pup has received and when they were given so they can set up a vaccination and deworming schedule (see Chapter 13).

What Kind of Health (Or Show) Guarantee Do You Offer?

Most reputable sellers offer some type of immediate health guarantee with their pups, giving you a certain amount of time (usually 24 to 48 hours) to take the dog to your vet for a complete physical to make sure they're not sick. When buying a show-potential puppy (one you plan to exhibit in dog shows; see Chapter 12), find out if the breeder will offer a replacement pup if the dog isn't show quality at adulthood. For any puppy, show or pet, reputable breeders typically include a guarantee in the sales contract against some or all heritable conditions or genetic defects for up to two years.

Is This Pup Eligible for Full or Limited AKC Registration?

A filled-out and signed registration application should accompany every breeder's AKC-registrable dogs. The form also has a section for you to complete when you purchase a pup. Do it ASAP, enclose the required fee, and send it to the American Kennel Club (the address should be on the form). A registration certificate will soon arrive in the mail. Then, and only then, do you own a registered dog!

If you plan to show your pup in conformation or compete in certain AKC dog sports (see Chapter 12), registration papers are a must. They can also serve as a record of ownership. Otherwise, you can simply file them away and put the cost of the registration fee toward your pup's pet health insurance, first vet visit, or puppy kindergarten class.

If your puppy has limited registration, that means they aren't a show dog (although it can still compete in obedience, agility, and other sporting events) and their offspring won't be eligible for AKC registration (see Chapter 4 for more).

Will I Receive a Registration Application When I Buy?

If you want an AKC-registered dog and the seller doesn't have a registration application ready to go with your puppy, proceed with caution. Yes, it's possible that the paperwork is still at the AKC offices and will arrive soon. If you trust the seller enough to take the puppy with papers pending, you should request a bill of sale signed by the seller that includes your dog's breed, date of birth, sex, and color — as well as the registered names and AKC numbers of the dog's sire and dam, and the full name and address of the breeder. If the important paperwork doesn't show up in a week or so and you want to contact the AKC, you'll be able to identify your dog with all the information from the bill of sale.

TIP

Most breeders automatically offer a copy of the puppy's pedigree. The *pedigree* is your Chihuahua's family tree, and it gives more information than just names. If any of their ancestors were illustrious in the show, obedience, or agility ring, abbreviations of their titles may be included, too. For details, check out Chapter 4, or ask the breeder to explain what the letters mean.

What Dog Clubs Do You Belong to and Recommend?

Most good breeders belong to a dog club or two. For example, U.S.-based Chihuahua breeders are often members of the Chihuahua Club of America, and possibly local all-breed dog clubs as well. Canadian breeders might belong to the Chihuahua Club of Canada. Breeders in the UK might be a part of the British Chihuahua Club. Chihuahua clubs exist around the world, including in Australia, Japan, Mexico, New Zealand, South Korea, and most European countries. Membership in a dog club is a good sign that you're dealing with a serious breeder, but not everyone is a "joiner." So don't pass up a puppy that makes your heart sing just because the breeder didn't join a dog club.

May I Call or E-mail You for Advice After We Get Home?

Make sure the breeder you choose is willing to be a source of information after the purchase — someone who can give you advice about the breed, training, and so on. A caring breeder may ask *you* to keep him or her posted on the puppy's progress. Steer clear of any breeders who hem and haw when you ask if you can use them as resources to help you raise your new puppy.

Chapter **17**

Ten Fascinating Facts About Chihuahuas

This book includes a lot of information on the Chihuahua breed and plenty of advice on how to give your Chi a great life. But in this chapter, we share ten tidbits that are just for fun. Want to know why Chihuahuas are popular or more about their history? Maybe you're intrigued by their tiny size or other anatomical features, or you want to know some of the activities in which they excel. This chapter gives you the scoop on all that, and more. There are a lot of myths and misconceptions about Chihuahuas, and it's our goal to give you the real lowdown on these charming little dogs with the great-big attitude.

Chihuahuas Are a Top 40 Breed

Modern Chihuahuas have been known since the mid-19th century, and people began to exhibit them in dog shows in 1890. A dog named Midget, owned by Texas Ranger and Chihuahua breeder Hamilton Polk Rayner, was the first Chihuahua registered with the American Kennel Club (AKC), in 1904. By 1908, the breed had its first champion, a dog named Beppie. The Chihuahua Club of America was founded in 1923. (Interestingly, the Chihuahua's homeland, Mexico, didn't recognize the diminutive dogs as a breed until 1942.) The little dogs had a slow but steady rise to popularity in the United States. In 1964, they were the 12th most popular breed registered by the AKC, and at one point they climbed as high as number five in the rankings. The 1960s were their heyday, but they have remained well known since then. In 2021, Chihuahuas ranked 37th among the breeds registered by the AKC, putting them in the top 40. Worldwide, though, Chihuahuas rank eighth in popularity and are particular favorites in Mexico, Guatemala, and Puerto Rico.

On Instagram the Chihuahua is a star — the number-one most hashtagged dog. They are so well loved that there is even a holiday celebrating the Chihuahua! International Chihuahua Appreciation Day is May 14.

Chihuahua Ancestors Were Guides to the Afterlife

Before there were Chihuahuas, there were little dogs called Techichis, who date to the time of the Toltec civilization in Mexico, some 1,100 years ago. The Toltecs carved images of dogs that resembled Chihuahuas on the walls of the pyramids they built. The Toltecs were eventually conquered by the Aztecs, who also appreciated the little dogs. They appreciated them so much that they considered the small dogs essential for a safe journey to the afterlife. That was kind of hard on the dogs — they were sacrificed in order to take on the wrongdoings of the deceased, as well as to guide them safely over the Nine Waters of Danger to the underworld.

Chihuahuas Are Soft-Headed, Literally

You might have a soft spot for Chihuahuas, but did you know they have a real soft spot — on top of their head? It's called a molera, also known as a fontanel, and it's a soft spot on the head that is there at birth (human babies have them, too). Its purpose is to help the head move easily through the birth canal, as well as to allow for growth of the brain and skull in those early formative months. Some moleras are open, meaning there's a hole in the head — basically a gap between the skull's growth plates. It's super-important to handle a Chihuahua puppy's head carefully and to make sure they don't run head-on into a piece of furniture, for instance.

TECHNICAL
STUFF

A molera is seen in many small breeds, not just the Chihuahua, and it's not the same as the medical condition hydrocephalus, or water on the brain.

Chihuahuas Are the World's Smallest Dog Breed

There are lots of little dogs in the world — Maltese, Pomeranians, Yorkshire Terriers, to name a few — but Chihuahuas hold the official title of world's smallest dog breed. A Chihuahua named Milly, who stands less than 4 inches tall, currently holds the Guinness World Record for smallest dog. The smallest Chihuahua by length is Brandy, 6 inches long from nose to tail tip, and weighing in at 2 pounds. Although some end up being bigger, Chihuahua breed standards around the world call for the dogs to weigh no more than 6 pounds.

Chihuahuas Descend from Ancient Dogs of the Americas

In April 2017, a study published in the journal *Cell Reports* found that Chihuahuas were among a group of dogs with large amounts of DNA unlike that of other American breeds. Other breeds included the American Hairless Terrier, the Peruvian Inca Orchid (a South American sighthound), the Chinese Crested (not actually from China), the Rat Terrier, the Toy Fox Terrier, and the Xoloitzcuintli (also known as the Mexican Hairless). Archaeological evidence of a canine subspecies existed, but the DNA evidence backed it up, with living evidence in modern breeds.

For the study, researchers examined gene sequences from 1,346 dogs representing 161 existing breeds from North America, Europe, Asia, and Africa. With the results, they assembled a canine evolutionary tree. We now know that, at least in part, Chihuahuas descend from the first dogs who populated the Americas 10,000 or more years ago!

Chihuahuas Are Flyball MVPs

Is your Chihuahua crazy about their ball toys? Are they smart? Fast? You might have a flyball star in the making. The relay race involves teams of four dogs racing each other over four hurdles, stomping on a pedal to release a tennis ball, and taking it back over the hurdles so the next dog can run. The fastest team with the fewest penalties wins. Chihuahuas can be prized members of flyball teams because the jump heights are set for the smallest dog. A flyball team with a Chihuahua on it has easy-peasy hurdles to cross. Active Chihuahuas who love to run, play fetch, and play with other dogs could have flyball in their future.

In January 2022, Chihuahua Lalo, now retired at 12 years old, earned the North American Flyball Association's Iron Dog title, awarded to dogs who earn flyball points over ten consecutive racing years. See Chapter 12 for more dog sports in which Chihuahuas can excel.

Chihuahuas Live Long Lives

Little dogs have a reputation for living longer than large dogs, and Chihuahuas are no exception. They typically enjoy a long lifespan, up to 18 years and sometimes more if they're blessed with good genes, good nutrition, and good veterinary care. In fact, a 21-year-old Chihuahua named TobyKeith currently holds the Guinness World Record title for oldest living dog.

According to a white paper by pet insurer Nationwide, Chihuahuas are among the breeds at lowest relative risk for a cancer claim.

Chihuahua Ears Act as Air Conditioners

One of the noteworthy physical characteristics of Chihuahuas are those ears. Large and erect, they are an evolutionary adaptation that helped Chihuahuas and their ancestors the Techichis withstand the heat of their environment in Mexico.

The large surface area of the ears helps the body to release excess heat. The thin, exposed skin of the outer ears contains many blood vessels that can dilate or widen, depending on the weather, quickly dissipating heat through the ears.

Chihuahuas aren't born with pointy ears, though. At birth, the ears are floppy, and it can take some months before they reach their erect state — and some never do!

TIP

You can learn to read your Chihuahua's ears to understand what the dog is feeling and thinking. Ears held forward mean your dog is interested in something. The ears may twitch if they're listening to something intriguing. Gently held back and accompanied by a happy tail wag? Your pup wants to be petted or cuddled. Ears pinned back tight signal that your dog is nervous or afraid.

Chihuahuas Are Named After the Mexican State of Chihuahua

Chihuahuas are from desert country. If you've ever been to the border town of Juarez, just across the Rio Grande from El Paso, you've visited the state of Chihuahua — or the "Free and Sovereign State of Chihuahua," as it's formally known.

The area is also known for an important archaeological site, the Paquime ruins, the Sierra Madre mountain range, and the home of revolutionary leader Pancho Villa. The capital city of Chihuahua has a beautiful pink baroque-style cathedral.

This is the place that gives the pooches, who first attained popularity there with tourists, their name. And rumor has it that in some places, you can still see packs of feral Chihuahuas roaming the land of their ancestors.

Chihuahuas Can Be Working Dogs

When you think service dog, you probably picture in your mind a Golden or Labrador Retriever acting as a guide dog or a German Shepherd helping a person with mobility issues. But have you ever heard of a Chihuahua service dog?

Little dogs like Chihuahuas can act as service dogs in a number of different ways. They can alert people with hearing loss to important sounds such as fire alarms, doorbells, timers, or crying babies; can warn people with diabetes of low blood sugar; or act as psychiatric service dogs for people with autism, post-traumatic stress disorder, or depression, interrupting self-harming or repetitive behaviors, reminding them to take medication, waking them from nightmares, and more. Chihuahuas might be tiny but they're mighty.

Chapter **18**

Ten (Or So) Famous Chihuahuas

Thanks to television and movies, most of today's pop culture enthusiasts admire, or at least are amused by, famous Chihuahuas. Sure, some are film and commercial stars, but others have won glory in other arenas.

In this chapter, we tell you about diminutive dog stars as well as Chihuahuas who have earned fame for their kind actions, sports prowess, and literary associations. But choosing only ten of them was just too hard, so we might have cheated a little and stuffed a couple of them under one heading!

MacKenzie: American Hero Dog

A four-pound Chihuahua named MacKenzie was named 2020's American Hero Dog, a title conferred by the votes of almost a million dog-loving Americans, for her contribution to the rescue of baby animals who require special medical attention. MacKenzie, who lives in Rochester, New York, helps her handler, Sue, care for young animals with birth defects by cleaning and cuddling them and teaching them how to play and have good manners.

The now-ten-year-old Chihuahua is perfect in this role because she herself was born with a cleft palate. She had to be tube-fed for nearly a year and overcame multiple bouts of aspiration pneumonia before she could receive surgery to correct her condition.

When she's not caring for young animals who need help, Mac-Kenzie visits local schools, demonstrating the importance of kindness toward both animals and humans with physical differences. Students learn that anyone can make a difference in the world, no matter how small they are.

Bruiser

In the movie *Legally Blonde*, Elle Woods, played by Reese Witherspoon, attends Harvard University with her plucky Chihuahua Bruiser (whose real name was Moondoggie). Bruiser/Moondoggie also was featured in *Legally Blonde 2*, where he was present in the courtroom while his mistress pleaded cases! He lived a long life, even for a Chihuahua, making it to the age of 18.

Gidget

Gidget, Taco Bell's talking dog star, retired from the advertising business in 2000 after a long and successful career as chief spokesdog for the fast-food chain. But it seems like only yesterday!

She played a cool-guy role and did her own stunt work, which included riding on Godzilla's tail, running up a fire escape, riding a skateboard, and jumping on a taxi cab. She loved riding in limos, and she had her own line of drinking cups, T-shirts, and talking toys. She even had two male stand-ins! But despite all her fame, this diva was easily pleased and willingly worked for chicken and steak bits. Ay, Chihuahua!

Gidget was born December 8, 1994, and lived with animal trainer Sue Chipperton, who acquired Gidget as a pup and trained her for stardom. Her expressive face appeared in a print campaign for The Limited, and she had a "carry-on" role in the movie *The Fan* with Robert De Niro before becoming the hottest commercial canine since Spuds McKenzie. Following her Taco Bell adventures, Gidget appeared in another movie. She played Bruiser's mother in *Legally Blonde 2*!

Chipperton tells the stories of Gidget, Moondoggie, and more in her book *A Famous Dog's Life*, a fun and fascinating read that covers not only movie-dog life and training but also pet adoption and training tips.

Mojo

Perhaps you fell in love with the gutsy Chihuahua called Mojo in the action movie *Transformers*. His name was Chester in real life, and he was quite the spark plug. One of his several scenes included him lifting his leg and relieving himself on an evil transformer's foot! Mojo also appeared in *Revenge of the Fallen*.

Wheely Willy

The subject of two best-selling children's books, *How Willy Got His Wheels* and *How Willy Got His Wings* (Doral), by Deborah Turner, Wheely Willy was a real-life paraplegic Chihuahua who got around via a canine "wheelchair" that allowed him to move freely on his front legs while wheels rolled on behind him.

Originally found abandoned in a box with a cut throat and spinal injuries, Willy was eventually adopted by pet groomer Deborah Turner. She tried to rig something that would give Willie the gift of autonomous movement, but she failed until she saw an ad for the K-9 Cart.

Willy's can-do attitude inspired others as he visited hospitals and institutions around the globe and participated in local events (he's from Long Beach, California), such as the Los Angeles Marathon and the Cystic Fibrosis Fun Walk. Willy also made several appearances on the Animal Planet television network!

Desmond

Which Chihuahua has the most dog sport titles? A flashy four-year-old long-haired Chihuahua named Desmond is well in the running. His full name, titles and all, is MACH2 Cupcake's Ob-la-di Ob-la-da Life Goes On BN, RN, FDC, MXG, MJC, MFB, T2B, TQX, BCAT, CGC. (In other words, he's a Master Agility Champion — ranking #1 Agility Chihuahua in 2021 and 2022); Beginner Novice in obedience; Rally Novice; Farm Dog Certified (yes, really!); Master Gold Agility; Master Century Jumpers With Weaves; Master Bronze FAST (another agility title); Time 2 Beat; Triple Q Excellent; Beginner Coursing Agility Test; and Canine Good Citizen (CGC).

Most of these titles are determined by the number of points the dogs earn in competition, but for the CGC, for instance, they must pass a test that requires them to perform certain behaviors flawlessly. (See more about the CGC in Chapter 12.) In the Farm Dog Certified test, dogs are required to show that they're comfortable around livestock, can navigate farm areas such as barns, and walk over unusual surfaces, to name just a few. Desmond's fans describe him as spunky, fun-loving, and energetic, a real show-stealer.

Pepito, Xavier Cugat's Dancing Dog

You might not be old enough to remember him, but Xavier Cugat, a popular Latin American band leader during the 1930s and '40s, liked to take his Chihuahua, Pepito, on stage with him. He often held Pepito in one hand while conducting his band with the other. Cugat had several Chihuahuas, and according to a popular (and possibly true) story, he once dressed a Chi like a baby, complete with a bonnet, so he could smuggle him into his hotel room.

Pepito was featured in the book *Pepito: The Little Dancing Dog*, by Mark Evans, and illustrated by Cugat himself.

Angel and Rusco

Before they won starring roles in the movie *Beverly Hills Chihuahua*, Angel (who played Chloe) and Rusco (who played Papi) were in rough situations. Angel had been given up to a shelter by her owners, and Rusco too was in a shelter. Both were fortunate enough to catch the eye of movie-animal trainer Michael Alexander. Rusco, in particular, had big ears and a winning expression, along with a bouncy personality, which sealed the deal.

Montecristo

This real-life jetsetter Chihuahua has traveled to Pisa, Italy, Florida's Everglades, and lots of places in between with owner Sonja Lishchynski. He has visited eighteen countries and counting! Even better, Montecristo, with some help from Lishchynski, has written a book about one of his adventures: *Montecristo Travels to Pisa*. And he's now accompanied by a sister, Pompadour, also a long-haired Chihuahua. Rumor has it that more books are in the works, so keep an eye out. A portion of the profits from the sale of Montecristo's books helps to support Veterinarians Without Borders, a nonprofit organization that helps to feed, vaccinate, and care for animals around the world.

TobyKeith

A seven-pound Chihuahua named TobyKeith is currently the world's oldest living dog at age 21, as verified in May 2022 by Guinness World Records. TobyKeith was adopted by owner Gisela Shore when he was four months old. His days involve sleeping interspersed with running up and down the stairs and noshing on his favorite treat, a little bit of deli turkey.

Index

L

lactose intolerance, 109
Lap of Love, 282
latent learning, 186
leashes, 80–82, 152
leather, 84
Leave it cue, 192
leptospirosis, 242, 245
level bite, 28
licking, 148
lifespan, 299
limited registration, 70, 293
litter box method, 168
littermates, 44, 55, 63
Lone Star tick, 260
long coat, 11
  brushing, 121–122
  comparing smooth and, 43–44
  grooming, 131
  tools for caring, 82
loose dogs, 95–96, 152
loyalty, 19
luxating patella, 278
Lyme disease, 245, 260–261

M

macadamia nuts, 115
MacKenzie, American Hero Dog, 301–302
magnesium, 99
majors, 220–221
males
  clothing for, 87
  traits, 44–45
Malta, 27
manganese, 100
marking, 45, 189–190
massage, 120

mat splitter, 82, 121
matches, 224
mats, 121
Mayans, 33
meat source, 103
medications, 12, 200
  administering medicine correctly, 246–247
  following dosages, 236
memory, 137–138
merle pattern, 26
Mexico, 27, 33, 141, 300
microchips, 88, 250–251
mineral oil, 129
minerals, 98–100
miniature Chihuahua, 65
mites, 263–264
  ear mites, 264
  follicular, 263–264
  sarcoptic mange, 263
  walking dandruff, 264
mobility, 280
Moctezuma II, 141
Mojo, 303
molera, 22, 27, 276–277, 297
Montecristo, 305
morning, housetraining, 169
motion sickness, 157
motivation, 205, 211–213
mounting, 148, 193–194
munchkin in the middle, 139
muscle, 31
muzzle, 28
myocardial parvovirus, 243

N

napping, 89
National Dog Registry, 251

natural dog, 17
neck, 28–29
neglection, 18
neutering, 12, 45, 190, 193, 249–250
nipping, 179–180
noises, 154
non-core vaccines, 241
nose work, 208
nutraceuticals, 280
nutrition, 98–100
  deficiencies from generic brands, 103
  needed nutrients, 98
  vitamins and minerals, 98–100
nylon chews, 83

O

obedience, 208
obesity, 114
obstacles, 207
odor neutralizer, 171
Off cue, 196–197
Official Standard for the Chihuahua, 23
off-square bodies, 26
omnivores, 101
onions, 114–115
online purchases, 64–65
online resources
  AAHA, 232
  acupuncture, 278
  Center for Pet Safety, 86
  cheat sheet for book, 4
  Chihuahua Clubs, 52
  dog health information, 64
  dog sport organizations, 208
  Lap of Love, 282

urinary tract infection, 148

USDA (United States Department of Agriculture), 64

V

vaccinations, 204, 241–246

DAPP, 242–244

extra precautions for Toy puppies, 241–242

other diseases, 245–246

puppy kindergarten, 155

rabies, 244–245

socialization and, 151

veterinarians, 231–251

asking about breeders, 52

being good client, 235–237

choosing, 232–234

choosing before homecoming, 88

considering long-term cost, 12

health certificate signed by, 158, 210

oral hygiene appointments, 124

preparing for first exam, 237–240

when to call vet immediately, 268–269

veterinary behaviorist, 185, 190

Veterinary Medical Teaching Hospital, 103

vitamins, 98–100

W

walking, 134, 159–161

walking dandruff, 264

warmth, 37, 43, 87, 89

wash-and-go breed, 17

watchdogs, 19, 178

waving, 214–215

weight

breed standards, 26

feeding guidelines

adult dogs, 110

performance diet, 110

reduced-calorie diet, 110–111

senior dogs, 111–112

well let down hocks, 31

well-laid-back shoulders, 29

Western Mountain wood tick, 260

wheat, 103

Wheely Willy, 303–304

whipworms, 255–256

withers, 26

World Small Animal Veterinary Association (WSAVA), 123

X

xylitol, 115, 124

Y

Youth of Moses, The (Botticelli), 27

Z

zinc, 100

Zoom Groom, 120

About the Author

Kim Campbell Thornton: Kim is an award-winning writer with 30 books and well over 1,000 articles to her credit. With her veterinary partner, Dr. Marty Becker, and dog trainer Mikkel Becker, she writes the weekly feature Pet Connection, which is offered through Andrews McMeel Syndication and appears in newspapers across the country, as well as online. Kim is also content manager for Fear Free Happy Homes, which promotes education on pet behavior and care; relief of fear, anxiety, and stress in pets; and building a great relationship with animals. She's an Elite Fear Free Certified Professional who has taken continuing education courses in puppy and kitten behavior and avian behavior and care.

Jacqueline O'Neil: Jackie is an award-winning author of more than a dozen books and a few hundred magazine articles on animal care and training. Previously, she worked as a dog breeder and trainer, handling her own dogs to top awards in the show and obedience rings.

Dedication

To Gemma, the first, best little tiny dog. —Kim

To my daughters, Peggy and Sunny Fraser, who served as mommies to a munchkin named Manchita. —Jackie

Author's Acknowledgments

Many thanks go to veterinarian and Chihuahua lover Diane Walker, who performed the technical review of the manuscript; the Chihuahua fanciers who shared their experiences with and photos of their beloved dogs: Andrea Kuska, Amelia Darby, Rachel, and Elle from AllThingsChihuahua.com; Bridget Kennedy, for providing information about and photos of Desmond, her top-performance Chihuahua; Allynid "Lynnie" Bunten, president of the Chihuahua Club of America; and Julie Ellingson, dog groomer and Chihuahua fan extraordinaire. —Kim

My husband, Tom O'Neil, took some of the photos for the original edition of this book. My daughter Peggy Fraser, who hates posing for pictures, did it anyway. Thanks, honey. Taco Bell Corp. provided information about Gidget, once the world's most recognizable Chihuahua, and included photos of its superstar.
—Jackie

Publisher's Acknowledgments

Acquisitions Editors: Kelsey Baird and Jennifer Yee

Development Editor and Project Manager: Victoria Anllo

Copy Editor: Amy Handy

Technical Editor: Diane Walker

Managing Editor: Kristie Pyles

Production Editor: Mohammed Zafar Ali

Cover Image: © otsphoto/ Adobe Stock Photos